Jenny

Jenny

A Father's Story

Gerald R. Lishka

1998
Galde Press, Inc.
Lakeville, Minnesota

FIRST EDITION
First Printing, 1998

Library of Congress Cataloging-in-Publication Data

Lishka, Gerald R.
    Jenny : a father's story / Gerald R. Lishka.
       p.   cm.
    ISBN 1–880090–38–4 (trade pbk.)
       1. Pivaral-Lishka, Jennifer Marie, 1988–1991—Health.
    2. Abnormalities. Human—Patients—Biography.   3. Fathers—
    -Biography.   4. Fathers and daughters—Biography.   5. Bereavement—
    -Psychological aspects.   6. Adoptive parents—Biography.   I. Title.
    RG627.L57   1996
    616'.043—dc20
    [B]   96–31037
                                                                        CIP

Galde Press, Inc.
PO Box 460
Lakeville, Minnesota 55044–0460

This book is dedicated to all of those who
have experienced the death of a child.

Other Books by Gerald Lishka:

A Handbook for the Ballet Accompanist

Darkness Is Light Enough

Contents

Prologue   ix

I Meet Jennifer   1
   A Revelation   1
   Becoming Father and Daughter   5
   Homecoming Strategies and Preparations   14

Jenny Comes Home   21
   Medical Procedures and Problem-Solving   21
   Routines at Home   33
   Medical Visits to the Hospital   39
   The Lizards Find New Homes, Birthdays, and Other Memories   42
   Storm Clouds   51
   A Battle Line Is Drawn   59
   We Are Alone   61

Last Days   63
   Alarm   63
   Our Last Night   70
   Jenny Is Gone   72
   Jenny's Message   77
   Funeral Preparations   79
   Holy Family Church   87
   Gethsemani   93
   I Return to L. A.   98

Later Things   101
   Emptiness   101
   Looking for Support   104
   The Compassionate Friends   109
   Beyond the Physical World   113
   A Medium   117
   An Astrologer   123
   Treasures   134
   My Return and Lifelong Commitment to Meditation 135
   A Birth and a Channeler   138
   I Meet Jessica   147

A Crisis 148

Self-Realization Fellowship 149

Brother Anandamoy 150

A Dead End 152

Thanksgiving, and a Baptism 153

Heartfelt 154

Dr. Ribe 155

Year's End 158

I Return to Jenny's Grave 162

Through the Winter 167

Films of Jenny, and a Tibetan Lama 170

A Fast, an Initation, Dreams, and a Bonding 176

Sebastian Dies 179

Father's Day, and a Birthday 184

Rosa 184

The First Anniversary 187

Dreams, and a Strange Occurrence 187

A Desecration 190

Jenny Protects Me from a Fraud 193

Dreams and Visions 198

The End of a Marriage 204

A Birth 207

I Am Alone 207

Jerry Alber Arrives—and Leaves 208

Meditation for Jessica, Jenny's Footprints,
     an Odd Occurrence, and an Insight 209

I Begin Writing Jenny's Story 211

Mementos—a Last Look 213

Jessica 217

Advice to Bereaved Parents 225

Jenny—My Final Thoughts 237

Epilogue 245

Prologue

Nestled in the rolling hills and farmlands of Kentucky, at Trappist, south of Bardstown, on 2,400 acres in Nelson County, lies the beautiful Abbey of Our Lady of Gethsemani, the oldest in North America, a monastery inhabited by brothers of the Trappist order, and the burial site and former habitation of Thomas Merton, the great Catholic monk, scholar, and writer. Just inside the entrance to the main grounds and within a few hundred feet of the burial place of Thomas Merton and other brothers lies a very old, small, private cemetery, lovingly tended by the religious ascetics who live in the Abbey.

Many of the graves are generations old. Some can probably no longer be identified. Among them lies a small, relatively new grave. Its gray headstone reads:

Jennifer Marie
Pivaral-Lishka
June 24, 1988
August 9, 1991
Our Precious Baby

The beautiful child who lies there changed me forever. This book is the story of her short but remarkable life, and the unforgettable way in which she touched so many people.

Jenny at home

I Meet Jennifer

Then some children were brought to Him so that He might lay His hands on them and pray; and the disciples rebuked them.

But Jesus said, "Let the children alone, and do not hinder them from coming to Me; for the kingdom of heaven belongs to such as these."

And after laying His hands on them, He departed from there.

—*Matthew 19: 13-15*

A Revelation

I was living in Los Angeles. It was Saturday, November 3, 1990, and it had not been a very good day, but I had decided in the afternoon that I would try to make it end on a better note. The circumstances were not unusual. I was upset and resentful of my wife, Suzanne, and although I have no idea why now, it was probably over money, or what in my eyes was her extreme self-reliance and the feeling I lived with daily that she did not love me or need me. I went out and bought groceries and wine to prepare a first-class dinner for Suzanne and myself.

When Suzanne came home late, I was standing at the stove. She sat down on a dining room chair a few feet from me and began to talk about something that immediately got my attention.

1

Suzanne had an extensive background in nursing, and at that time was Director of Quality Improvement at Huntington Memorial Hospital in Pasadena. She had often come home from the hospital and related to me, as all spouses do, things that had happened at work. Over the past months she had mentioned a little girl named Jennifer, with a serious medical condition, who was living on the pediatric ward, but I had no real understanding about the nature of Jennifer's case, except that it was a very serious one.

Suzanne and I had no children. We had never made any specific plans to have children, since neither of us seemed interested, and a surgery several years earlier had made it impossible for Suzanne to have them. In fact, although I liked children, I had never felt any desire to become a father. Neither I nor anyone else could ever have predicted my reaction when, out of the blue, Suzanne said, "You know, we could have Jennifer if we wanted her."

My eyes became wet with tears. As I stood looking down at the stove, I felt that the whole inside of my mind had suddenly become flooded with light. Without ever having shown any unusual interest in Suzanne's stories about Jennifer, and without ever having laid eyes on her, I knew deep in my soul that Jennifer was mine. I never doubted it, I never questioned it. I asked Suzanne when we could go visit Jennifer. We agreed to go the following day.

The following afternoon, after an organ recital at St. Vibiana's church downtown, Suzanne and I drove to Huntington. We took the elevator to the fourth floor and entered the pediatric ward through its large swinging doors. I saw a little girl, almost two and a half years old, with black hair and large, dark, liquid eyes, sitting in a red wagon. As Suzanne and I stood talking to the nursing assistant, Jenny did not seem to notice me. But when I looked at her, my first impression, an unforgettable one, was that she was a very serious little soul. She looked kind of sad. Her hair, frankly, was rather a mess.

I remember having no noticeable reaction to seeing Jenny. I simply looked at her and did not speak, and she paid no attention to me. But as I picture that moment in my mind, my heart aches deeply, my eyes become filled with tears, and I am filled with longing for her, wishing an impossible wish that time could be turned back and our time together could start over again from that moment. Suzanne and I stayed only a short while. After we left, we talked things over, and the next afternoon, Monday, after work, I drove to the hospital, spoke for a while with Fran, one of the medical social workers, and told her to start the paperwork that would make Jenny our foster child.

The story of Jennifer Janeth Pivaral—her birth, her medical condition, and the circumstances under which Suzanne came to know about her are remarkable. I moved to Los Angeles in September 1985, and after we were finally able to sell our condominium in Louisville, Kentucky, Suzanne joined me in the spring of 1987. Her first nursing job was at Los Angeles County U.S.C. Medical Center, Women's Hospital, one of the busiest medical centers in the area, and one which provided extensive care to the indigent and economically disadvantaged.

A Hispanic girl named Rosa Pivaral came to the hospital, probably looking for drugs or going through withdrawal. She was pregnant, had never had any prenatal care whatsoever, and gave birth to two girls on June 24, 1988. These two infants were Jennifer and her sister, Wendy, born as Siamese twins, about ten weeks prematurely. Wendy was dead at birth, her head attached to Jennifer's abdomen. In a matter of hours she was surgically removed from Jennifer, who survived. I have no idea what became of the body of Jenny's dead twin.

It is my understanding that Rosa had spent much of the past couple of years living on the streets, taking drugs, and hanging out with gang members. Rosa's lifestyle, her use of drugs, her complete lack of prenatal care, and the fact that she wore tight jeans and belts to hide her pregnancy explained, at least to me, the medical condition of her twins. Yet, to my surprise, I know of no medical professional involved with Jennifer who definitively acknowledged a link.

In addition to being a Siamese twin, which is very rare, Jennifer was also born with some of her organs outside of her body, a condition that occurs more frequently and which is generally correctable through surgery, as was the case with Jennifer. By the time I first saw her, when she was almost two and a half, she had had about five major surgeries, and at the time I met her, she was in the process of recovering from a nearly fatal bout with sepsis.

From birth onward, Jenny was unable to eat. That is, she could take food and water by mouth, but her digestive tract was damaged in some way so that practically nothing she ingested could pass from her stomach to her intestines, both of which were functional. The first time that the Huntington staff actually attempted to get Jenny to ingest food by mouth was on April 13, 1989, almost ten months after birth. This experiment was not successful, and although I do not know how many follow-up attempts were made, I can conclude that nothing significant came from them. From time to time Jenny did take small amounts of nourishment orally, especially when she developed infections in association with her feeding line. Nevertheless, since long before I had known her, she had not eaten, except to drink water and Pedialite.

For Jenny to receive nourishment, various surgical procedures were performed on her after birth and also later at various points during her life, whereby a catheter for feeding was introduced into one of her internal organs. After talking with Suzanne and even with her pediatrician, Dr. Laurance, I was unable to get a precise picture of Jenny's medical history. A Broviac catheter had been permanently placed in her chest for feeding her. Through this catheter, various kinds of liquid nourishment could be pumped directly into her heart, which then delivered them to the rest of her body by means of her circulatory system.

There were other problems. The bile and other excretions produced by Jenny's stomach, and whatever liquids she took by mouth that were not absorbed into her digestive system needed to be eliminated. To accomplish this, she was given a gastrostomy tube. By means of a hole made in her abdomen, one end of this tube could be inserted directly into her stomach. Although this tube could be removed and reinserted when necessary, the end inside her stomach had a mushroom tip so that it could not fall out. This tip, which could be elongated to make insertion easy, expanded once inside the stomach. Finally, Jenny was born with an imperforate anus. Although her backside looked normal, she had no rectal opening. Therefore, in order for her to be able to eliminate whatever waste products built up in her intestines, which were much shorter than normal, she was given a colostomy. Through surgery, a small portion of her intestine protruded through the skin on her left side, a few inches from the site of the gastrostomy tube, and she used a small colostomy bag.

Since I have no medical training, I suppose it would seem presumptuous of me, particularly to doctors, to draw conclusions about Jenny's medical condition. Still, I have drawn my own conclusions, which are: Rosa's lifestyle was a contributing factor. And, while in the womb, Jenny was deprived of nourishment that might have helped to ensure her normal development due to the fact that the other twin, who was attached to her by its head, appropriated some of that nourishment for itself. However, I am only guessing.

Nevertheless, in spite of all her medical complications, Jenny would develop to look quite normal, except for her catheter, tube, and bag, and a lot of scar tissue on her abdomen, the result of several extensive surgeries. And when I came to know her two and a half years later, Jennifer was, in fact, extraordinarily beautiful. She was the loveliest, most light-radiating child one could ever imagine. And she was brilliant.

After Jenny's birth, Rosa was in no condition physically, emotionally, or psychologically to take care of her. It is my understanding that, after being released from the hospital, Rosa returned once or twice. I suspect that she felt utterly inadequate to the task of taking care of her child, and she probably felt a great deal of guilt. She never saw Jenny again. Jenny's father, a member of one of the most violent and drug-involved Latino gangs in Los Angeles, either saw Jenny once in the hospital, or, at least, heard of her medical condition and promptly absolved himself of any future involvement or responsibility.

No one else either in Rosa's family or the father's family was able to take responsibility for Jennifer. This fact, along with her extremely serious medical condition, made her a ward of the state and a permanent hospital resident. Jennifer was subsequently transferred from Women's Hospital, and Suzanne lost track of her. Suzanne continued to work at U.S.C. Later, she worked at another hospital, and eventually took the position of Director of Quality Improvement at Huntington. Remarkably, one day, as she was making her rounds of the pediatric ward, she encountered Jennifer.

This amazing coincidence would turn our lives upside down. Suzanne became interested in Jenny's case. If Suzanne had ever thought seriously about trying to bring Jenny to live in our home, I had had no indication of it. But Suzanne had recently had a conversation with a friend of hers who seemed to have considerable financial resources, and who had suggested that he could make bringing Jenny home a reality.

Suzanne's friend, a film director, had a lover who died from AIDS. Prior to moving to Huntington, Suzanne had taken a deep personal interest in this patient's case. He was in the hospital where she worked, and she had been of great support emotionally and spiritually both to this patient and to the film director. After the patient's death, the friendship remained between Suzanne and the director, and they got together occasionally to have lunch and talk. Suzanne told her friend about Jenny's story, and as a result, this friend had offered to back us financially so that we could take care of Jenny. As it turned out, her friend was unable to offer us the financial support he had hoped to due to serious financial reversals in his own life. Fortunately, however, we discovered later on that there was financial help available elsewhere.

Becoming Father and Daughter

After meeting Jenny and returning to the hospital the following day to talk to the social worker, I started visiting Jenny on the pediatric ward on a regular basis. Suzanne would often go to the pediatric ward during work, where Jenny would be playing near the nurse's station or in her room, or in the large playroom just down the hall. Suzanne would often load Jenny into her little red wagon and take her to the first-floor cafeteria while she had lunch. Jenny, a long-time resident of the hospital, would always be greeted by everyone, since she was known to virtually the entire staff at Huntington, and although she ate nothing, she enjoyed the socializing.

I would come to the hospital after work, arriving either in the late afternoon or early evening. I went back to see Jenny a day or two after speaking with the social worker, and had in mind that I would go to the hospital every three or four days to visit. However, after only a week had passed, I totally abandoned this plan, having quickly realized that I was thinking about Jenny from morning to night every day, and that my day meant nothing to me unless I knew I was going to see her after work. There were only two occasions over the next three and a half months that I missed a single night of visiting Jenny. Once, probably in early December, when I was so sick with the respiratory flu that I could hardly stand up, I nevertheless determined that I would go to see her. However, probably in everyone's best interests, and exercising the common sense that I lacked on that occasion, the nurses on the pediatric ward would not let me onto the floor, and told me kindly but firmly that if I came back while I was so sick, they would have a security guard escort me out of the hospital. It was only about two or three days until I was able to come back, having made every effort to get well as quickly as possible, or at least to appear well enough to fool the nurses. At Christmas, I went to Illinois to be with my mother, and although I was gone only four days because I wanted to get back to Jenny, I found it almost unbearable to be away from her even for that short time. After that, I resolved never to be away from her again, not even for a single night, as long as she lived at the hospital.

If Suzanne knew I was coming to the hospital, she would wait for me so we could spend time with Jenny, who quickly came to think us of as a couple. Sometimes, I would go home from work, attend to my mail, and so on, take a shower, and then go to see Jenny so that I could stay late. After a time, I almost invariably put her to bed and returned home only after she had gone to sleep. In addition, I always saw Jenny on Saturdays and Sundays, either in the afternoon or at night, so that we were always together on a daily basis.

I vividly remember the first thing that Jenny and I did together. After meeting her for the first time on Sunday and talking with the social worker the following afternoon, I returned a day or two later. At that time, Jennifer was just recovering from a terrible bout with sepsis that had almost killed her and had kept her in the pediatric intensive care unit for some time. I think God kept her alive so we could find each other. During the time she had been sick, a condition had developed wherein her blood would, as I understand it, literally seep out of her veins. In order to combat this, she had been given extensive medication, the result of which was to make her severely, although temporarily, arthritic. Therefore, when I went to see her, the little thing was literally, and with some difficulty, just getting back on her feet. She was sitting in the hallway, in a t-shirt and diaper, barefoot, entertaining herself. I spoke to her and, offering her my hand, which she took without hesitation, we started slowly down the hall together, her long gastrostomy tube and the drainage bottle attached to the end of it dragging along on the floor behind her. Although I could see that walking was difficult and somewhat painful for her, she never complained. Jennifer was a trooper. I was glad that, within a few days, she had recovered her mobility and was moving about without pain.

Jenny seemed to take to me right away, which I found deeply gratifying. Although I had not spent a lot of time around children, I had always liked them and was very good with them. The nurses were also very pleased, and told me that Jenny did not generally warm up well to men. I remember being a little taken aback when, one night after I had starting visiting the hospital, one of the nurses asked me if I would like to put Jenny to bed. It seemed simple enough, I suppose, but my experience with putting children to bed was nonexistent.

The nurse and I took Jenny to her room, and they went through the nightly routine of getting her ready for bed, putting a fresh diaper on her, and so on. I will never forget the experience I had with Jennifer that night. There was a large, comfortable rocking chair in Jenny's room, which the nurse placed by the side of Jenny's bed. I sat down in the chair, held Jenny, and after turning out most of the lights so that there was just a pleasant glow in the room, the nurse said good night and quietly closed the door behind her.

As if she and I had done this every night of our lives, Jenny put her head on my shoulder and I held her close. After a moment or two, she raised her head and pointed toward something. Although Jenny was almost two and a half years old, and could talk, she generally did not say a lot, but was very good at expressing her needs and desires with gestures. Surprised, I asked her what she wanted, and she pointed again. There was a partially folded towel lying on one side of the sink. "Do you want that?" I asked, and she nodded. I handed it to her. Very methodically, which made the whole thing so sweet, she folded up the towel and placed it on my shoulder as a pillow, put her head down and quickly fell asleep as I gently rocked her.

That night, in that room, I experienced something I had never felt in my life. I was forty-one years old, and over the years since my youth I had been no stranger to mystical experiences. That night, holding Jenny in my arms as she slept, in the soft, glowing light and quiet of her room, and away from the chaos of the world, my soul came to rest. I was filled with an absolute peace I had never known from being so close to another human soul. For the first time in my life, through this beautiful baby, I had been touched with the kind of love that I had believed could only exist on a cosmic level, beyond everyday human experience. Revelations need not last long to turn one's life upside down. That evening, in the space of a few quiet moments, God was revealed to me in that child. From that moment, I became forever bonded to Jenny. And in contrast to most of my life until that moment, I no longer felt alone.

If I could have stopped time and remained forever with Jenny in my arms, sleeping on my shoulder, I would have done so. I had no more desires; I felt fulfilled, happy, and at peace. At that moment I became Jenny's father, and she became my daughter—my very own daughter. Time passed, and eventually I arose and carefully put Jenny into bed. As quietly as I could, I raised the bars on her crib so that she could not fall out and left the room.

Not many days passed before the nurses became aware that Suzanne and I were making application to become Jennifer's foster parents. If not, why would I be there night after night? But since nothing was definite in an official sense Suzanne did not discuss it openly with most of the nursing staff, which was understandable. I, however, made no secret about our intentions, and in my mind, the possibility that Jennifer would not be ours was unthinkable.

Never did I feel like these visits were a chore or an obligation. Besides building my relationship with Jenny, I was also able to become friends with many of the wonderful staff who took care of Jennifer, and I got to know a number of people throughout the hospital. Huntington soon began to feel like my second home. In my heart, it really was home, because that was where Jenny was, and no place could be home without her.

One person whom I came to know well was Jenny's pediatrician, Dr. Laurance, whose private practice was located near the hospital. I saw him almost every day. He had taken a deep personal interest in Jennifer and had grown to love her. Had Suzanne and I not come along, Dr. Laurance and his wife, who had several children of their own, would perhaps have considered becoming Jenny's foster parents. Jenny's residence at Huntington was because Dr. Laurance was willing to take her as a Medicare patient, which meant that he was paid virtually nothing for all the care he gave her. Medically speaking, Dr. Laurance had been looking after Jenny for most of her life, and I am sure that he pulled her through some episodes which would have made other doctors give up hope.

Dr. Laurance was very happy that Suzanne and I came into Jenny's life. I had heard from Suzanne, and from Fran, one of the medical social workers at the hospital, and others, that efforts had been made on many fronts to get various families to take Jennifer as a foster child. However, and somewhat understandably, in spite of the fact that some of these people showed an interest and seemed to come fairly close to making a commitment, in the end they backed away, given the extensive medical issues involved and the inescapable reality that Jennifer's life span was, to say the least, a question mark. Personally, I thank God that they backed out, because Jenny has enriched my life in a way that is utterly inexpressible. I am the lucky one—the one who got the treasure that others passed by.

When I first starting seeing Jenny, I noticed that she called many of the nurses "mommy" (who, in turn, referred to her and addressed her occasionally and affectionately as the Piv, Miss Piv, or Pivy). She also started calling me Mommy. Quite early on, but certainly not prematurely in my eyes, some of the nurses taught her to call me Daddy. If this was a ploy to tug at my heartstrings, it was deeply appreciated by me, although totally unnecessary, given the fact that I was already a completely hopeless Jennifer addict. Without my daily fix of seeing her, life would have seemed meaningless. Since she was calling most females "mommy," this is also how she addressed Suzanne. I thought it was very sweet of the nurses that, after it became apparent that Suzanne and I had planned to take Jenny home with us, they began gently to coax her into calling each of them by name, so that only Suzanne was Mommy. In this way, and in a short time, Jenny had one Mommy and one Daddy.

One of her favorite things was to be pulled about in one of the red wagons that were always parked in an alcove on the pediatric ward. Before my arrival, her trips in the wagon were confined largely to the pediatric ward. The reason I say this is because the first few times we went beyond the large swinging doors at either end of the ward she would get very concerned and want to go back to more familiar territory. As in most all matters, I readily acquiesced to her wishes, since there was nothing to be gained in frightening her. (And besides, my training—that is to say, Jennifer's training of me—was coming along quite well, and in a very short time she was able to program me to respond to her subtlest of wishes with a mere look from her—a nod, a pointing of the finger—or in cases where I seemed unusually dense, a word or two.)

Before heading out in a wagon, I always covered the bottom and sides with soft blankets and propped up a couple of pillows at the back end. Sitting or reclining comfortably, bottle of Pedialite in hand and her gastrostomy tube and bottle tucked in next to her, Jenny was ready to go. Gradually, by venturing a little further with her each time, I was able to overcome Jenny's fear of going beyond pediatrics. Huntington was an enormous, sprawling hospital; I became lost in it many times. The construction of a huge new wing was being completed, and it was open to travel long before it was occupied. Thus, Jenny and I would go forth on long excursions that seemed to stretch into miles, through endless corridors, inhabited and uninhabited wings, basements, elevators, and ramps. Sometimes, when I went to see Jenny at night I was fairly tired, and would have preferred to stay off my feet, but I quickly abandoned trying to weasel out of the wagon rides, because she loved them so much and always insisted on going. Therefore, off we would go, with Jenny usually indicating her preferred route for that evening by a nod or a finger when we reached any kind of intersection.

The next step in terms of excursions was going outdoors. On most weekends the weather was warm, sunny, and beautiful—typical of southern California, even in the middle of winter. The hospital grounds had several lovely courtyards, eating areas, lawns, and paved footpaths, and there was always the option of circling the entire hospital on the sidewalk. Thus, I began to take Jenny outside. She was not used to being outdoors, and as was the case when we had first ventured beyond pediatrics, Jennifer was apprehensive about leaving the familiarity and security of the hospital. But her inquisitiveness and eagerness to experience new things, and, I think, her trust in me, quickly won out, and after a few times she really looked forward to going outside.

I learned how most of us take ordinary things for granted. Since she had spent almost all of her life traveling about on hard, tiled floors, Jennifer was at first, much to my surprise, extremely reluctant to walk on grass or even to be pulled over it in the wagon. As with other things new and untried, she would give me that incredibly adult look of concern and doubt, that unmistakable frown of disapproval. But the strangeness of grass was quickly overcome, and its feel, texture, and sponginess ceased to be a mystery.

The option to going about in the wagon, I should mention, was a wheelchair. There were also a number of those on the pediatric ward, with comfortable seats and backs. So each night I would say to Jenny, "Wagon or wheelchair?" and she would make the choice. Thus, we were seen regularly making our way from one part of the hospital to another, through the cafeteria, down passageways, across lobbies, courtyards, and lawns, and around the sidewalks, stopping here and there to say hello to one of Jenny's many admirers or to observe some aspect of hospital life.

Jennifer's walk was a little bowlegged. It was nothing serious, and it somehow made her even more adorable. My heart would melt every time I saw her toddling around the corridors of the pediatric ward. (As she grew older, she outgrew this condition.) I always encouraged her to walk as much as possible, especially at first, after she had been bedridden from her most recent episode of sepsis. Walking, of course, could not hold a candle to being chauffeured about in a wagon or wheelchair. However, Jenny loved to climb up and down stairs, with deep delight. I held her hand, of course, so I also got a lot of exercise—more than I wanted, in fact. But I could never turn her down, since this activity made her so happy. She would often ask to go to the stairwell just outside the pediatric ward, and we would slowly make our way up and down several flights at a time. It was always deeply rewarding to see her look of enthusiasm, her smile, and her satisfaction and pride when we did this.

Throughout the hospital there were vending machines for coffee, soft drinks, candy, and so on. Jenny was fascinated with what happened to coins inserted into them, so stopping at these machines was a must when we went on our excursions. We would park at the bank of vending machines just outside the hospital cafeteria.

I would hold Jenny in my arms, hand her some coins, and she would insert them into the slot. When we first started doing this, I noticed that she had some difficulty getting the coins in, since she did not quite grasp that the coin had to be held vertically to fit the slot, but she figured it out with a little practice. She was not interested in getting anything out of the machines since she had no taste for candy or soda, but she was in shoving the coins in again and again; if I had been willing, we probably could have stayed at a machine for half an hour while she made a game of putting in the quarters, dimes, and nickels. After she inserted some money, I would push the coin return lever, she would listen to the jingling as the money went through the machine and landed in the coin return, and, holding her with one arm, I would retrieve the coins with my free hand. Although Jenny sometimes seemed a bit puzzled why potato chips and candy bars did not come out of the machines as they did when other people put in money, her primary interest was in inserting the coins and listening to them jingle and then reappear. We would repeat the procedure indefinitely, usually until my arms were aching from holding her. Then I would put her back in the wagon and we would continue on our trip until we encountered another vending machine. Sometimes I avoided these locations if I felt tired, but often Jenny would remind me that we had missed a stop.

Another favorite stop was the fountain in the lobby of the new wing of the hospital, where people often tossed coins. Since throwing in my own money would have become very expensive, I would reach down to the bottom of the fountain, scoop up a handful of money, and lay the coins on top of the little brick wall that encircled the water. With delight and with her typical total absorption, Jenny would throw the money back into the water a coin at a time or in handfuls until the supply was exhausted, whereupon I would reach into the water and fetch more coins. As with the vending machine game, we would usually continue this until I got bored and coaxed her into moving on.

There were many things do to on the pediatric ward. In her own room, in addition to her own little dresser, were her personal toy box, toys, games, crayons and coloring books, dolls, stuffed animals, and story books, most all of which had been given to her by the staff. In the daytime, the playroom right across the hall from Jenny's room was open and supervised by a child life therapist. Jenny could spend many hours in there with other children playing games, painting, working puzzles, cooking on the child's play stove, and so on.

When I visited Jenny in the evenings and we were not riding around the halls, we usually played out in the hall of the pediatric ward, sitting on a blanket on the floor near the nurse's station. One sure-fire form of entertainment was a paper airplane; I did half the throwing and almost all the retrieving. One night I brought a deck of cards to the hospital, which became the nightly inspiration for many games. Jenny's favorite activity with the cards, and mine, was for me to build a house of cards as high as I could and then let Jenny stomp on it. She loved this game, but she would get so excited that I was rarely able to complete any ambitious architectural endeavor before Jenny would raise her foot and stomp my construction into oblivion with ferocious enthusiasm and a grin of deep delight. After wrecking my project, she would always look at me to get my reaction, particularly if she had been a little premature, and we would laugh together.

Jenny also loved being involved in whatever the nurses were doing; she occasionally pushed their nearly inexhaustible patience to the limit by insisting on being involved in things which, contrary to her own opinion, were beyond her medical expertise. (My experience with children has shown me that they often prefer participating or helping in whatever the adults around them are doing in preference to playing with toys. In this way they feel needed and are reassured that they belong.) Jenny, therefore, often helped with the paperwork at the nurse's station, filling out and stamping forms, and the supervision of the various prescriptions that appeared suddenly through the vacuum tube.

The pediatric intensive care unit was housed in a large room just behind the nurse's station and accessed by various doors at each end of the station and by a small hallway on one side. If there were no medical emergencies in progress, this unit was also part of Jennifer's territory, and she could enter and exit pretty much at her own will. While in the PICU, she was well supervised and, there too, enjoyed participating in the routine.

During the months that I visited Jenny, I saw many moving things on her ward, like a small boy in the PICU who had been in a coma for a long time, and who eventually died. There was a young girl with cancer who stayed for some time, and who I got to know. Other patients came and went—children who had fallen into swimming pools or had drunk some kind of poison, sick children, and children who had failed to thrive through lack of attention. Jenny and I saw all of them. Most made it, but some did not.

Early on, Suzanne and I began taking Jenny's clothes home and washing them. Prior to this, the nurses who had taken such wonderful care of Jenny, who had loved her and bought her clothing and toys, had taken turns taking her laundry home. They would have continued to do this, but Suzanne and I thought that it was only right that we begin doing it.

I had gone to see Jenny one evening and, since I was especially tired, I had decided that I would go home a little earlier than usual, before Jenny had gone to bed. We were sitting together on the little child's bench along the wall, a few feet from the nurse's station. I had announced my attention to leave, kissed Jenny, said goodbye to the nurses, and was walking away toward the exit. As I looked back, Jenny burst into tears and began wailing as only a small child can. Her wet, sad face stopped me in my tracks. It was obvious to me and to all the nurses, who were watching this scene with some amusement, that Jenny was deeply upset at my leaving. I retraced a few steps, said something like, "Well, I guess I'm not leaving yet," and sat back down with her. From that night on, I rarely left without putting Jenny to bed, although when I did she was usually very good about it.

In December, I left Los Angeles to fly to Bloomington, Illinois, to visit my mother, who was 79 and living alone. But that year, because of Jenny, I could hardly tear myself away from Los Angeles, and went to Bloomington for a much shorter period of time than I normally would have.

When I returned, my first and only thought was seeing Jenny again. I arrived late in the evening, so the next night, after work, I went straight to the hospital, filled with the anticipation of a joyous reunion. When I got off the elevator on the fourth floor and approached pediatrics, I could see Jenny standing alone about halfway down the corridor between the doors and the nurse's station. I eagerly went through the doors and approached her with a big smile, but there was something different about her whole demeanor. When she saw me, she looked at me in a way I will never forget. Instead of the beaming smile and shining face that I had expected, she regarded me as if I had betrayed her. There was something odd, almost vacant, about her eyes. There was hurt there, but also resentment. Her look pierced my heart like a spear. She turned away from me, ignoring me completely. I was stunned, but I realized immediately that she thought I had abandoned her.

I let Jenny take her time. She continued to go about her business, aware of me, but not wanting me to know it. After a few minutes, we found ourselves near the nurse's station, and I maneuvered her into sitting with me on a blanket. She chose to appear absorbed in whatever it was that she was doing, so I spoke to her gently, gradually insinuating myself back into her world. It was only about ten minutes before we were friends again and my transgressions were forgiven. I can still see that look she gave me; I can feel deeply the pain that was in my heart because I had hurt her. Then and there I resolved that I would never miss a night again. I could not do it to her or myself.

When I told Suzanne, she explained that children often reacted this way toward their parents in similar situations. As an example, she cited kids hitting their parents upon being picked up by them at camp, after being away from home for a few days, and other similar behavior. I felt much better, because I saw that Jenny's behavior toward me showed how much she loved me. However, despite the relief I felt from this insight, the anguish I had experienced from Jenny's look left an indelible impression, and my resolve never to leave her at the hospital again remained as strong as ever.

On December 15, 1990, Suzanne and I took Jennifer on her first visit to our home. She did not stay overnight, of course, since the paperwork for us to become foster parents was still in progress and since we had no medical equipment or supplies in our house at that time. But from the moment she walked in the door, she accepted our townhouse at Vallejo Villas as her home, without question. She knew intuitively that she belonged. In addition to getting a feel for the place and being shown where her room would be, next to our bedroom on the lower level, she got to meet the other members of the household—two cats, Sarada, a sort of tortoise-shell mixed breed, and Sebastian, the Manx; and also, three terrariums full of my lizards, Rima and Brahma, the Chilean collared lizards, Negoya, the iguana (then several feet in length and having his own three hundred gallon terrarium), and Ananda and Maya, the Egyptian agamas.

In addition to Jenny's relish and ease at being in our home, we were pleasantly surprised at her attitude about riding in the car. Given the tentativeness that she had shown weeks earlier about such new experiences as the outdoors and grass, we wondered how she would react to sitting in the car, in front, strapped in her new car seat. But she never even commented on it, and acted as if she had been doing it all her life. Prior to that, one of the nurses had taken Jennifer out of the hospital and in her car once, not enough time for any real acclimatization. However, in that case, as in ours, Jennifer was with someone she loved and trusted, and this made all the difference.

Jenny was also entirely comfortable about going back to the hospital after her excursions to our home. I am glad that it did not make her sad. We continued these trips on a regular basis, also going to parks and restaurants, which Jenny loved. Suzanne and I delighted in giving her these new experiences.

A week after Jenny's first visit, Suzanne brought her home over Christmas, while I was away visiting my mother. Although I wanted to see my mom, I deeply missed being with Jenny on Christmas day, and we had our Christmas celebrations together before and after my return.

There were a couple times when Jenny got sick. Although neither episode turned out to be terribly serious, one was very frightening. It began by Jenny not feeling well, and after a day or two she began to show symptoms that indicated a possibility that she was getting septic. I had never seen Jenny really sick but Suzanne had; and the hospital had almost lost her more than once. I got really concerned when I saw how worried Suzanne was.

A couple of days had passed during which Jenny was not feeling well and was just not herself when I went to the hospital one night. I had looked forward to visiting her all day, and I was sure that seeing me would cheer her up. When I arrived in the pediatric ward, I saw Jenny down the hall, lying in her wagon near the nurse's station. Suzanne was sitting next to her. I walked up, looked down at Jenny, smiled, and said hello. She did not move or say a word, but only lay there, looking up at me. Her face was empty and expressionless, and although I did not detect pain in her eyes, it was obvious that she was totally wiped out.

The lifelessness in Jenny's face stunned me. I had never seen her like that. Deeply shaken, I remained with her and Suzanne for a few minutes, and then went a few steps down the hall into her room to get something. At one moment, I found myself standing still and silent by the window, realizing—deeply, and really for the first time—that Jenny could get sick and die. Tears came to my eyes. When Cindy, one of Jenny's primary caretakers and a favorite nurse of hers, walked into the room, I shared with her what was going on inside me. I saw right away that she was also concerned. There was, as well, a disturbing note of grim acceptance in her face and voice when she said something about the inevitability of Jenny getting sick periodically, and—what concerned me even more—a feeling I got from her that one day Jenny would get something from which she would not recover.

Fortunately, that particular episode of illness was caught and treated in time, and in a few days, to my great relief, Jenny was her old self again. And although of course I proceeded with all of our short- and long-term planning for Jenny, and in the hope for her long future with us, it was that brush with the possibility of her becoming seriously ill again that really awakened me to that fact that the precious creature whom I loved and adored so much was in some ways very vulnerable. The experience had shaken and sobered me, and from then on, I had a much more acute awareness—one that I lived with daily—that Jenny really was a fragile child, and that the balance for her between health and sickness, and life and death, was a delicate one.

Homecoming Strategies and Preparations

As time passed, Jenny's anticipated move home with us proceeded along several parallel paths. First, Suzanne and I had to become her official foster parents. The bureaucratic procedures which this entailed were handled largely by the State of California and the County of Los Angeles. Actual licensing of foster homes was overseen by the State of California, Health and Welfare Agency, Department of Social Services, Community Care Licensing; everything else was done by the County of Los Angeles, through the Department of Children's Services and their Children's Social Workers (CSWs). Second, and in conjunction with the state and county requirements, Suzanne and I had to set up our home in order to care for Jenny. Third, since Suzanne and I both worked full time, we had to find a day care facility of exceptional quality, with policies that would permit accepting Jennifer, and with an absolutely first-rate staff that could address her special needs. In addition, we had to find special back-up day care facilities that could take care of Jenny if she were sick or under the weather and unable to attend regular day care, the only alternative to which was either Suzanne or myself staying home from work with her. Fourth, we were also strongly encouraged to line up highly qualified individuals for home respite care and babysitting. Fifth, Suzanne and I both had to be thoroughly oriented and trained in the use of all of Jenny's medical equipment and supplies, and in the numerous procedures required to take care of her properly. And finally, in whatever ways appropriate and necessary, Suzanne and I needed to prepare ourselves, individually and as a couple, physically, emotionally, and spiritually, for the responsibilities of caring for Jennifer.

The assignment of our first children's social worker through the County Department of Children's Services was, in my opinion, guided in some way by fate or the hand of God. When I say that, for some totally subjective reason of my own, he reminded me immediately and always thereafter of Prince Myshkin, the central character in Dostoevsky's *The Idiot*, I am deeply sincere in saying that I mean this as a compliment to him. I do not mean to imply for a moment that he was in any way unprofessional or incompetent. On the contrary, he was articulate, handled himself very well, and seemed to know exactly what he was doing. Therefore, my comparison of him to the Dostoevsky character lies rather in a certain quality or charm he projected that is very difficult to put into words, but which might be described as almost otherworldly, or even angelic.

While addressing all the practical details, he gave one the impression, at the same time, of having one foot in another world. One might almost imagine him being guided from time to time by voices that not everyone heard. As I try to recall my intuitive impressions from that time, the practical result of this seemed to be that he did something which, although in no way improper or unheard of, he did not necessarily have to do; namely, he arranged things so that Jenny could move home with us prior to our having completed the voluminous, time-consuming paperwork and procedures necessary to have our home licensed as a foster care facility. Normally, the entire licensing application process had to be completed and the license granted before a home could even be considered for the placement of foster children.

Things eventually worked out so that Jenny would actually move home with Suzanne and me permanently on February 22, 1991. However, my completed application to have our home licensed as a foster care facility was not mailed to the State Department of Social Services until April 9, and the completion of that process took some time. Our home was finally licensed effective July 9, 1991, almost five months after Jenny came to live with us, and we did not actually receive the license until October 4. Therefore, it was indeed fortunate for us that the children's social worker from the county effected Jenny's move home in advance of the state licensing procedures.

Another significant issue was preparing our home for Jenny. Suzanne and I lived in a comfortable but modest two-bedroom condominium a few minutes northeast of downtown Los Angeles. A winding driveway led to our garage on ground level, along with the living room, den, dining room, kitchen, and a half bath. Downstairs were two bedrooms and two baths below ground level. The side of our unit opposite the garage looked out into a steep canyon. Although the unit was anchored on bedrock, it was set against a steep hill, with the driveway behind it at the upper, ground level. Off the living room was a small balcony with a superb view looking south.

We had the same problem many of our neighbors had—little extra space, with the only real storage area being the garage. Our fully carpeted house was packed with furniture, including the three terrariums for my lizards, one of which was eight feet long with a three-hundred-gallon capacity. The second, smaller bedroom, which I had been using for a den and which needed to be converted into Jenny's room, was loaded to capacity, including the terrariums. I did not see how the problem could be solved until Suzanne suggested that we would park our cars on the street and use the garage for my den. The street was not particularly safe for cars, given the vandalism and thefts, and in addition, this created some inconvenience, since parking on the street meant walking several hundred feet to the condo. However, we made the best of it.

I cleaned the garage thoroughly and reorganized its contents. I disconnected the electric door opener, locked and barred the door, and insulated the cracks and vents. The final arrangement was quite spacious, and included a large throw rug, the terrariums, and all the rest of the den furniture, including a television. It was a little dark during the day, but at night, with the lamps I had placed, it was quite cozy.

The lizards thrived on heat, so I was not concerned about high temperatures. At night, if it got too cool, the lizards had their electric hot rocks, and, I placed a couple of space heaters about for cold weather so I could adequately control the environment in the garage and keep the reptiles healthy. Also, from early morning until the middle of the evening, each terrarium ran its own set of incandescent and full-spectrum lights, all of which I had put on automatic timers. Having seen to the happiness and comfort of the reptiles and myself, I could now turn to Jenny's room.

In Jenny's room, we cleaned the carpeting, painted the walls, added some nice wallpaper bordering, and had new window curtains made. We bought a beautiful, bright red metal crib with high sides (one of which could be raised and lowered), which after a month or so we placed against a different wall to prevent a draft on Jenny and to avoid tripping over the pump stands at night. (How happy it made me to go shopping for Jenny's crib with Suzanne, since it symbolized her homecoming. On a traumatic but amusing note, this was also my initiation into the price of children's furniture!) There was also an attractive sofa bed, which we had had recovered earlier, shelves for toys and books, a nightstand, lamps, and plenty of space for Jenny's dresser and toy box, which would stay at the hospital until just before the move. There was room left over for the pumps, stands, medical supplies, and a small refrigerator for feedings. The finished product was beautiful—a perfect room for a two-year-old girl—warm, bright, and cozy, with plenty of closet space for Jenny's clothes. This room totally changed the character of our house; it made it into a home, in which would live with us the most wonderful little being I had ever known.

Other important issues were addressed to ensure compliance with the licensing requirements and to protect Jenny in our home. Medicines and other dangers were put out of reach. A retractable gate was placed at the top of the stairs, and we assembled a proper first aid kit.

The issue of day care for Jenny was critical, and it weighed heavily on us. Originally, Suzanne and I had envisioned in-home care—someone qualified and medically trainable coming to the house five days a week. But as time passed, we determined that, even though all of Jenny's medical equipment and supplies would be paid for from other sources, the monthly check that we would receive for Jennifer's various other needs would fall short of paying for in-home care. Without an alternative, we did not see how we could bring Jennifer home. Thus, the idea of traditional day care surfaced. Everyone involved, including the medical social workers, thought that this would be a viable idea, and good for Jennifer's social development. Suzanne and I agreed, but where were we going to find an agency within reasonable distance with the exceptional staff who would be both capable and willing to take care of a child like Jennifer?

I think that forces beyond the ordinary were working for us. After Suzanne and I had wrestled with this problem for a while, a colleague of Suzanne's at Huntington told her about All Saints Children's Center in Pasadena. This outstanding church-affiliated facility, one of the best of its kind in the Los Angeles area, was only a few minutes from the hospital. Its staff was highly trained, well-credentialed, managed by a lady who was thoroughly professional, and, to our great relief, willing to take Jenny. Inquiries were made to the Center from various sides, and after thoughtful consideration—and some real soul-searching—the management and staff decided that taking Jenny was something that they should do, and something that they wanted to do. Jenny would be the first child with unusual medical problems to be accepted by the Center.

Suzanne and I began to take her to the Center for short periods prior to her moving home. Jenny became gradually accustomed to the routine of going there and got to know the staff and kids, and the staff got to know Jenny and became familiar with her special medical needs. Suzanne was often able to take Jenny over from the hospital on predetermined days. At first, Suzanne stayed with her. A little later, she would leave Jenny there with the staff for longer periods until she was comfortable staying for several hours. This would make it possible for Jenny to go to the Center full-time, with ease, starting on the Monday following her first weekend home with us. The staff was wonderful—caring, patient, and interested. Jenny grew to love going; and, I think, she came to love some of the staff. I know they loved her.

Just prior to Jenny's move home, the staff at All Saints Children's Center made a videotape of Suzanne and Jenny at the Center. In this instructional video, which the Center kept and copies of which are now in my possession, Suzanne went step-by-step through the various procedures that the staff would have to learn: cleaning the colostomy site and changing the bag; cleaning and dressing the gastrostomy site and emptying that bag; and, ensuring that Jenny's Broviac catheter was kept clean, safe, and securely taped to her skin inside her clothing. We provided the Center with a box containing all the various kinds of medical supplies that the staff would need for Jenny, and we replenished it periodically.

By the time Jenny came to live with us, Suzanne and I had both been trained and certified as qualified in all the areas relevant to her care.

Finally, during the weeks prior to bringing Jenny home to live with us, Suzanne and I prepared ourselves physically, emotionally, and spiritually, as individuals and as a married couple, for the impact that the responsibility of caring for Jennifer would have upon us. Although Suzanne and I had many similar interests in music, literature, art, and aesthetic issues, we were different in terms of temperament and background. Although we were both spiritually minded, Suzanne had come to embrace the Catholic faith, whereas my philosophical outlook was Eastern and deeply influenced by Hindu and Buddhist teachings.

While we were preparing to bring Jenny home, I was doing work as a contracts administrator for a consulting firm in Los Angeles. My background included extensive training and work as a professional classical pianist. Suzanne was in nursing management and she was an avid supporter of the arts who had experience in commercial interior design. After we were married in August 1981, Suzanne and I operated a small consulting practice in interior design. Eventually, she returned to nursing. Before meeting Suzanne, I had published a book in the music field, and after we were married I finished a manuscript on metaphysics, which was finally published by Galde Press in 1996. I fell into my current field only after sampling a number of other things, including real estate and sales work, none of which suited my temperament.

Suzanne and I had a serious talk one night, about two or three weeks after I had met Jenny. Each of us acknowledged to each other for the first time that the question of how long Jenny might live had no answer. And although we were to discuss this subject with many people, including Dr. Laurance, over the coming weeks, nothing could be known for certain. Unquestionably, the technology used to feed Jenny had not been intended to replace entirely a normal manner of eating, at least not for a period of years or an average lifetime; and, there were side effects, some known, others perhaps not. There were serious medical issues. Whereas the potential dangers were not fully evident to me for many months, Suzanne, given her medical background, was more informed than I was, and more troubled. Dr. Laurance was optimistic about Jenny's future; Suzanne and I chose to be as well.

Nevertheless, we admitted that Jenny could die at any time—in a year, a month, or a week. Therefore, we asked ourselves in earnest if, given the possibility that Jenny might die in a short time, or if in fact we knew that Jenny would die in a short time, would we feel differently about becoming so deeply committed to her and bringing her home? My answer was immediate and unequivocal. It required no reflection. Even if I were to learn that Jenny would have only a day or even an hour to live in our home as our child, I was resolved to giving her that day or that hour. In my mind and heart, Jennifer was my child. My love for her was such that any course of action other than bringing her home was unthinkable. Something deep in my soul had made a commitment even before I had met her, and after the first couple of days of being with her I was utterly beyond changing my mind. Suzanne agreed that she was also committed, regardless of what might come to pass.

As the date of Jennifer's move home came closer Suzanne began expressing some conflicts about her ability to commit totally to taking care of Jenny, and this created a profound inner turmoil for her. It also caused me deep concern. After much soul-searching and an interview with her pastor, Suzanne expressed to me again her commitment to taking Jenny. I sensed, however, that she remained troubled; and, since her state of mind and ability to see this through, in addition to affecting her, had a potentially enormous affect upon Jenny and me, I could only hope that she would find the strength to remain firm.

Sometime within a few weeks before Jenny was to move home with us, I got word that Jenny's biological father, the gang member who had quickly deserted Jenny and Rosa shortly after Jenny's birth and was never heard from again, had heard that Jenny was going to be our foster daughter and was making noises to the effect that he was not going to allow his daughter to be raised by any white family. Shortly after hearing this news, I had the opportunity to share it with Fran, the medical social worker at Huntington. I also told her, quite matter-of-factly, that if he ever tried to come between Jenny and me, or threatened us in any way, I would kill him. And, I explained to her exactly how I would do it and get away with it. Soon after that, Father Toni, one of the priests from Suzanne's church, came by Huntington to visit us or to confer some kind of blessing on Jenny. At any rate, although I do not remember why, I chose that occasion to tell him the same thing that I had told Fran. Although he actually said nothing in response and did not seem especially upset by my remarks, I noted surprise in his eyes. It occurred to me later that my statement had been so direct that he could think of nothing to say. Perhaps, I thought, it was not that common, as a priest, to hear someone make death threats. At any rate, I was not about to let some irresponsible gang member, the very thought of whom I despised, threaten my relationship with Jennifer. He did not know it, but by shooting off his mouth he was walking into a minefield. He did turn out to be all mouth, and made no subsequent attempts to interfere.

On February 16, 1991, just six days before Jenny was to move home with us, I had to put one of my lizards to sleep. By that time I had accumulated an over-ambitious collection of reptiles. In July 1989, I got the urge to get a lizard. Thus, I bought Rima, a female Chilean collared lizard a few inches in length, and installed her in a modest but comfortable terrarium, which I soon upgraded to a 40-gallon one. In October 1989, I got a companion for Rima, a male Chilean collared lizard whom I named Brahma, and who lived with her. Then, in February 1990, I fell in love with iguanas, in spite of knowing how much they grew, purchased a sixty-gallon tank, and bought a baby iguana (sex unknown, but assumed to be male), whom I called Negoya. I nursed his bruised nose back to health (a malady common in lizards who continually bump head-first into the glass sides of tanks) by applying salves and giving him injections of antibiotics.

In a short time I saw that Negoya would quickly outgrow his tank, and unwilling to have him cramped, I ordered a custom-made, three-hundred-gallon terrarium, eight feet in length, which, like my others, I outfitted handsomely. After installing Negoya in his new home, I found myself left with an unoccupied sixty-gallon tank and, instead of exercising good sense and limiting my reptile collection, I gave in to my compulsion to fill it with something. In July 1990, I bought two Egyptian agamas, whom I named Ananda and Maya. Thus, I had five lizards in three terrariums, totaling four hundred gallons. The iguana ate fruits and vegetables, but the others were insectivorous, so in addition to purchasing crickets and worms weekly at the pet store, I would catch butterflies, caterpillars, and small spiders for them. Combined with keeping their tanks clean, this became quite a responsibility.

Then, in February 1991, Brahma got sick. He ate and drank little, started losing weight, became aggressive, and began to lose his motor coordination. Most vets knew little about reptiles, and even the ones who specialize do not know a lot about obscure ailments and the methods for treating them, especially when it came to the smaller lizards. Thus, I did the best I could by following their advice and by employing the things I had read. When it became apparent that Brahma had stopped eating entirely, I fed him water with a medicine dropper with limited success, and tried to entice him into taking a cricket or worm offered with tweezers, but to no avail. After that, for several days, I would soak him in a solution of warm water and honey, in an effort to offer him some nourishment and hydration.

When it became clear that my efforts were not going to help, and that he was dying and uncomfortable, I decided to put him to sleep. In the wild, the law of survival would have quickly taken care of the matter, but in captivity, he could linger for a long time, which would be unkind to allow. Thus, reluctantly and sadly, but for his own sake, I decided that I had to bring Brahma's life to an end. I placed him in a large plastic container with plenty of air, put on the lid, and set it in the freezer portion of the refrigerator. Being cold-blooded, reptiles do not shiver and shake, as would mammals under similar circumstances, in an effort to maintain their body temperature. The metabolisms of reptiles are governed solely by their environments. Therefore, when Brahma was placed in the freezer, his body temperature quickly dropped, he went to sleep painlessly, and died.

I removed his frozen body a few hours later. I felt deeply sad and touched with compassion at the sight of his small, still form. Life seemed so fragile and so easily lost. Indeed, he was a reptile, and far from having any feelings for me. But nevertheless, the death of this little creature that I had cared for, and the fact that I had had to be the one to end his life, caused me heartache. I took his body outside and, in the little landscaped area just outside the front door, I dug a grave for him. Now, even years later, I rarely walk by this spot without remembering that he is there.

The reason that I mention Brahma's death is that, given that it was so near to the time Jenny was to come home, I felt a little superstitious. I was uncomfortable that this loss had occurred just before Jenny was to leave the hospital. To say that it seemed like a bad omen is perhaps overstating it; but it certainly was not a good one. I did not dwell on it, but I clearly remember how I felt at the time. At any rate, wherever his feisty little spirit was, I hoped that he was happy, perhaps in some reptile paradise, sunning himself on a hot rock and snapping at insects.

Just four days before Jenny was to come home, I went to the pet store and bought another Chilean collared lizard as a companion for Rima—this time a female, Alexandra.

Because of my love for animals and my experiences in caring for them, I have come to revere the teachings of Buddha. Unlike Christianity, which does not even acknowledge doctrinally that animals have souls—which of course they do—the Buddhist philosophy teaches the love for, and redemption of, all creatures. Thus, Buddha, in his infinite compassion, pledged himself not only to come into incarnation again and again for mankind, but for all living things. I remember this when I contemplate the infinite variety of life, and I am especially mindful of it at those times when I witness the death of some small, fragile creature like little Brahma.

Jenny Comes Home

Hush little baby,
Don't you cry...

Medical Procedures and Problem-Solving

On Thursday, February 21, 1991, all the paperwork got signed and Suzanne and I officially became Jennifer's foster parents. The following day, Jenny moved out of Huntington for good and came home to live with Suzanne and me. It was one of the happiest, most exciting, and apprehensive days of my life. All the medical equipment and supplies were in place, and only a few of Jenny's personal belongings remained at the hospital. I had taken the day off from work and met late in the morning at our home with a representative from the company that would be supplying us with Jenny's pumps. She provided me with a hurried orientation regarding their programming and operation, which would later prove to be a disadvantage.

Later, I arrived at the hospital full of anticipation and exhilaration, and met Suzanne and Jenny. The staff of the pediatric ward gave a wonderful going-home party for Jennifer in the play room, and many of the staff from all over the hospital stopped in. There were balloons, cake, and refreshments, and Jenny received many wonderful gifts and wishes of good luck. I have several snapshots in Jennifer's photo album of the party, and in every case Jenny looks a little dubious. It was typical of her to be reticent around large, noisy gatherings of people, even when the atmosphere was a festive one. Even at this party, where she was the center of attention, or perhaps *because* she was the center of attention, she had a serious look on her little face most of the time. Much later, I was glad to see some snapshots taken by others in which she was smiling radiantly.

After the party, Suzanne, Jenny, and I said good-by to everyone, collected the rest of Jenny's things, and headed to our place. Also in Jenny's photo album are some wonderful photos of her in her room at home that afternoon. She is wearing her dark blue, white polka-dot dress, standing in the center of the room, or sitting on the little red wooden baby chair that I gave her, which had been mine as a child. She is looking up at the camera, beaming from ear to ear, surrounded by armies of stuffed animals, dolls, toys, and books; on one side of the room is her new bright-red crib, and on the other the sofa bed and her three little cardboard dressers that we brought home from the hospital.

Although, as I have said, Jenny loved many people at the hospital and was deeply loved and cared for by the staff, I was amazed that, from that afternoon forward, she never again mentioned the hospital. During her first night at home, she lay down in her crib and went to sleep as if she had done so every night of her life. I was deeply relieved that Jenny experienced no separation anxiety whatever after she left Huntington, and I can only believe that this was so because she knew how much Suzanne and I loved her and that she belonged there with us. Never a night passed but that I looked into Jenny's crib with wonder and happiness, awed by the realization that this sleeping child was now my daughter.

Jenny's first couple of weeks at home were nerve-racking for Suzanne and me—obviously not because we did not love Jenny or want her there, but, to put it simply, because we were scared. Here, in our home, was a medically fragile little girl, just over two and a half years old, who did not eat, whose survival depended on a battery of medical equipment and supplies, and who, until recently, had depended upon a large hospital staff to take care of her. Suzanne and I knew that Jenny's happiness, health, and survival depended upon our meticulous care, and that mistakes could make her critically ill or even kill her.

In the beginning, the programming and operation of the three pumps that fed Jenny nightly and the use all of the ancillary tubing and supplies were intimidating. I cannot forget the first night Suzanne and I pieced together the three sets of tubing for the bags of total parenteral nutrition (TPN), liquids, and saline solution, attached them to the bags, got all the tubing routed into one main line, ran each line through its respective pump, and attached the main line to Jennifer's Broviac catheter. The instructions I had received that afternoon now seemed vague, and not to have addressed certain problems at all. Although I was somewhat familiar with the system that had been used in the hospital, I had never done it from start to finish, and besides, the pumps designed for home use operated differently.

Suzanne and I found ourselves in a state which I would best describe as controlled panic, and because of this more than anything else we were ready to go for each other's throats. Jenny remained absolutely calm throughout the affair, in the total faith that we knew exactly what we were doing. We did have in our possession the phone number to a kind of assistance hotline, but we would come to discover that help was often obtained only after waiting for a call back from whatever individual was on duty and subsequently reached that night; and besides, it was very confusing to try to understand telephone instructions with one's hands full of tubing and attachments, parts of which must be kept absolutely sterile in order to prevent contamination and its very serious consequences.

Jenny in polka-dot dress

We got through that first night and Jenny slept like a log. After a few nights, the procedure became easier, and in a short time it was automatic, except that doing the setup required one always to be careful to avoid dangerous mistakes. Suzanne would often assist me in attaching the line to Jenny's Broviac catheter, which was more easily done by two people than one. Then Suzanne would usually read Jenny a bedtime story, after which I would come back and lie on the floor next to Jenny's crib and hold her hand through the bars until she fell asleep. After some weeks had passed, I got into the habit of doing most of the setup right after coming home from work, so that all that needed to be done at Jenny's bedtime was hook her up and turn on the pumps.

One of the biggest problems in the beginning was the pumps, which were programmed to sound a highly audible alarm in case of problems or malfunctions. The alarm also sounded to indicate when the programmed feeding cycles were completed. From the first night Jenny slept at home, and for at least two or three weeks thereafter, the alarms went off constantly during the night because of air bubbles in the lines. By "constantly," I mean five, ten, even fifteen times each night. For me, an hour or two of uninterrupted sleep got to be a real luxury. Fortunately for Jenny, who had learned to sleep soundly through all kinds of nocturnal noises at the hospital, she was never awakened when the alarms were activated.

If a bubble of air, other than a very small one, were to get through Jennifer's Broviac catheter and into her bloodsteam, the results could be extremely painful or even fatal. Therefore, if any air bubbles formed in an upper line above where it came into contact with the pump, they would be detected and blocked from further passage when they reached a sensory membrane on the exterior of the pump over which the line was clamped. When the lines were set up at night, it was critical to make certain, through bleeding the lines, that no air bubbles were present anywhere in the lines, either between the points where they were connected to the bags of TPN, lipids, and saline solution which hung on hooks above the pumps, down to the pumps themselves, or between the pumps and the point at which the lines were connected with Jennifer's Broviac catheter.

During the period when Jenny first came home, although we always made certain that the lines were initially clear of air each night, any or all of the three pumps would sound their alarms repeatedly during the night. I would get up, turn off the alarms, clear the lines of bubbles, restart the pumps, and go back to bed. Thirty minutes, an hour, two hours later, an alarm would go off again—night after night. Finally, after several conversations over many days with advisors from the company providing the pumps, we were informed that air bubbles often formed in the various bags of liquids as they warmed up to room temperature. Until use, all of the feedings were kept in a small refrigerator in Jenny's room. We were therefore advised, finally, that it was normal and safe to remove a bag each of the TPN, lipids, and saline solution from the refrigerator each morning and let them warm up during the day for use that evening. Thus, by evening, all of the carbonation processes had exhausted themselves and the bubbles had dissipated. When we adopted that practice, the problem of alarms going off all night was almost completely alleviated, except for an occasional uncooperative bubble.

We programmed the pumps to deliver the various feeding solutions into Jennifer's system based on the number of cubic centimeters of feedings and the number of hours over which the feedings were to be pumped. The pumps automatically computed the rates. Depending on when we started the pumps at night, Jennifer's feedings were normally finished around 6:30 or 7:00 o'clock the following morning, usually simultaneously or within a minute or two of each other, at which time Suzanne or I would get up and turn off the alarms. We then had the option of going through the procedure of disconnecting Jennifer at that time, or going back to bed and disconnecting her later, when she awakened and was ready to get out of bed.

An episode related to Jenny's lines occurred during the first few days she was home that really frightened us because, had we not become aware of the problem in time and interceded, the consequences could have been fatal. The lines of flexible plastic tubing that delivered Jenny her feedings had several junctures at which they were connected to something else. A separate line was connected to each of the three bags of TPN, lipids, and saline solution. Each of these three lines then had to be attached to a connecting piece that routed all three formulas into a single line, which was then joined with the tip of Jenny's Broviac catheter. We worked for a long time with a system that required us to route two of the lines together and then route that joined line and the remaining line into a single conduit, since the juncture apparatus was designed to connect only two lines, rather than three, to the single tube leading to the Broviac catheter. Eventually, we were able to order a three-pronged juncture piece that simplified things. Some of the tubing required extender lines in order to give Jenny enough freedom of movement in her crib. I usually checked on her during the night because she would become completely entangled in the lines as she shifted and rolled over in her sleep, something which was always of concern to me, but completely unavoidable.

At the beginning, all of the lines delivered to us were equipped at their ends with a device that permitted us to screw the tubing tightly together at junctures—all except one line that was used for one of the three formulas. For some reason, this line did not have the screw-type end; rather, it was fitted with an open-ended, hard plastic tip that was meant to be jammed tightly into the tip of the next line—a kind of funnel arrangement, and one we had seen used often in the hospital.

One night soon after Jenny came home, we hooked her up as usual, put her to bed, and turned out the lights in her room. Later in the evening before Suzanne and I went to bed, Suzanne's intuition prompted her to take a glance into Jenny's room, whereupon she noticed a dark spot on Jenny's bedding. Suzanne turned on the lights to discover to her deep dismay that the dark spot was a combination of formula and blood. The funnel-type connection had come apart. Formula was being pumped onto Jenny's bedding, and in addition, blood was slowly seeping from the Broviac catheter in her chest out into the blankets and sheets. I heard Suzanne's cry of alarm and came at once.

The immediate problem was easily corrected by reconnecting the lines. Fortunately, Suzanne had discovered the situation early in the evening, so no real harm was done. But Jenny could have bled to death that night if the problem had remained undetected. In addition to being appalled, I was furious at what seemed to me to be the stupidity of such an equipment design flaw. To prevent any possibility of such a thing happening again, I heavily taped all of the connections along the lines, including the screw-type ones, every night. In addition, I always made sure that, besides being heavily taped, the funnel-type connection was jammed as tightly as possible into the next line. Even after I was eventually able to procure all lines with the screw-type connections, I never abandoned the practice of taping them. The taping also helped to ensure that Jenny would not disconnect something by playing with it. We were adamant in training her not to tamper with the lines and equipment, and she really seemed to understand the seriousness of the situation and to respond to our direction most of the time.

One other issue of special concern was the connection of the line to the end of Jenny's Broviac catheter. In the beginning, this was done by attaching the line and the catheter with a screw-type device like the ones used on other parts of the tubing. The only problem was that this meant unscrewing and removing a cap on the end of Jennifer's Broviac catheter before the screw-type end of the feeding line could be attached. First, it was necessary to make absolutely certain that there was no air in the end of the line before it was screwed onto the Broviac catheter. Second, unscrewing the tip of the Broviac catheter meant a brief but unavoidable exposure of the end and interior of the catheter to the air, and therefore the possibility of contamination from airborne viruses and bacteria.

Eventually, we discovered and employed a better procedure for connecting Jenny's Broviac catheter with the feeding line. Her Broviac catheter was fitted with a cap that had a small, tough membrane that could be punctured with a hypodermic needle. The end of Jenny's feeding line was then fitted each night with a screw-on hypodermic needle, which was then inserted through the membrane on the tip of her Broviac catheter. Once connected, the needle and Broviac catheter were held together by a kind of cradling device made of lightweight plastic. Although this device seemed a bit clumsy at first, we got used to it, and it offered a distinct advantage in that Jenny's Broviac catheter was not exposed to contamination on a nightly basis. Each night, before inserting the hypodermic needle, we carefully disinfected the membrane with alcohol. The same membrane-type cap could be used many times before being replaced.

With either method of attaching the line to the Broviac catheter—screw cap or hypodermic needle—it was, as I have said, absolutely necessary first to purge the lines of any air. After setting up the lines and clearing them of any detectable bubbles, the pumps were actually turned on just prior to attaching the main line to Jenny's Broviac catheter. Once the formula was seen to begin slowly dripping from the end of the main line (either from the screw cap or from the needle, depending on the type of apparatus used), it was safe to make the connection.

This connection procedure required planning, timing, mental concentration, and physical coordination. It was easier, of course, with two people working together. However, one person could do it alone, and in time I got quite good at it. Essentially, if one worked alone, while making sure to keep Jenny quiet and still, one would have to hold both the Broviac catheter and the end of the main line in one hand, making sure not to contaminate them by touching anything, while working quickly with the free hand to activate all three pumps one after the other. Then, once the main line began dripping from the end, the connection could be made. Speed was essential, in that it minimized the danger of anything becoming contaminated. With practice, Jenny became quite skilled and cooperative at holding her own Broviac catheter without contaminating it, up until the moment of connection. In fact, she was enthusiastic about participating.

After the connection between the main line and the Broviac catheter had been made, it was taped heavily and securely, particularly in the case of the needle and cradle arrangement, since only proper cradling of the needle prevented it from coming out of the membrane on the catheter. If the needle were to fall out, no harm would come to Jenny, but feeding would be wasted, and a new needle would have to be attached in order to avoid the danger of contamination through rein-serting the used one. Conscientious taping of this connection was also paramount since, despite our admonitions to her, Jennifer occasionally got the idea in her head to play with this connection or partially unwrap the tape.

Finally, with respect to the Broviac cather, the cap with the membrane was preferable because, when Jenny was sick, it permitted us to administer antibiotics hypodermically at home, without using a vein, and avoiding daily trips to the doc-tor's office. An antibiotic administered through, for example, a shot in the arm, is distributed gradually thoughout the body. However, since the membrane on the tip of the Broviac catheter led through nine or ten inches of tubing directly to Jenny's heart, any antibiotics administered by this method had to be injected very slowly, timed over several minutes, with great care and control, in order to avoid suddenly flooding her heart, and consequently her circulatory system, with the antibiotic and thereby causing a severe or possibly fatal reaction.

Jenny's medical supplies were delivered weekly. I kept a careful inventory and made sure we had enough of everything. Jennifer experienced deep delight and satisfaction in helping me unpack and organize these supplies. I had to make sure that she did not take anything sterile—which was most everything—out of its packaging. Home supplies (in addition to the refrigerator and three pumps, which were permanent) included bags of TPN, lipids, and saline solution; numerous sets of tubing and attachments; hypodermic needles and syringes; Broviac catheter caps; gastrostomy tubes; colostomy bags; spray adhesive; special medicinal sur-gical tape and other types of tape; gauze; surgical gloves; iodine swabs; and so on. Suzanne and I, of course, never could have afforded any of this; vendors were paid by the state. The annual cost for the rental of Jennifer's home medical equip-ment and the purchase of her medical supplies was about $180,000. Costs for doctor and hospital visits, drugs, and so on, were in addition to this, and could eas-ily bring the total to $250,000 a year.

I have been asked if I thought such expenses were justifiable. I was called upon to weigh Jenny's medical needs and her very life against the huge sums of taxpayer money expended to support her through Medicare, Medi-Cal, and so on, especially in light of all the "needy children in the world, and other social prob-lems." How could I possibly respond to this, except to hope that anyone asking such a question might one day have occasion to look deeply into the eyes and soul of some beautiful, needy child, and experience what I felt when I looked at Jenny? When I ponder the incalculable, heartbreaking waste of money in this government on things beyond absurdity, how can I take anyone seriously who asked if I thought Jennifer's life could be weighed in dollars?

Another problem that quickly surfaced after getting Jenny home was her colostomy bag. It would fall off up to several times a day. Each time this happened, a new bag would have to be used. I had to go through a considerable amount of bureaucratic red tape several times to get our allotment of colostomy bags increased sufficiently to keep pace with Jenny's needs. Having once fallen off, a bag could not be reused, since the seal portion of the old bag had lost its adhesive properties. In order to affix a new bag to Jenny's colostomy site, which was on her left side, a few inches from and level with her naval, she had to be cleaned up, since the old seal usually leaked some of the contents of the bag. In addition to thoroughly cleaning the area around her colostomy so that a new bag would adhere, the dressing around her gastrostomy site would often have to be changed, and sometimes a whole new set of clothing would be required. For obvious reasons, this was problematic if we were out in the car or in public. At home, there was the probability that some of the bag's contents would spill onto furniture and carpeting.

I recognized that Jennifer's colostomy bag fell off for several reasons. She was far more active at home than she had been in the hospital. She was going to parks, restaurants, stores, and day care; she was running, jumping, and clambering up on furniture—things that normal children do. In addition to the moving and twisting about, she was sweating more. Also, whether a medical oversight, or out of some medical necessity I did not understand, the site of her gastrostomy was only a few inches from her colostomy, so that the inevitable leakage of bile from her stomach out onto her skin and into her gastrostomy dressings eventually found its way under the seal on the colostomy bag.

The acidic stomach bile did quick work on the adhesive seal, and the resulting mess was a foregone conclusion. For this reason, Suzanne and I tried to empty the bag into which the bile drained as often as necessary. Otherwise, it would become full, the tube from Jenny's stomach would back up, and the bile would spill out onto her skin and dressings. We also strongly encouraged the staff at her day-care center to be vigilant about this, since draining a gastrostomy bag was a lot easier and less time-consuming than dealing with a broken colostomy seal. Finally, I felt that the seals on Jennifer's colostomy bags were the wrong shape and that the adhesive surfaces were not large enough.

Fortunately, the passage of time proved all the problems with colostomy bags to be correctable. This was fortunate indeed because, in addition to the time and physical inconvenience involved in getting Jenny reorganized several times a day, I would on occasion experience an agonizing sense of desperation, a fear that I might be facing problems that had no solutions, that we were destined to live like this forever. I was commited to doing that, if necessary, but was determined that, if these problems had solutions, I would find them. I must say that it was the love which Jennifer was capable of inspiring, and giving, that enabled me to maintain an attitude that expressed itself in terms of determining how a problem could be solved and that it must have an answer, rather than whether or not it could be solved. The irrevocable bond that I felt with my daughter demanded and inspired total commitment, and provided me with the necessary drive to solve these kinds of problems.

One day, Suzanne found herself discussing the colostomy bag problem with a staff person at Huntington. We were given some sample bags that worked far better than the ones we had been using, and which we were able to order in place of the old bags. The new bags had larger, differently shaped seals that were far more effective. Even if some bile from the gastrostomy site did seep under the new bag's seal, it held much longer because it was larger. Also, we were able to obtain a special spray adhesive that was applied to the already sticky surface of the bag's seal before placement. The result was that Jennifer could wear a bag far longer. With practice, Suzanne and I refined our techniques of placing the bag so that it needed to be replaced only once or, at the most, twice a day. Sometimes, Jenny even got through the whole day on one bag. Of course, the new bag also made life much easier for Jennifer and for the staff at the day-care center. Naturally, Jenny was always given a fresh colostomy bag after her bath at night, before going to bed. Usually, but not always, the bag was replaced in the morning.

The gastrostomy bag, which collected bile and other liquids that drained through the tube inserted into Jenny's stomach, was little problem. Neither the colostomy nor the gastrostomy site were of concern in terms of infections. The tube from Jennifer's stomach to the gastrostomy bag was only about a foot long, so the bag was pinned either at full length or folded in half inside of her dress, where it was not visible. Jennifer almost always wore dresses rather than pants or shorts, since access to the bag was more difficult with pants. Also, when tucked or pinned inside of pants, the bag created a bulge and was generally just more troublesome.

The gastrostomy bag and tube were very durable, and could be cleaned and reused for some time. The only catch with the gastrostomy bag was that it had to be drained frequently—a simple procedure. Regular emptying of the gastrostomy bag was necessary for two reasons. First, most of the bile that Jennifer's stomach produced had no place to go. If it could not drain, she would throw it up—something she often did and which seemed to trouble her very little. The bile had no unpleasant odor. Second, Jenny drank a fair amount of water and fluids during the day, especially when it was hot. Only a portion of what she drank was absorbed through her stomach or got through into her intestines. The rest drained readily into the colostomy bag, making it necessary to empty it several times daily. The bag had a spigot-like feature which made emptying easy—in fact, a little too easy for Jenny, so we usually taped the spigot so that she would not play with it.

The dressings around Jenny's gastrostomy site were more problematic and required some skill and practice in order to be done effectively. Out of necessity, Suzanne and I refined the procedures over time, thereby making Jenny's life and ours more pleasant. The dressings consisted of a medicinal ointment, absorbent gauze, special surgical tape which did not damage the skin over long use, and a small piece of adhesive material which was placed around the gastrostomy site. In addition to damaging the seal on Jennifer's colostomy bag, the excess bile that inevitably leaked out around the gastrostomy tube that was inserted into her stomach irritated and burned her skin, soaked the gauze, loosened the tape, and soiled her clothing.

Before the application of a fresh dressing to Jenny's gastrostomy site, which was done in the morning, at bedtime, and any other time during the day that was necessary, the skin around the site was gently but thoroughly cleaned and dried. A medicinal ointment was often applied to her skin, especially at bedtime, and whenever any signs of irritation or blistering from bile were evident. Then, a two-by-two-inch square would be cut from a larger piece of flexible material similar in composition to Jenny's colostomy seal, one side of which had adhesive properties. We would slit this small piece and cut out a small hole in the center, so that the square could be slipped around the gastrostomy tube and applied to the skin, leaving no skin exposed around the site to prevent irritation from bile. Next, absorbent gauze was applied around the site to soak up bile. Suzanne developed a technique of rolling up the gauze which, in addition to maximizing its absorbancy, enabled it to add stability to the gastrostomy tube at the entry site. Finally, surgical tape was liberally and strategically applied to the gauze so that it would stay securely in place, and to the gastrostomy tube so that it would not easily be dislodged from Jenny's stomach. If the dressings were applied properly, and the gastrostomy bag drained regularly, the dressings might last the whole day or require only one changing.

If the gastrostomy tube was not securely taped to Jenny's skin, it could be pulled out of her stomach. The mushroom tip, although expanded once inside the stomach, was flexible enough so that it could be inserted and removed with relative ease. Therefore, once in a while, the tube would accidentally come out. Perhaps the tape would come loose, or she would catch the tube on something in the play yard at day care. When this happened, the tube had to be reinserted and new dressings applied. Reinserting the tube was simple, but it required training and great care. Therefore, Suzanne and I were the only ones who reinserted the tube. If the tube should become dislodged at day care—something that happened very rarely—Suzanne would be called at Huntington, which, again fortunately, was only a few minutes drive from the day-care center, and she would drive over and reinsert the tube.

To reinsert the tube into Jenny's stomach, the rounded end of a slender surgical steel device several inches long had to be inserted into the mushroom tip on the end of the tube. The steel device was used to stretch the end of the tube and the mushroom tip, elongating and narrowing them. The tube, with the steel device inside the mushroom tip, was then slowly and carefully inserted through the opening of Jenny's skin and pushed directly into her stomach. When the steel device was slid out, the mushroom tip automatically expanded. The trick was to know how far to insert the steel device into the stomach. If it were pushed in too far, the stomach wall could be damaged or punctured. Naturally, this procedure, although simple and quick, required training, control, and common sense. Jenny was a real trooper—amazingly cooperative, understanding, and brave. She would lie still on her back, we would tell her to take a deep breath, and the procedure worked in a few seconds. For her, the gastrostomy tube and bag, like the Broviac catheter, seemed like a natural, more or less permanent part of her anatomy. When the gastrostomy tube occasionally fell out, it seemed to cause her some concern, and she was anxious to have it reinserted.

For the night, we devised a special arrangement to drain the bile and other liquids from Jenny's stomach, similar to what had been done at the hospital. Since Jennifer's system received almost all of its nourishment at night, in liquid form, while she slept, in addition to her bladder processing and passing a lot of urine, her stomach drained a large quantity of fluids. The daytime gastrostomy bag would not have been sufficient to hold all of it. Therefore, at night, after we put Jennifer in her crib, we removed the gastrostomy bag, attached an additional piece of tubing several feet in length to the short tube coming from her stomach, fed it through the vertical bars on the crib, and attached the other end of it to the inside of a baby bottle. The end of the tube was run through the nipple of the baby bottle and the tubing taped to the outside of the bottle to keep it in place. The nipple was slit sufficiently in order to prevent the buildup of air pressure inside the bottle, which would in turn cause the bile in the tube to back up. The bottle itself was then taped to the inside edge of a large plastic pan that was placed on the floor beside the crib. This way, anything that spilled or overflowed out of the bottle would not end up on the carpet. This arrangement worked very well, even when Jenny managed, as she often did, to get tangled up in the several feet of tubing.

In addition to the colostomy bag, and the gastrostomy tube and bag, there was the Broviac catheter. Although in some ways the easiest to take care of, the Broviac catheter was at the same time the most important feature—critically important—in terms of hygiene, and Jennifer's very existence. This thin piece of rubber tubing, one capped end of which extended eight or nine inches out of Jenny's chest, had been surgically implanted into her heart. Jennifer was completely dependent upon this device for her nourishment and hydration. Without it, she would die. I was unable to understand exactly how many access sites there were in the body for such a device. I did understand, however, that these sites were limited, that they wore out in time, and that, apparently, they could not be reused. Therefore, the care of the Broviac catheter and the access site in Jenny's chest were of paramount importance.

About every three days, after her nightly bath, we would have Jenny lie on her back while we cleaned the access site on her chest. Wearing surgical gloves, we would hold the Broviac catheter away from her skin, dip a sterile swab stick into a special antiseptic solution, and clean the access site and the surrounding area, using a circular motion, beginning at the site and working outward, and always being careful not to go backwards. Like all procedures with Jenny, this was done more easily by two people, but could be handled by one person provided that they were organized.

The caps for the tip of the Broviac catheter could be replaced as desired. Naturally, they came in sterile packaging. If the caps were the type that had a membrane, they were replaced on a fairly regular basis, perhaps every couple of weeks. The top of the cap and the membrane were disinfected nightly, prior to the puncturing of the membrane with the hypodermic needle that was connected to Jenny's feeding line. Jenny was never allowed to play with her Broviac catheter. It was almost the only thing that I would strongly scold her about—for her own sake. When Jenny was not connected to her feeding line, the Broviac catheter was always rolled up a time or two and securely taped to her skin.

In terms of hygiene, the Broviac catheter was by far the most sensitive issue. The area of Jenny's chest immediately around the site where the catheter had been inserted had to be kept clean and free of infection—thus, the disinfection procedure every few days. The other end of the catheter, that which was connected to Jenny's feeding line, was equally important, if not more so. One had to take great care when removing an old cap and replacing it with a new, sterile one. And, as I said, the membrane on the cap had to be thoroughly disinfected before being punctured with a sterile hypodermic syringe. We were advised to keep the Broviac catheter, especially the tip, out of Jenny's bathwater—a task easier said than done. Although we tried various techniques, nothing ever worked to our complete satisfaction. I suspect that one or two of Jenny's bouts with infections after coming to live with us were due to the Broviac catheter coming into contact with her dirty bathwater. Dr. Laurance did feel, however, that it was safe for Jenny to go into the swimming pool at our condominium complex, given the heavy amounts of chlorine in such pools.

Gradually, Suzanne and I made headway dealing with Jenny's medical equipment and supplies. In time, the teachers at her day-care center became comfortable and more adept with respect to the things they sometimes needed to do for her, which included cleaning Jenny up after things leaked, replacing colostomy bags, changing gastrostomy dressings, and emptying the gastrostomy bag regularly. Any time that Suzanne and I took Jenny on excursions, we were prepared for emergencies, because we carried a bag that contained towels, scissors, surgical tape, gauze, spray adhesive, and other supplies. To be caught unprepared away from home was to be avoided.

Taking care of Jenny required time and knowledge of many procedures, but things got easier. Problems were solved, fewer surprises and emergencies occurred, and Suzanne and I became seasoned and settled into a routine far different from the one we'd had before bringing Jenny home. Jenny was a joy. Everything about her was delightful. It was preferable, in my opinion, to dispose of a used colostomy bag or empty a gastrostomy bag than to change a diaper filled with excrement.

To see Jenny playing in the park or strolling down the sidewalk, one would never suspect that there was anything unusual about her. Her Broviac catheter, colostomy bag, and gastrostomy tube, bag, and dressings were undetectable under her dress. The only thing that one might occasionally notice would be the gastrostomy bag, if the bottom of it happened to be hanging a little below the hem of her dress. It used to amuse me to see the looks of interest and perplexity on people's faces when they would catch sight of the bag. Their attempts to be discreet were always a failure. If the bag had any bile in it—and it usually did—it would be light green or sometimes yellowish. I am sure people wondered what on earth it was.

Routines at Home

Jennifer not only looked normal, but came across as healthy, precocious, and exuberant. She was inquisitive, loving, and playful; she smiled and laughed, and had beautiful, deep, intelligent, sparkling eyes. Her hair, which was black and radiant, beautifully complemented her exquisite features and dark, glowing skin. When we were out in public, it was common for people to compliment Jenny on her exceptional beauty and radiance. Given her physical appearance and general demeanor, Jennifer's medical history would have shocked anyone who did not know her.

We had a full household when Jenny came to live with us, even though I had relocated my den out into the garage. In addition to Suzanne, Jenny, and me, there was Sebastian, the white male Manx cat; Sarada, the tortoise-shell female mixed-breed cat; Rima and Alexandra, the two Chilean collared lizards in a forty-gallon terrarium; Ananda and Maya, the two Egyptian agamas in a sixty-gallon terrarium; and Negoya, the iguana, in a three-hundred-gallon terrarium. (Thank God I had gotten rid of the gigantic, homemade bird feeder on the balcony long ago—a structure which attracted everything from mountain blue jays to migrating water fowl. The problem of bird excrement had gotten totally out of control.)

The lizards lived in their own worlds in the garage-become-den, so Jenny's only contact with them came from an occasional impulse of hers to watch the "lizzies" through the terrarium glass. The lizards would sit for long periods without moving; then, occasionally, one of them would make a sudden motion and startle Jennifer. Negoya, the iguana, who had grown to more than five feet in length from head to tip of tail, could be particularly startling when he made a violent move. Once in a while, Jenny would be standing in front of Negoya's tank or one of the smaller terrariums, and a lizard would unexpectedly come alive. Jennifer would instinctively jump back, look at me, and, usually with a smile on her face, say "Scare me, Daddy!"

Sarada and Sebastian (whom Jenny called "Bast") were not very available either—at least for handling by a three-year-old. Sebastian, a gentle and loving cat, was tolerant if he happened to come within Jenny's range, but he usually circumvented her to avoid the hair pulling. Sarada, on the other hand, whom I had had since before meeting Suzanne, was utterly intolerant, if not downright hostile, toward anyone but Suzanne and me. She did not like other people, and, during her six-month contact with Jenny, was aloof at best, and sometimes nasty. Fortunately, both cats, who spent all of their time indoors, were fixed and declawed. Sometimes at night, after Jenny had gone to bed, I would place Sebastian in the crib with her. He would sit for a short time, then leap out and exit before he could be recaptured.

After Jenny moved home, one of the routines that quickly became established was the weekend shopping trip to the grocery store and Price Club (which Suzanne joined so that we could buy diapers and other things in bulk and at large discounts), something that Jenny and Daddy did together. Jenny got into the shopping, and her company made the excursions fun instead of a dreaded chore. I had never enjoyed going to the grocery store, and venturing into the pandemonium of Price Club on a Saturday morning would have turned me into an animal were it not for the soothing effect Jenny had upon me. I felt a deep satisfaction in knowing that she got so much out of just doing things with me, in seeing that she felt included and important, and in observing her "seriousness."

Jenny would always sit in the cart, facing me in the child's seat, and together we would go down the aisles and select things we wanted. Nothing ever got put into the cart without first being handed off from me to Jenny. She was an integral part of the production line. At Price Club, she always became especially alert when we approached the section which she knew housed the large boxes of "baby diapers," as she called them, and she never failed to remind me to stock up on these.

Sometimes, we would be going down an aisle and she would spot something and point to it, having decided that we needed it, even though she often did not know what it was. And if we could use it at all, I gave it to her to put in the cart. I felt that this would really make her feel important. And she was. Children like to puncture plastic bags and soft containers with their fingers. This turned out to be especially problematic with items like dried beans or peas, trail mix, or pasta. After a couple of gentle reprimands, Jenny cooperated. At the checkout line, Jenny always took charge of loading our purchases onto the conveyer belt. I would either hand her the items first, or, especially as the cart got emptier and there was room, I would stand her inside of it and she would do the unloading herself. Then it was home to unpack.

At home, Jenny enjoyed stroller rides around the hilltop we lived on. I got a lot of exercise that way. Someone from Huntington had been kind enough to give us a nice stroller, as well as a high chair and a car seat (so that I only had to buy one car seat in order to have one in each car). However, the wheels on the stroller seemed to be designed to do everything imaginable except make it easy to push a child in the direction one wanted to go. I had a little more patience with the thing than Suzanne did, being more mechanically inclined and having the added advantage of more muscle power. Eventually, I concluded that all strollers, regardless of price or manufacturer, had wheels designed so as to be as unresponsive and as difficult to steer as possible. Nevertheless, Jenny, Suzanne, and I covered many miles doing laps around the summit of Monterey Hills, the neighborhood where we lived, observing other children in their strollers, people walking their dogs, and the little gardens of flowers ("fowers," to Jenny) that adorned each complex.

I gave Jenny a little, red, wooden chair that had been mine as a child. My parents kept it after I grew up, and at some point my mother gave it back to me. It was just Jenny's size, and I remember that she used to drag it around the house from place to place. Over the years, I have been tempted at times to repaint it, since it is fairly well scuffed up, but I have overcome the inclination, and it is obvious to me now that to have done any kind of refinishing would have marred its charm. Even today, the are a few reminders around the house that attest to the chair having been dragged past a particular piece of woodwork. As long as I live in the house, I will not remove the beloved traces of red paint left on one of the white, wooden doors below the sink in Jenny's bathroom—precious evidence that she really lived there and transformed our lives. Now, years later, the chair sits in my bedroom, and every time I look at it, I see it not as my chair, but as Jenny's. And, in my mind, it is a link between her childhood and mine. It is the only object I have that both of us used as children; therefore, it is very special to me—something unique, and deeply treasured—a symbol that reminds me I was once a child like Jenny, and that we both lived for a time in innocence.

After Jenny came to live with us, it was necessary for me to modify a few of my behaviors. Jenny noticed and, in some cases, picked up my undesirable traits. I am referring chiefly to my use of profanity, especially in the car, and my dislike of driving in general. Once I had realized that Jenny had absorbed two new words into her vocabulary, I corrected the situation. First, I completely stopped using the words, at least around her. Second, when I heard her use the words, I would not let on at all as if there were anything wrong, but rather immediately suggest a harmless substitute word. To my great relief, and Suzanne's, this approach was successful, and in a short time the use of the objectionable vocabulary ceased. It seems Jenny forgot the original terminology.

In one case, Jenny adopted a word I tended to use with great flourish and, since she had difficulty in pronouncing it correctly, it came out as "fut!" I was shocked the first time this happened. I was in her room and she was a few feet away in the bathroom, when she got upset about something and came out with the word in question. The first thing that flashed through my mind was the likelihood of her saying it in front of Suzanne or her teachers at day care. What would their first assumption be about where she had heard it?

Panicked, I said, "Phooey!" Jenny got the idea right away. I only remember a couple of times when I had to supply the substitute word; after that, Jenny used "phooey" on the rare occasions when her frustration about something seemed to need verbalization. Even the substitute word fell out of use after a while.

When I got frustrated at a red light that seemed as if it would never change, or when I was confronted by another driver who seemed exceptionally stupid, I would mutter the phrase "son of a bitch," sometimes half under my breath, sometimes more audibly. Jenny picked up on this right away, and the fact that I was upset.

One time when Jenny and I were in the car, I got upset about something and blurted out the phrase. Repeating the whole phrase seemed too much for her, so, looking at me very seriously and supportively, she simply said, "Bitch!" Although it was amusing, I realized that another favorite expletive would have to bite the dust. Although I discontinued using the phrase, it was not long after that when, on another trip in the car with Jenny, I got perturbed about something. I did not say a word, and although I thought I was concealing my irritation, Jenny tuned in on it immediately. Turning to me to offer her total support once again, and as if I had forgotten what I was supposed to say, she said, "Bitch, Daddy, bitch!" Thereafter, if I got worked up enough that I felt I had to say something, I used "phooey"— not as satisfying, of course, but necessary. And Jenny dropped the "b" word.

Although I was a good driver and did not take chances, I did tend to be short-tempered behind the wheel. Over the years, various girl friends, and finally my second wife, Suzanne, tried to change this behavior. Not only were their attempts to no avail, but they sometimes made the situation worse, since men in general are, of course, not receptive or appreciative when it comes to being told by women how to drive and what attitudes are appropriate. Suzanne would some-times tell me that my driving scared her. I found this difficult to take to heart, regarded it as unwarranted criticism, and usually just got madder.

When I began driving regularly with Jenny in the car, she picked up on it right away when I got angry about something. Even when I made no comments, she read my emotions like a book. Although I had curbed my tongue while behind the wheel, my occasional frustrations were still apparent to her, and one day when I flared up, I was very surprised when Jenny turned to me with concern and said, "Stop, Daddy, stop!" But what really struck me was that she herself was not upset or afraid, or critical; I could see that she was genuinely concerned about me! She loved me and wanted me to be happy.

I was so deeply moved by this that, from that incident on, my whole posture toward driving changed permanently. My years of fierce resistance to female crit-icism about my driving were broken down in a moment by Jenny's words. I responded to her love. And, how could I continue do something that made her unhappy? How could I say no to her? From then on, it was not necessary to hide frustration; it was no longer there. Jenny's love, which was stronger, had melted it away.

In fact, my driving habits were affected even when Jenny was not with me. Somehow, she had reached me in such a way that my general hostility toward all driving was diffused. My attitude was better; I drove more slowly and carefully. Why should I not do everything in my power, behind the wheel of a car and oth-erwise, to make sure that Jenny was safe, secure, and happy, and that I was safe and healthy so that I could take care of her?

Whereas Suzanne had formerly criticized my frightening and erratic dri-ving, she began to complain that I drove "like an old man!" I found that easier to live with.

One other little phrase that Jenny picked up from me was one that I had started to use back in the days of visiting her in the hospital. Sometimes, for instance, if I did something incorrectly, inefficiently, or clumsily, such as apply surgical tape to Jenny's gastrostomy tube in a manner that was less than satisfactory, I would jokingly say, "Dumb Daddy!" Naturally, after a while, Jenny starting offering the comment herself when it was apparent that I had messed something up. I never cared, and actually thought it was cute. However, I discontinued saying it (and therefore she did, too), because I felt that if other people heard her, they might think that she was being deliberately disrespectful to me, especially if she continued to say it as she got older. Besides, Jenny might start calling other people dumb, perhaps her teachers at day care or other adults.

Jenny loved it when Suzanne and I sang to her. Several of the nurses at Huntington had sung to her a great deal, especially at bedtime. I had also begun singing to her at bedtime at the hospital, at her insistence, and sang to her more as time went on. Perhaps one reason I became more relaxed in the car was because, whenever Jenny and I drove anywhere together (and I think the same thing was true of Suzanne and Jenny), she would ask me to sing to her.

The song Jenny knew best and which she almost invariably asked for was "Hush, Little Baby." On the mornings that I drove her to All Saints Children's Center, she would unfailingly request "Hush, Baby." Even though I heard this song nightly, since it was on one of Jenny's favorite bedtime cassettes that she had brought home from the hospital, I did not know the real words. Therefore, I mostly made up the lyrics, which Jenny never minded, and which as time passed covered a universe of subjects, including Sebastian and Sarada, pizza pies, the weather, my job, Daddy and Jenny, and whatever else popped into my head at the time. I got a great deal of practice at this (and overcame a lot of inhibition about singing in front of others), since any trip in the car warranted a song.

Often, after Suzanne and I had gotten Jenny ready for bed, including getting her hooked up to the pumps and starting the feeding, Suzanne would hold Jenny in the rocking chair near the crib and sing to her. After we had put Jenny in her crib, however, I usually took over and read her a story. Although she had a great many books, she preferred a select few, and of those, the one which she usually insisted on hearing was "Good night, Moon." She never got tired of having it read to her, and actually, I never got bored with it either. It was soothing to both of us. Jenny even had the tape of it, but nothing could substitute for live reading.

After reading was finished, I put on one of the bedtime cassette tapes and, lying down on the floor right next to Jenny's crib, I would reach through the bars and hold her hand until she fell asleep.

Children love routines. The one at bedtime was important to Jenny. Although she might overlook skipping the rocking chair segment if Suzanne was tired, the sequence of what happened thereafter was a ritual that permitted little tampering. A reading of "Good night, Moon" or something else was hard to get around. And, if I, too, was especially tired on a given evening, although I might manage to bypass the reading, lying on the floor next to Jenny and holding her hand was sacrosanct.

If Jenny even suspected that I was thinking of leaving her room without lying down next to her, she would quickly point to the floor by the crib and say, "pillow," since I always placed a pillow on the carpeting before lying down. She even saw to it that the pillow was next to the proper end of the crib—the end where she was going to lay her head.

I can still see Jenny's face one night when I tried to get her to go to sleep without doing this. I was really tired, and had made up my mind. I was just going to turn out the lights and get ready for bed. Suzanne was also still in the room and was trying to help convince Jenny about my doing this. Reasoning was a total failure. Under no circumstances was Jenny going to buy it. Finally, Suzanne and I decided that we were just going to leave the room, that I was going to bed, and that was that. As I started to go, Jenny, who had already gotten up and was standing on her mattress, holding onto the edge of the crib, started to cry—really cry. Huge tears began to roll down her face, and she pleaded with me to stay. Her huge, dark eyes, her wet face, and her quavering voice were so inexpressibly sad that I simply said, "Okay, it's all right," and stayed with her.

I was glad I stayed. I never tried to walk out on Jenny again. What were a few more minutes? They meant so much to her; and they meant as much to me, too. Was she blackmailing me, manipulating me? Some of the child-life therapists probably would have said yes, and that I should not have given in. But I thought, as I still do, "Who cares?" Jenny was no ordinary child! She was a baby who had spent the first two and a half years of her life in a hospital, often sick, and with no mother or father! And how long did she have with us? A month? A year? I did not know. If Jenny should die one day, did I want to remember a night that I walked out of her room, knowing how much she wanted me to stay? Or did I want to be able to look back and say to myself that I did everything in my power to make her happy and feel loved? Looked at in that way, some little contest of wills or authority seemed utterly petty and ridiculous.

So that night, like the others before and after it, I turned out the lights, put on a soothing tape, and lay down on the floor next to Jenny. She reached out from between the bars of the crib and waited for me to hold her hand. Clasping her hand in mine, I guided it back inside the bars so that her hand and mine could rest on the mattress. I held her hand until she was asleep. If I let go too soon, she would awaken, and we would have to begin again. But that would be okay, too. Finally, I cautiously pulled my hand away, rose, and turned off the tape. But before I left the room, I stood by her crib and looked at her, with no doubt that I had the most beautiful daughter in the world.

Suzanne often called Jenny her "precious baby." She would pick Jenny up, hug her, and ask, "How is my precious baby?" I quickly adopted it too, often calling her "precious baby," or "Daddy's precious baby." Sometimes, then, Jenny would also refer to herself as "precious baby" (I think her version of it was "presh baby"), which, in my eyes, was adorable. Sometimes, Suzanne or I would say to Jenny, "Who's our precious baby? Is it Sarada?" Or, "Is it Sebastian?" Jenny would smile and say no. "Who is our precious baby, then?" we would ask. And, with a big grin, Jenny would say, "Me!" And indeed, this sweet child was the most precious thing that could ever be imagined.

Mostly on the advice of the Huntington medical social workers and child therapists, we did not take Jenny back to the hospital to visit for a while, once she came home to live with us. They felt that a clean break would be best both for Jenny and for the hospital staff. I did not necessarily agree with any of this, but I cooperated. Jenny did not mention the hospital after moving home, so I do not think she missed it. However, after a few weeks, we did start to take her back for occasional visits. and she really enjoyed seeing the nurses. They were delighted to see her, and Jenny did not seem confused.

Once I took Jenny by the pediatric ward for a quick hello, and she became concerned while we were there. We were by the nurse's station, and she was in her stroller. Dr. Laurance made an appearance, and when Jenny saw him, she became worried that I was going to leave her at the hospital. She liked Dr. Laurance very much, but she linked seeing him there with the idea that I might be taking her back to the hospital to stay. She looked at me with a worried expression and pointed insistently at the doors to the ward several times, saying, "Home!" I was touched by her concern that I might take her back to the hospital and leave her, and I assured her that we would be going home. She was not totally convinced, so we soon left because I did not want her to be worried in any way. She brightened up as soon as I wheeled her toward the elevator.

During one of Jenny's social calls to the hospital with me, a nurse on the pediatric ward mentioned how odd it looked to her when Jenny came in wearing a jacket. Suzanne and I had bought several jackets and coats for her, and that day she had on a light nylon jacket with sporty colors. She probably had her sunglasses on also, which she wore now and then just for effect, since she thought she looked so cute in them (which was true). The nurse told me that, after seeing Jenny in nothing but diapers, T-shirts, and dresses for so long, it was strange to see her dressed for outdoor weather. I understand how this would have made a startling impression the first time.

Medical Visits to the Hospital

Unfortunately, not all of Jennifer's visits to Huntington Memorial Hospital were social calls. After she moved home with us, there were several times when we had to admit her to the pediatric ward for a couple of days or more. Invariably, these episodes would begin with a very high fever. A high fever would be cause for worry for any parent, but in Jenny's case it was reason for deep concern and immediate action, since such an elevated temperature could be an indication of the onset of sepsis, the presence of disease-causing organisms or their toxins in the blood or tissues, and in Jenny's case a condition brought on most likely by the contamination of her Broviac catheter. If Jenny became septic and did not receive medical attention right away, she could get terribly sick or even die.

In Jenny's photo album, I found a snapshot of her with the following caption: "March 28, 1991. Huntington Memorial Hospital. Jenny with nurse, Carol Schwaerzler. Getting ready to go back home to 694 Vallejo Villas after being in Huntington Memorial Hospital for a few days for treatment." The photo is of Jenny, standing in the hallway of the pediatric ward near the nurse's station, beaming happily at one of the nurses, and hooked up to some pumps mounted on a portable stand. I think that this was the first time we had Jenny back in the hospital—only about five weeks after she had moved home. And since there were several more such visits over the next few months, the issue that had been raised of keeping Jenny away from Huntington for a time for psychosocial reasons—both with respect to her and the pediatric nurses—turned out to be beside the point.

Typically, when such episodes occurred, Suzanne and I would discover late in the evening that Jenny had suddenly developed a high fever. Depending on the severity of the fever, Jenny's behavior, and Dr. Laurance's advice, we would either try to ride it out, while giving Jenny children's aspirin in the form of vaginal suppositories (something which she did not at all care for), or disconnect her from her feedings, put her in the car with her partially used bags of TPN, liquids, and saline solution, and rush her over to the Huntington emergency room, where she would be admitted and transferred to the pediatric ward. There, she could be closely monitored and treated with intravenous antibiotics until the danger was over.

The first time Suzanne and I went through this, it was deeply upsetting. As other episodes occurred, although our concern and vigilance naturally remained at a very high level, we adjusted to these emergency visits. No matter how scrupulous we were in caring for Jenny, bacteria, and so on would from time to time find their way into her system. It seemed unavoidable. After all, even under hospital conditions, Jenny had become septic on various occasions.

Oddly, and especially in the beginning, these periodic bouts with high fever and resultant trips to Huntington did not generally seem to upset Jenny at all. She actually seemed to enjoy going. She liked seeing the nurses, they liked seeing her, and she gave Suzanne and me the definite impression that she understood completely that she was going to the hospital in order to get well, and that she would be coming back home soon. In fact, Jenny would sometimes become a little bit delirious from the fevers, and at such times would talk to herself or to us about things she was imagining that seemed to be very pleasant fantasies for her.

On the occasions that Jenny got admitted to the hospital, Suzanne would of course visit her frequently during the day, and I would come right after work. If the situation seemed especially serious, I would sleep in Jenny's room on the pediatric ward with her all night.

As time passed, it seemed as if Jenny got more cantankerous about having to stay overnight in the hospital. She would sometimes throw fits of violent temper, and cry for long stretches loudly enough to deafen anyone within fifty feet. On the occasions when she had to share a room with one or more other children and their attending parents, I do not know how they endured some of Jenny's scenes, except to say that they showed remarkable patience and understanding. As some of the nurses who knew Jenny moved on to other jobs and new staff came on board, Jenny would sometimes find herself under the care of someone she did not know. Some of these new nurses were completely intimidated by her temper tantrums. I could not fail to find a touch of humor, from time to time, in seeing a three-year-old baby completely get the upper hand with these young women. Of course, it was especially difficult for these poor girls to try to control a child who, in addition to behaving like a bull in a rodeo, was hooked up to intravenous feedings or antibiotics and needed periodic changes of dressings, colostomy bags, and so on.

Under such circumstances, Suzanne and I were sometimes the only ones who could placate Jenny and restore order. I remember especially well one night that Jenny was in the hospital for observation and medical treatment, some time after she had moved home with us. The pediatric ward was very crowded, so for this visit Jenny had to be in a large room with three other beds. She was acting like a wild animal. (Looking back, I am asking myself if perhaps her blood sugar was way out of balance.) Even with the door to the room closed, one could hear her crying and screaming way down the hall. I do not know how the other children and parents in the room were able to cope. The whole pediatric ward seemed disrupted by her behavior.

Later in the evening, we got Jenny hooked up for her feedings and tried to settle her down to go to sleep. She screamed and thrashed about, and all attempts to quiet her were in vain. Finally in desperation I asked her if she would like me to get in the crib with her. She said yes, and her tantrum immediately subsided. Hospital cribs are the same size as the standard ones found in the home, except that the hospital versions are higher off the floor and have sturdy steel bars all the way around. For the child's protection, the bars on either side can be slid up and down and secured, creating, in effect, a cage. Even the tops have some kind of covering. I climbed in next to Jenny, slid the bars in place to keep us safely in, and curled up as best I could. Jenny maneuvered herself around for a minute and found a comfortable position with her head on my chest. She was happy and completely satisfied, and we both went to sleep. As far as I remember, I stayed in the crib with her all night, and she awoke in the morning in a much better frame of mind. Actually, it was fun, and now that I think of it, it was probably the only time that Jenny and I were able to sleep in the same bed.

The Lizards Find New Homes, Birthdays, and Other Memories

On April 9, 1991, almost seven weeks after Jenny came home, and after uncounted hours of exhausting paperwork that encompassed every kind of personal and financial information imaginable on Suzanne and myself, I submitted a completed application for foster home licensing to the California State Department of Social Services. The entire process, which included both Suzanne and me being fingerprinted (this material to be placed on permanent file in Sacramento) and a thorough criminal background check, was lengthened even further due to requests from the department for additional data. By the time I had finished, my record copies included well over fifty documents, some quite extensive and detailed. I never could have imagined so much was involved, and I was greatly relieved to put it behind me. And I was also grateful that the children's social worker from the county department of children's services had made it possible for Suzanne and me to bring Jenny home before going through this very time-consuming process.

On the morning of June 2, 1991, a Sunday I recall very clearly, I awoke with an alarm going off inside my head. I had to get rid of my reptile collection as soon as possible. I had given my reptilian pets the finest homes, care, and attention. I had managed all the work, even after Jenny had come to live with us. That Sunday morning, as I lay in bed, my feelings were not that all the work was so demanding that I could not keep up with it, although that was close to the truth. Rather, it was an urgent voice warning me to divest myself of this responsibility and the time it demanded every day.

Once it was clear to me that I had to do this, I wanted to do it immediately. After the pet store where I bought all of my reptiles and supplies opened that morning, I called the manager. He accepted my offer, which was that I would gladly donate my lizards to the store as long as they would resell them to responsible new owners. It was a great business deal for him, and I was not interested in profiting from it. I only wanted the animals to get good care, and I felt that he would see to that.

By early afternoon, I had safely transported all five lizards—the two Chilean collared lizards, the iguana, and the two Egyptian agamas—safely to the pet store. With some sadness, regret, and a streak of guilt, I returned home and began to dismantle the equipment in the tanks.

I did not return to the pet store again, either to learn the fate of my pets or to be tempted by anything new. It would only be in the next months that I would understand the import of my powerful intuition to divest myself of these pets and their demands on my time and energy.

On June 8, 1991, I turned forty-two years old. With Suzanne's help, Jenny gave me a knit shirt and a pair of shorts. Since they were the right size and color coordinated, I assumed that Suzanne had picked them out. However, Suzanne told me that when she and Jenny were shopping for a present, Suzanne found herself in kind of a quandary about what to get, so she asked Jenny, who toddled over to a certain display and selected my outfit without hesitation.

Despite the passage of time, when I see that shirt in my closet or those shorts in my dresser, I think lovingly of Jenny and of that day. I treasure those two items of clothing, and after they are worn out, I will keep them forever. I wish very much that there had been years and years of other birthdays—both Jenny's and mine—that we all could have shared together.

June 8 was also someone else's birthday, a friend of Jenny's from All Saint's Children's Center named Maggie Rascoe. In the afternoon, Suzanne, Jenny, and I drove to Maggie's house in Pasadena to attend the birthday party. I remember it so well because it was Jenny's social debut, the first time she had been an invited guest to a party with her peers. Jenny wore her beautiful black dress with the floral design, and her fancy socks and black patent leather shoes. She shared in all the festivities and games, and had Mommy push her for a while on Maggie's swing. It was sunny and very hot that day, and Jenny drank a lot of fluids (probably just water, since she would not touch any kind of soft drink). Her gastrostomy bag, which was pinned under her dress, got very full at one point, so I discreetly took her around to the back of the garage and drained it into the dirt at the edge of a little garden. How strange the scene would look to anyone who might happen to see us, if they did not know us!

Jenny was highly intelligent and perceptive, and intuitive. Sometimes, her intuition seemed more like mental telepathy. On another occasion, Jenny, Suzanne, and I were sitting at the dining room table having dinner. As usual, for Jenny, this meant enjoying watching Suzanne and me eat, although she might take a few minute nibbles from the little bit of our food that we would always put on her plate in order to include her and encourage her to try to eat. Suzanne and I had been talking about one thing or another, and, during a lull in the conversation, Sue Collins, Jenny's former child therapist from Huntington, who now lived in Las Vegas, popped into my head. Nothing we had been talking about related to her in any way. After a few minutes of silence, during which I had wondered to myself when Sue would be coming to visit us again, I said, almost as if to myself, "I wonder..."

Suddenly, Jenny looked at me with a big smile and twinkling eyes, and said loudly, "Sue!" I was amazed. The simplest explanation is that Jenny was reading my mind, and I believe it. Just as I had begun to speak, my mind seemed to go blank for a second or two, and I am totally convinced that, during that brief lapse when my conscious mind relaxed, Jenny's subconscious mind came into contact with mine and she read my thought. After retrieving my thought, she smiled at me triumphantly, just the way she would have if she had just successfully written something on a piece of paper or stomped on one of my playing card houses. There was no doubt that on many occasions Jenny was very attuned to Suzanne and me.

Another time Jenny showed me an act of love I will never forget that touched me deeply. We had all finished eating dinner, and I was lying on the floor in the living room a few feet from the dining room table. Jenny took a pillow from a nearby chair, and walking up to me with that big smile of hers, placed it under my head. I thanked her warmly, after which she went to the dining room table, brought back my cloth napkin, and with great attention and care spread it out on my chest like a blanket, just like we did for her every night when she went to bed. The kindness and concern for me, which she expressed through such touching gestures, made me feel warm and loved, as she felt.

One evening we were eating spaghetti. Suzanne had placed a small amount in a bowl and had given it to Jenny. As the meal neared completion, it was obvious that Jennifer was, as usual, going to eat little of what was in front of her. Assuming, naturally, that she was finished with it, Suzanne innocently reached over, took Jenny's bowl, and prepared to pour its contents onto her own plate.

In a flash, and with the most indignant expression imaginable on her face, Jenny reached over, grabbed the bowl, yanked it away from Suzanne, and set it on the table with a loud thud. She did not utter one word, but the adult, histrionic scowl of intimidation and disapproval she gave Suzanne was priceless, as if to say, "How dare you presume to remove my bowl and help yourself to its contents!" Suzanne was speechless. Although Jenny's behavior was not exactly good social etiquette, the way she had gotten her point across was so funny that it was all I could do to keep a straight face. After Jenny had reclaimed her bowl—none of which she ate—none of us said another word. It was, however, probably the last time Suzanne or I removed any food from her without asking permission.

I deeply admired and respected the spunk that Jennifer often showed. It went with her amazing bravery and will to overcome physical adversities. This spirit should never be squelched or met head-on, especially in children, and its expression is vital to the development and health of the personality. Naturally, such impulses need proper direction. It has always seemed to me that this energy—this assertion of will and of the Self—should be nurtured in youth by guiding it adeptly into creative channels; that the manifestation of this kind of energy and will is important, and that, again, especially with young children, it should not be met with disapproval, but with gentle correction and teaching. The energy that comes from within cannot be plugged. If it is frustrated, it will turn to poison and violence; hence, our deeply sick society. Such forces which rise up from inside us must be recognized and accepted as utterly unamenable to being dammed up. Rather they must be dealt with in the only way possible—by finding creative outlets for them.

Among the vivid recollections I have of Jenny being with us are some that stand out for no apparent reason. Like hundreds of others, they are everyday scenes that are not linked in my mind with any intense emotional content that would explain their lasting impression. But they have come to mind again and again, haunting me, and at times they well up in my memory out of the blue.

I remember so well the Saturday morning I washed the large throw rug on the garage floor with Jenny's "help." I laid the rug on the driveway, in the shade just outside the garage. Soaking it first, I then squirted dish detergent on several areas and began to work up a lather. It was a pleasant, sunny morning, not too hot, and Jenny and I were both barefoot. Jenny helped me scrub the rug for a while, and sometimes held the hose. I cannot remember why, but there was an empty box of powdered laundry detergent and the scoop that came with it lying around. Jenny made a game out of scooping water into it from the plastic bucket, pouring it out, and starting over again. She was deeply absorbed in this activity and totally self-entertained, content to be near me. Perhaps the scene links me with the magical parts of my own childhood—the parts when I was happy, and not lonely.

My mother told me that, as a child at Christmas, I was far more interested in the boxes than the toys that came in them. I can recall the cardboard shoebox that was a rocket ship or jungle boat; the concrete bench in the back yard that was a canoe or dock in the middle of an imagined lake or the Amazon river; the lush green grass that became a trackless jungle for my small plastic animals, cowboys, Indians, army men, and knights. In the house, the three rooms upstairs were all mine, and I remember the register in the floor, through which I could peer down into the dining room that, with the imagination, could be turned into a gigantic cavern or undersea cave. Although my mother and father did not approve, I used to lift the removable grating and lower one of my soldiers or rubber scuba diving men on a string through the bottom metal grid that was flush with the dining room ceiling toward the carpeted floor that seemed hundreds of feet below. Hearing one of my parents coming, I would quickly haul my man up again before they discovered what I was doing.

I think often of another time when Jenny and I went to a shopping mall for me to buy some shoes for myself. We were standing together in front of a display window at a shoe store. I had my hands clasped behind my back, and was moving back and forth slowly, perusing the merchandise. I happened to look down at Jenny, who was right in front of me. Her hands were clasped behind her back also, as she slowly paced this way and that, evaluating the shoes. I had to laugh to myself, amazed at the mannerisms—and everything else—that children pick up.

Once, Suzanne, Jenny, and I were out in the car late one weekend afternoon. We found a Chinese restaurant that looked nice, parked, went in, and ordered carryout. The three of us waited outside for about fifteen minutes near the front door, where there were statues, some shade, and a long strip of grass. Nothing at all happened. Jenny played and frolicked around the statues, and up and down the little shaded lawn. I see the scene clearly in my mind's eye now, just as it has come to me so many times over the past few years. I recall taking the food home and eating it at the dining room table. I can see the tiny little ears of corn among the other vegetables. Why do I remember all of this, and with such passion?

Jennifer was not generally fussy. One time, she, Suzanne, and I stopped to eat dinner at an indoor-outdoor Mediterranean restaurant on Lake Street in Pasadena. Jenny was being cantankerous; she complained, shifted her chair all over the place, and almost tripped a couple of people walking by the table. Two Middle

Eastern men sitting nearby noticed her behavior, and one of them, by way of teasing her a little, made some remark to her about behaving herself. The utterly foul glare that he received in return from Jenny was hilarious, and typical of her sometimes histrionic and adult-like expressions. The message in her eyes was unmistakable. "Who in the hell do you think you are to tell me how to behave?" This must have happened around the end of July 1991, because I believe that it was the last time that Suzanne and I had the opportunity to take her out to eat.

On Monday, June 24, 1991, Jennifer turned three. We'd had a birthday party for her the day before at home. Many friends came, including Dale and Jim Roggenkamp, our friends from Kentucky who were visiting us.

For several reasons, I remember this birthday party as one of the happiest times we had with Jenny. Most of the many friends who came loved Jenny very much and had been an integral part of her life, or at least knew all about her from Suzanne and me. In addition to Dale and Jim, and Dora Anne Mills, a pediatrician from Huntington, other celebrants included Zippy, a nurse and very close friend of Suzanne's, and her family; Juliane Schmidt, another nursing friend of Suzanne's and a godmother of Jenny's; several pediatric nurses from Huntington, including one of Jenny's all-time favorites, Carol Taylor; and Father Michael, from Holy Family Church, Suzanne's parish in South Pasadena.

The party is also memorable because, at one point, Suzanne, Julie, Father Mike, Jenny and I, and others, went downstairs to Jenny's room and Father Mike baptized her. This ceremony was, I believe, one of several such baptismal rites performed for Jenny. She had received baptism at least once while she lived at Huntington, and I think there were also other occasions. Certainly, she should have been a very holy child by her third birthday. One reason that I still see this ceremony so clearly in my mind is the hilarious look of suspicion that Jenny had on her face while, as we all stood close around, Julie held her in her arms like a baby. I remember that there seemed to be some short delay in the actual sprinkling of the water, during which, as well as it being obvious to me that Julie's arms were about ready to fall off, Jenny grew more and more doubtful as to what was going on and whether or not her voluntary docility was really in her best interests. Everything got done before anyone fell apart; all ended well, and Jenny's sanctification was ensured yet another time.

As I look at the photos of Jenny on this occasion, I am also deeply gratified because they show graphically her remarkable development in just the four months since she had left the hospital to live with us. The first pictures I ever took of Jenny were in November 1990, while she was living at Huntington. I was surprised when I went back and counted forty-one photos of Jenny at the hospital during this month! These pictures bring back many powerful emotions. They are especially touching because, although Jenny's inner beauty shines through in typical fashion, one cannot fail to note in these early photos a kind of heavy sadness in Jenny's face and eyes.

Jenny and Carol Taylor

Jenny was not unhappy at the hospital. She was well cared for there and deeply loved by many wonderful people. But when she came to know Suzanne and me as her mother and father, and especially when she came "home," she changed—rapidly and astonishingly. The November 1990 photos often show a baby with a somewhat sad face and eyes that communicate something is missing in her life; and that something, in my mind, was the cohesion, security, and happiness that can only come when a child has two parents who love it. Her adorable little face and body are heavy-looking due to the substantial amount of lipids (fats) in her diet (actually a wise precaution on the part of Dr. Laurance, in the event that Jenny should become sick and need the reserves). Her hair is bushy and in need of a good stylist.

Around mid-December 1990, when Jenny began to make home visits, a change started to occur in her appearance. In the photos taken of her in our home during visits in December 1990 and January 1991, her whole aura changed remarkably. She often had a joyous smile; she looked deeply happy and content. And in looking at these pictures, one could not fail to read in Jenny's face that she felt she belonged there with us. Photos of Jenny in March, a month or so after she moved home with us, show a radiant child. Between November 1990 and March 1993, a somewhat melancholy-looking baby had been transformed into a glowing little girl.

Photos of her at her birthday party testify that a dramatic and beautiful metamorphosis had occurred. Jenny's face and body, her expression, and her whole demeanor appeared radiant. She had slimmed down and was beautifully proportioned. She had grown like a weed, and was noticeably taller. Her skin was beautifully tanned and glowing, and she had a short, stylish haircut. She was wearing a beautiful little light-colored dress that accentuated her rich skin tone. The short sleeves on the dress puffed out a little, like small wings, so that one notices a remarkable coincidence. Jenny had become a beautiful summer butterfly. The caterpillar had transformed herself into a shining, vibrant, winged creature.

On Sunday, June 30, 1991, Suzanne and I took Jenny on a major outing. At the invitation of Dolores Guerrero, a volunteer from L.A. Youth Programs who occasionally provided respite care, and her husband, Suzanne, Jenny, and I spent the day at Rancho Calamigos in Malibu, a large, western-style ranch in the foothills. The event was held especially for children with various physical handicaps and included a sumptuous barbeque, entertainment, games, swimming, and pony rides.

At the barbeque, Suzanne ate moderately, I stuffed myself, and Jenny ate nothing. But she had a good time. We all did. The temperature, however, was scorching.

Among the things that stand out in my mind about this day are a conversation Suzanne and I had with a woman who ate at our table. She was with her daughter, who was around seven or eight years old, and who, like Jenny, had a Broviac catheter. I do not remember why this child had the catheter, since she seemed to eat normally. At any rate, seeing that this child apparently had done very well on the catheter for a long time, Suzanne and I felt encouraged about Jenny. However, as I said, this woman's daughter took most of her nourishment by mouth, so her digestive system must have been much closer to normal than Jenny's. Therefore,

Jenny and Suzanne at Jenny's third birthday party

her heart and other internal organs were not subjected to the kind of strain put on Jenny's system by her abnormal means of ingestion, namely, receiving all her nourishment through the catheter over a period of years.

The photos I took of Jenny include ones of her petting a horse and riding on a pony. Being around horses was a new experience and, although the pony that we sat her on was quite docile and harnessed with other animals in a merry-go-round fashion, and in spite of the fact that Suzanne stayed right with her the whole time, the expression on her face is at best one of uncertainty.

The other pictures of Jenny are at the swimming pool. One is of Dolores holding Jenny at the top of a slide that goes into the water. This is somewhat amusing because, since Jenny did not have a swimsuit and we could not let her go in the water that day, Dolores found herself in a jam, on top of the ladder, unable either to let go of Jenny or to get her back down. I had to climb up and rescue them.

The other photo, especially meaningful to me, is of Jenny sitting in the shade at the edge of the pool, her feet dangling in the cool, refreshing water. We felt so badly that Jenny could not go in the pool that day, but none of us had brought swimsuits, and Jenny did not even have one. I could have gone in wearing my shorts with Jenny in a diaper, but there were all of her tubes and dressings to be concerned about, and I did not have a change of dry clothing. I do not think we knew if Jenny should be allowed in a swimming pool for health reasons. Therefore, she had to be content with dipping her feet in the water, even though she wanted to get in. She would have gone down the slide in her clothing in a second if we had let her, and, probably because she did not know the danger, it did not appear that she had any fear of water.

At the end of the afternoon we drove home on the 134 freeway, which was a furnace with bumper-to-bumper traffic. My car was not air conditioned, and Suzanne, who was very sensitive to heat, did poorly. Jenny seemed to hold up pretty well, but she became fretful toward the end of the trip. She was very hot, and I suspect that she became somewhat dehydrated, since most of the water she drank ended up in her gastrostomy bag.

The following day we talked to Dr. Laurance about Jenny going in the swimming pool. He saw no problem, since, in his opinion, the heavily chlorinated water would kill any infectious organisms. I bought a pretty blue one-piece swimsuit for Jenny.

Thursday was the Fourth of July. The caption next to a photo in Jenny's album reads, "July 4, 1991, Jenny and Sue Collins, 694 Vallejo Villas, first time at pool." Jenny, smiling at the camera, is sitting with her feet in the water on the steps at the shallow end of the pool next to one of her favorite and most loved people, Sue Collins, her former child-life therapist from Huntington, who had stopped to visit us.

From then on, I tried to take Jenny to the pool whenever I could, as long as the weather was good and she was in good health. She loved the water. I bought a kick board and a large raft for us to play on. Oddly, what she seemed to enjoy even more than the pool was walking over to the nearby outdoor shower and having me turn it on just enough so that the water would fall gently onto her head and shoulders.

I had no idea at that time what significance the July 4, 1991, photo of Jenny and Sue Collins at the pool would later come to have for me, for I had no way of knowing when I took it that it would be the last one I would ever take of Jenny.

Storm Clouds

Not long after Jenny's third birthday party, the Children's Social Worker (CSW) from the Los Angeles County Department of Children's Services, our second CSW by that time, had stopped by our home on one of his periodic visits to see how Suzanne, Jenny, and I were doing. It was late in the afternoon on a workday, and Jenny was home from day care. We were all sitting in the living room talking. Jenny was playing and busying herself here and there in the room, and I was sitting on the floor, with my knees tucked under me, helping to keep her occupied.

At one point during the conversation, the CSW, who had always received very positive feedback from us about Jenny, casually turned to Suzanne and asked her how she was doing with the situation. Suzanne looked at him. As if she were making an announcement, and in a tone of voice which communicated an ominous ambiguity and doubt, she said she was having a lot of emotional difficulty coping, and that she was unsure of her feelings with respect to a long-term commitment to caring for Jenny. It seemed to me almost like she was trying to warn us, as if her mind were more made up than she wanted to let on, and that this was her way of "getting our feet wet" with the issue.

There was dead silence. In our midst, Jenny continued to entertain herself. The CSW was visibly taken aback. His face showed concern, but he kept his poise. I was stunned. Clearly aware of the emotional tension in the room, the CSW subtly shifted his demeanor to that of a counselor.

After a few moments, he turned to me and asked quietly, "How do you feel about this?"

I felt my face get hot with indignation. I felt betrayed and angry. Defiant and totally resolved, but controlled, I looked at him and said simply, with unmistakable conviction, "I will die before I will give her up!"

I shot a glance at Suzanne. It was her turn to be taken aback. I have no idea what she expected me to say under such circumstances, but I do not think that she had anticipated my response. Again, there was silence.

At some point during this exchange of words, Jenny did something odd I am certain no one noticed but me. She had been playing, and suddenly she stopped doing whatever she was doing and came to me. I was still sitting on the floor with my legs tucked under me. She stood right in front of me, put her face very close to mine, and looked into my eyes for a moment. I can still see her face almost touching mine, but I cannot describe her unusual expression.

She was smiling and seemed ecstatically happy. But there was something else in her face. Intuitively, unmistakably, I caught an underlying meaning in her gesture and expression. Although I do not believe that Jenny consciously heard and understood the import of what Suzanne had said, I knew then, as I do now, that something registered in her soul. And when our faces came close and our eyes met, something deep within her being spoke to my being. It is just now that I actually realize what it was in her look that I could never put into words before. It was unequivocal trust. Jenny was placing herself totally in my hands.

The interview ended on a less than reassuring note. Acting as an arbitrator, the CSW acknowledged our difference of opinion and, expressing his sincere hope that we could work things out, recommended strongly that we go into counseling. In a gentle way, he was insisting on it. I watched him make notes about the visit and about our agreement to get professional help.

Leaving my own feelings completely aside for a moment and looking at his, I could see his dilemma. Here was a couple who had taken responsibility for a baby whose medically fragile condition had until recently made it impossible to place her in a home. In the past, all of the other prospective parents had backed away. Now an element of doubt had been introduced about the present couple's ability to continue together to care for the child, who, in addition to having found a home, had become bonded to her foster parents and had grown to love them deeply and trust them completely. He and I must have been thinking the same thoughts. Where would this child go if we abandoned her? Into an institution? Back to live the rest of her life in a hospital? And, in addition to her overwhelming physical needs, what would this to do her emotionally? What would it do to her heart and her spirit? Could Suzanne really believe that it was even possible for us—for her—to hand Jenny over to someone else, like so much rejected merchandise? I could never accept such a thing. It was utterly unthinkable, and my emotions ran from disbelief to outrage—and fear. I loved Jenny with all my soul. She was my life.

Suzanne and I did not talk much for the rest of that day. I was almost beyond words, and it was probably for the best that I did not try to say anything. What I remember so powerfully is what happened after Jenny had gone to bed.

I lay on the floor next to Jenny's crib. As I held her small hand through the bars of the crib, I thought about what had happened that afternoon, what it meant, and where it might lead. In the quiet of the room, my concerns and anxieties caught up to me, but at the same moment I felt a powerful surge of love for Jenny. Tears filled my eyes. I raised myself up to a sitting position, and looked at her. There was still light in the room, so we could see each other clearly. Jenny knew I was deeply upset; I made no attempt to hide my feelings.

I looked into Jenny's eyes and spoke to her as an equal. My voice was soft, but full of emotion. I told her how much I loved her, more than anything in my life, with a power beyond any I had ever known, and that I would never give her up.

Jenny was sitting up also. As I spoke to her through the bars, our eyes were on the same level and our faces very close. Unblinking, Jenny's wide, dark eyes looked deeply into mine and into my soul. It was probably the most open, direct, and powerful communication between my heart and another's that I had ever known.

Jenny's soul was ancient. She understood. I could see it in her eyes—the clarity of her perception, the wisdom and comprehension, and her love and concern for me. She was not upset or frightened. She looked at me with love, like a mother would look at her child who was suffering. And at that moment, in the most loving, gentle, parental manner, she reached slowly through the bars and touched the tears that were streaming down my face.

I had come to her with my pain and she had comforted me. Her small hand gently stroked my cheek, brushing away the wetness. She never stopped looking directly at me, and she never spoke a single word the whole time. But she had understood everything I had said and had read my heart like an open book. In my whole life, no one, including my own mother, had ever looked at me in such a way—with such caring and love.

I awoke the next morning feeling the need to get things in motion. First, arrangements had to be made for counseling. During the summer of 1990, several months before I met Jenny, Suzanne had encouraged me to get professional counseling. Suzanne's primary concern was the frustration and anger that I felt in relation to my job and the individuals for whom I worked. I never focused this hostility directly at Suzanne, but, along with the other problems Suzanne and I seemed to have, my work made me unhappy and I often vented my frustrations at common, everyday things.

I had pushed away the idea of therapy for a number of reasons, including time, finances, pride, and the unwillingness to explore the real causes of the pain for fear that such a process might tear apart a marriage that could never be put back together again. And, since Suzanne clearly did not feel that she herself was in any need of counseling, but rather that the problem was mine, my ego was all the more resistant to the idea.

I remember a weekend during the summer of 1990 when Suzanne and I drove up into the mountains around the Mount Wilson Observatory north of Los Angeles to have a picnic lunch. The tone of our conversation was very uncomfortable because Suzanne had brought up the disturbing subject of therapy.

I looked around for prospective counselors. I had one session with another person who had been recommended by someone from Suzanne's church. After filling out some ridiculous paperwork which would supposedly reveal my psychological profile, I met with the counselor and described my problems and frustrations. When I had finished, he responded in an almost pastoral manner by asking me something along the lines of whether or not I had given enough thought to my relationship with the Lord or if I had shared my problems with Him. That was my signal to clear out as quickly as possible. I informed him politely that my area of concern was my relationship with my own self—not with the Lord. There was no resonance between us, and my first encounter with that therapist was also the last.

My neighbor, Lillian Evers, who was a therapist, recommended Ed Wortz. My first session with him was on September 5, 1990. In sharp contrast to my prior experience, Dr. Wortz and I resonated well. I found him empathetic, perceptive, and understanding. He was a Ph.D. psychologist who had extensive background in biofeedback and Buddhist meditation, and offered group meditation sessions at no charge to clients who were interested. He suggested techniques designed to deal with powerful emotions. His background in Eastern religions and philosophy, and his acceptance of reincarnation, made me comfortable and unreserved about revealing my inner self.

I talked to him at very great length, venting years of pent-up frustrations about the two most problematic issues in my life—my work environment, and my marriage with Suzanne, which had been plagued almost from its beginning in 1981 with struggles for control and power, incompatible styles of money management, and lack of intimacy and communication.

However, despite the progress I was making, I stopped seeing Dr. Wortz at the end of November, three months after I had begun therapy. There were several reasons for this. First, I met Jenny on November 4. She had a powerful effect on my life from the very beginning. Seeing her, loving her, and moving toward becoming her foster father gave me a whole new sense of purpose. My life was transformed, although underneath the problems I had talked about in therapy did not cease to exist. They did retreat into the background, given my all-consuming focus on Jennifer. I soon wanted to spend every weekday evening and every weekend with Jenny. Although I could have continued to fit therapy into my schedule, I chose to drop it rather than have it cut into my time with her.

I fell under an illusion common to many people who start therapy. In the beginning, due to the newness and the opportunity to vent repressed feelings, progress seems especially rapid, and one tends to believe that inner changes have taken place which are not as deep or lasting as they would like to believe. Much time and hard work are involved in obtaining real and lasting results from therapy.

I am conjecturing that Suzanne probably perceived things in a way somewhat parallel to mine. Although I would sometimes leave the therapy sessions feeling drained, I would come home and report, honestly, that I felt better and that I was making progress. And certainly this was true. But like me, Suzanne may have wanted to believe that things were getting "fixed" or at least significantly refurbished in relatively short order, and that long and arduous application was not necessary. I would not see Dr. Wortz again until July 5, 1991, this time with Suzanne, regarding her problems about Jenny and my profound concern.

In the meantime, it was necessary to address a deeply troubling matter: what were my options if Suzanne decided that she could not remain involved in Jenny's care and in her life?

The day after the meeting with the CSW left me in a state of uncertainty that became more unendurable by the moment. I felt that Suzanne had sabotaged me. Although that may not have been her intention, the result was much the same, and

I felt not only angry with her but as if she were my enemy. My sense of being deliberately betrayed centered on the fact that Suzanne had not discussed her feelings with me prior to the CSW's visit. I had had no opportunity to talk about the problem with Suzanne before it was laid in the lap of the CSW, and I was not prepared for what appeared to be a sneak attack.

I wondered if Suzanne's and my credibility as foster parents had been jeopardized, and if so, to the point that the county might remove Jennifer from our home. Such thoughts were probably an overreaction, but in my mind the stakes were so high and the prospect of such a thing so terrible that I had to consider how to handle even the most extreme possibilities.

What could I do if Suzanne became unwilling to care for Jenny any longer? I did not know what my options were, if any. I was utterly at Suzanne's mercy; whatever direction her whim might take would determine the outcome of Jenny's life and mine. If Suzanne stayed in the picture and we worked things out, our lives could go on as they had. But could they? Would she change her mind again? And when? Was it possible to live like this? If she decided that she could not care for Jenny any more, did she think that we could stay married, that I could even live under the same roof with her?

I wondered if that was how Suzanne saw the picture. Did she see herself holding all the cards? For a while, I had recognized only two possible options; namely, that Suzanne, Jenny, and I would stay together, or that Suzanne and I would have to give Jenny back to the county because of Suzanne's feelings, in which case I could not imagine remaining with Suzanne. I would hate her for the rest of my life. Were these the two options that Suzanne saw? And did she think we would remain together if she caused me to lose Jenny? Or was this her way of getting out of the marriage? Did she detest me that much? Or maybe, in the final analysis, she just could not keep her commitment to Jenny or to me.

I could not remain embroiled in this morass. Suddenly, a thought sprang up which I grasped onto instantly as a ray of hope and my only lifeline. Would the county allow me to keep Jenny, care for her and raise her, as a single parent? I had to know, and I knew what I had to do. If war came I had to be prepared. The way I saw it, war had been declared; I had been attacked. Now it was time to protect Jenny and myself.

I called Fran, the medical social worker at Huntington. I was reluctant to raise the issue with her, because I felt that doing so might make things worse by drawing attention to something not yet critical. However, I decided that this attitude was just a way of my sticking my head in the sand, and that I had to meet the situation head on.

After telling her what had happened, I confessed that I felt like I was in quicksand. I had no footing and could not take a stand because I did not know the possibilities.

Finally, I said, "Fran, if Suzanne and I separate or divorce over this issue, will the county let me keep Jenny? Can I raise her alone? I have to know!"

Fran perceived the depth of my concern and understood the issues involved. She assured me that, without delay, she would telephone her close friend who, in addition to having a senior position at the L.A. County Department of Children's Services, was a woman whom I had also come to know while getting Jenny into our home.

Not more than twenty-four hours passed before Fran called me back. The feeling at the county was that, if I could work out all the logistics in caring for Jenny myself, there seemed to be no reason why I could not keep her. I experienced an indescribable sense of relief. Although the storm around me was far from over and the road ahead would still be difficult, I now had a rock upon which I could stand. I knew that if things fell apart and Suzanne left, Jenny and I could go on together.

Fran and her colleague at the county recognized, as others would, that there was much to be said for Jenny remaining in my care, even if I were a single parent. After some of the shock and fear from this incident had dissipated, I realized that I was probably in a fairly strong position for arguing my case.

Jenny and I had bonded as father and daughter. Leaving aside what pulling us apart would do to me (something that the county would not consider one of their chief concerns), such a break in our relationship could be emotionally and physically devastating to Jenny. Furthermore, I had become an expert in caring for her medically. At that point in time, no one else in the world knew as much as I did about the day-to-day responsibilities, procedures, and nuances involved in caring for her. For the county to take Jenny from me and place her in another foster home, everything would have to start at ground zero. Jenny could not be placed with just anyone, not even for one night. And even the possibility of finding other parents who were both qualified and willing was in question. Then they would have to be extensively trained, certified, and so on, and, depending on where they lived and their financial resources, the problem of finding day care or in-home care would have to be solved all over again.

I thanked God that, at the time, I was not only the county's best bet—I was really the only game in town. Knowing now where I stood, I knew what I would do if I had to. I felt clear, resolved, and battle ready.

I admitted to myself that taking care of Jenny alone would be incredibly demanding. I would have to make all the decisions alone, provide one hundred per cent of the medical care, find time for visits to Dr. Laurance, provide all the transportation to and from day care, and so on. Working overtime at the office even occasionally would be almost out of the question, and I seriously wondered whether or not my managers would really be sympathetic or cooperative. Out-of-town travel or vacations were out of the question.

And what if I became ill? How would I manage? On the other hand, if Jenny got sick and had to stay home from day care, I would have to have plenty of vacation and sick time in reserve at the office to stay home with her, unless I could find a qualified baby sitter or professional nurse, possibly on very short notice. What if they really needed me at the office that day?

Then there was the big issue of finances. Without Suzanne's income, I would either have to sell our home and move into an apartment, or try to meet the mortgage payments and all the other expenses with the help of supplementary income the county provided for taking care of Jenny.

These and many other difficult questions went through my mind. When they sometimes confronted me all at once, I felt overwhelmed. I reminded myself often that, if it came to pass that I had to raise Jenny alone, not all of these issues would be critical on a daily basis—only some of them. I would simply have to be committed and determined, and take things one day at a time. Somehow, I would find a way to deal with all of it. I had to. The only other choice—that of giving Jenny up—was not a choice at all. It was unimaginable.

Meantime, during the few days that passed between my telephone conversations with Fran and the first counseling session with Dr. Wortz on July 5, 1991, the routines at home proceeded on an outwardly normal basis. I am trying to recall talks that Suzanne and I may have had about her issues with Jenny, but I remember essentially nothing, and I am thinking that we probably said very little to each other about it, preferring to postpone any involved discussions—or possible confrontations—until the first counseling appointment. Also by this time, another issue was coming to the surface.

Suzanne had previously begun the custom of a yearly trip to Trappist, Kentucky, about an hour drive from her home near Louisville, in order to make a retreat at the Abbey of our Lady of Gethsemani, established and run by a Trappist order of monks. This beautiful place, situated in rural Kentucky, had once been home to Thomas Merton, a renowned Catholic monk, scholar, and writer, now buried on the grounds, and whose writings Suzanne had studied avidly for years. After making a retreat there one fall, Suzanne had decided to make it an annual tradition. Suzanne had reservations to stay at the Abbey during the first week in August.

With the retreat, and Suzanne's wish to spend time with her family and friends in Kentucky, and to get some rest, the projected length of her absence from Los Angeles grew to almost three full weeks. I felt that this was a long time for her to be away, first of all because it would leave Jenny and me alone for a long stretch, and second, because, given Suzanne's recent doubts about Jenny, I felt that she should place a high priority on spending as much time in L.A. as possible, working with me in counseling with Dr. Wortz.

Frankly, I would have preferred for Suzanne to have canceled her trip entirely. This was probably not really necessary, and my wish was due in part, I admit, to my insecurity about her going, and therefore not based on entirely objective motives. But I did feel that I was being reasonable in asking that she not be gone for such a long time, and for the reasons that I have cited above. However, Suzanne and I were diametrically opposed on the subject, because one my my chief arguments for her not going, or at least not going for so long, which was that we should be spending that time in counseling together, and in trying to work things out, became her primary argument in favor of a long trip—namely, that she needed "space," and as much time away from Jenny and me as possible, in order to sort through her feelings and come to a decision about her ability to continue caring for Jenny.

Thus the differences that Suzanne and I had were now known to each of us. No immediate or easy resolution to the conflict was in sight, and the stage was set for our first counseling session together with Ed Wortz. Since Suzanne's proposed trip was only a month away, there was time for perhaps three or, at the most, four sessions prior to her going. I do not recall how many times we went during the month of July, but I do remember that, on at least one or two of these occasions, Jenny went with us because it was after day-care hours and we did not have a baby sitter for her. While Suzanne and I talked with Dr. Wortz, Jenny busied herself nearby with a pencil and drawing tablet or some other diversion, occasionally coming to one of us, as children do, to get our attention.

It did not seem to me that she paid much attention to what was being said, but who knows what a child hears and understands sometimes? Since I had already had counseling with Dr. Wortz between September and November of 1990, he already knew pretty well what I was all about and the nature of my past difficulties with work and the marriage. Now he needed to get to know Suzanne and develop an understanding of what it was that we were trying to deal with in coming to him. Over the next month, Suzanne and I aired our feelings and differences, and although I suppose that this constituted some progress in and of itself, nothing really got resolved.

Time passed, and whereas I made my desire strongly known that Suzanne not go to Kentucky, or at least shorten the length of her trip, she became more adamant about going for the full three weeks. It was difficult to tell what Dr. Wortz thought of all this. Obviously, part of his job was not to take sides, or if he did, at least not to show it. However, although he played his role of mediator well, I felt that sometimes he leaned in Suzanne's direction, and at other times, in mine.

It is likely that the CSW would have paid Suzanne and me a visit during the month of July, but I cannot specifically remember it. I do remember well, however, that he followed up to make certain that Suzanne and I were getting counseling, and that, hopefully, some progress was being made or that at least progress was possible. Suzanne and I had provided the CSW, at his request, with Dr. Wortz's name and telephone number, and Dr. Wortz subsequently informed us during one of our counseling sessions that the CSW had called him to verify that we were seeing him and to get a progress report. I was very appreciative that Dr. Wortz had given him positive feedback. And, after all, there was no reason for me to view the situation as entirely beyond hope. Nevertheless, my feeling that we were being monitored, or checked up on, made me feel a little uncomfortable and nervous, even though I understood that the CSW was just doing his job.

A Battle Line Is Drawn

In one of the July sessions, Suzanne and I came to the point that, based upon her unwillingness to make a new commitment regarding Jenny and her unrelenting position regarding her upcoming trip, I made it expressly clear where I had drawn the battle line. I had been asking her to cancel or consider shortening her trip, but she maintained her ground. She also maintained an ambiguous stance about whether or not she could "stay in the harness" with respect to being a mother to Jenny. Things had developed in such a way that, in Suzanne's mind, her upcoming retreat to the Abbey of Our Lady of Gethsemani was now the setting in which she would contemplate her relationship with Jenny and come to a decision.

I am aware that my words will have a deep impact upon Suzanne. She and others who know us will eventually read this. I had considered leaving out Suzanne's soul-searching with respect to Jenny and myself, and the conflicts and events that came about as a result of it. However, I am convinced that, if I do not write about everything I feel is essential, the book will fall short of what I deeply wish it to be—a beautiful and vibrant testament to Jennifer's life.

As time goes on, I have fewer and fewer illusions about my own strengths and shortcomings. Life has enabled me to discover inner resources I never knew I had. It has also offered me the opportunity to consider my weaknesses and even my ugliness. I could easily write a book on my own personality deficiencies—my obsessiveness, my need to control, my selfishness, and the inordinate amount of time I took to grow up and become a man, for starters.

I sincerely hope that Suzanne, whom I care for deeply, and all others who read this, will understand that I lay open some private and painful areas of Suzanne's life and mine not to be petty, but because to do less would discredit the depth and beauty of Jennifer's life. If Suzanne or anyone else were to write a book about Jennifer's life, its viewpoint would be understandably different than mine and equally as justifiable from its own perspective.

To continue the story—during the counseling session I found myself increasingly unable to hold back certain feelings. I resented the fact that, apparently, Jenny and I were supposed to remain in limbo about our futures until Suzanne found it convenient to make up her mind about us—until, in accord with her own schedule, she, the one-person jury, had time to arrive at a verdict. My indignation about Suzanne's continued ambiguity, which I saw as very convenient for her, entirely in her favor, and in complete disregard of Jenny and me, was steadily mounting. What clinched it for me was that my pleas for commitment or at least an indication of some definite direction in her thinking were met by an attitude that seemed to say, "Well, I just don't know how I feel, or how I'm going to feel. That's all I can say. Sorry about that."

Suzanne was probably just being honest. But honesty was not what I was looking for—unless it was coupled with commitment. I was not sympathetic to her dilemma, which was probably much more genuine than I was willing to admit. Indeed, I did not deem it in my best interests to be sympathetic, and I took Suzanne's attitude very personally. I saw it as a rejection of Jenny and of me, and the stakes were too high for me to remain totally objective.

Finally, frustrated with Suzanne's ambivalence, I took a stand myself.

Glaring at her, I said defiantly, "Fine! You do whatever you have to do! But I am going to raise Jenny, with or without you!"

For a moment, Suzanne looked startled. This was, in fact, the first time that I had told her unmistakably that I intended to take care of Jenny at all costs and that I would do it alone if I had to. I had made it clear that, if it came to my having to choose between Suzanne and Jenny, I would choose Jenny. I had already made that decision.

I never bluff in confrontations. I would back away (and often did) before saying something I did not mean. This was true in all of my relationships, professional and personal, and had always been true in my marriage with Suzanne. In the past, and as it would be for a long time, Suzanne and I would frequently avoid confrontations, each for different reasons—Suzanne, because she did not like unpleasantness; I, because I did not want to irreparably jeopardize the fragile balance of our relationship and perhaps have to eat my words at a later time.

Only once several years earlier had I laid down an absolute condition upon which the continuation of our marriage depended. In the early part of 1987, I had been in Los Angeles for a year and a half. Suzanne had been still living in Kentucky. Our condominium in Louisville, in which Suzanne had been living, had finally sold after being on the market since the fall of 1985, and Suzanne had come to L.A. in order for me to convince her to move here. During the time we had lived apart, Suzanne had developed misgivings about resettling in L.A., and when she flew out for me to give her my sales pitch, her second thoughts had come sharply into focus.

I explained to her that, although I loved her and wanted her to be in L.A. with me, I would allow her to return to Louisville alone rather than go back with her, even if it meant the end of our marriage, being alone, and losing my job, which at that time was partly under the auspices of her brother. Despite L.A.'s problems, I had found my independence and self-esteem there, which were essential to my sense of dignity, worth, and masculinity, and to have returned to Louisville would have robbed me of all that. I explained that, without my dignity and selfhood, I would be no good to myself and of no value to her or the marriage, either. Suzanne had responded positively to my quiet, firm declaration, and it was not until more than four years later, in Dr. Wortz's office, that I had delivered a second ultimatum.

Suzanne and I had not discussed the possible ramifications and consequences of her giving up her care of Jenny. There was no objective reason for me to think that Suzanne did not expect us to stay together. If she had felt that giving up Jenny automatically meant the end of our marriage, she had not said so. On the other hand, I had suspected more than once that giving up Jenny was Suzanne's way of getting out of a marriage she really did not want to continue. I did not know what Suzanne was thinking at that point, and apparently she did not know either.

Ever since meeting Jenny and talking with Suzanne about bringing her home, I had held onto the hope that having her in our lives would improve our marriage, make us a family, and turn our house into the home I had always wanted. Above all, I felt an irrevocable commitment and consuming love for Jennifer that had come into being from the beginning. Giving her up was unthinkable. I would have died before doing it.

The session ended, time passed, and August approached. Nothing changed. One day Suzanne made a comment that added to my concern, because the sadness in her voice left little doubt that her frame of mind was not very positive. I was lying on our bed and, as she was walking out of the room, she said to me, "If this doesn't work out, you can have the house. I'll just give it to you, so that you and Jenny can stay here."

We Are Alone

On Friday, August 2, 1991, the day after our tenth wedding anniversary, I went to work and Suzanne drove Jennifer to day care. Later that day, Suzanne boarded a flight to Kentucky. I was not expecting to see her for three weeks. In the late afternoon, after work, I drove to All Saints Children's Center to get Jennifer. When I got there, she saw me and in her sweet, touching way, dropped what she was doing, ran to me, and hugged my legs. I picked her up in my arms and we went home.

I parked in the street, and Jenny and I got out of the car. As we were walking into the entrance to our complex, Jenny happened to ask me where Mommy was. Just as I was considering how to explain the concept of an airplane trip across the United States, a jetliner helpfully passed by high overhead. Pointing to it, I said cheerfully, "Mommy's up there in the airplane. She'll be back in a few days." Jenny was satisfied.

That night, Jenny and I went through our usual routines. I gave her a bath, hooked her up to her pumps, and put her to bed. When she was asleep, I had time to ponder what the coming weeks would bring—what Suzanne was thinking and doing, and what she would decide about her life with Jenny and me. I really hoped that during her retreat, she would find new inspiration in her heart that would help to make us a family, and that she would be happy about the idea. Meanwhile, I really did not mind the prospect of Jenny and I going it alone for two or three weeks, except that I was a little nervous. If anything came up, I would be on my own. I hoped everything would go smoothly. I also reflected that if, in the future, things worked out so that Jenny and I were permanently on our own, now would be the time for me to get oriented to what that would be like. I went to bed and slept soundly.

Last Days

Now I lay me down to sleep.
I pray the Lord my soul to keep.
If I should die before I wake,
I pray the Lord my soul to take.

Alarm

On Saturday morning, August 3, the morning after Suzanne's departure, I was awakened around 8:00 A.M. by loud cries from Jenny's room. In alarm, I bolted out of bed immediately because I knew that something was not right. In all my past experience with Jenny, she had never sounded that way. She was not really crying; it sounded as if she were yelling out in pain, or maybe fear. My heart pounding, I ran into her room and stopped short, horrified, in front of her crib.

Jenny was up on all fours, in convulsions. She looked at me, and her eyes were wide with fright. Every few seconds, her entire body jerked with short, violent spasms. She was obviously frightened and disoriented, and I was terrified. The thought kept racing through my mind that bubbles had somehow gotten from the pumps and tubes into her circulatory system and were causing embolisms, possibly in her brain. Yet, during the first panicked seconds that I stared at her, I knew that Jenny was not in pain, but only deeply frightened. I had come to know Jenny and her behaviors intimately over the past months of caring for her, and I could tell when she was in some kind of pain. This was different.

Finally, after about a minute, the convulsions stopped abruptly. Still terribly shaken, I was nevertheless deeply relieved that Jenny then became calm and normal almost immediately. Suddenly, she was her old self, almost as if nothing had ever happened. Although my initial shock and fright were subsiding somewhat, I needed to take action immediately.

Dr. Laurance was not the only physician on Jenny's case. He had recently brought another pediatrician into his private practice on a trial basis, and this young woman was familiar with Jenny. Dr. Laurance was either on vacation or she was taking his calls at that time, and I reached her almost immediately by telephone.

Still shaken, I told her what had happened and was relieved that she at least ruled out the embolism theory. She told me to bring Jenny to the ER at Huntington and asked me if I wanted an ambulance to come and get us. I said that I felt better driving us myself, since the immediate crisis appeared to have passed. I got Jenny unhooked from her pumps, loaded her into the car, and drove her to the hospital.

When Jenny and I arrived at the ER, I parked the car and carried her inside. By this time, she had completely returned to her normal, ebullient self. No one would ever have guessed that, half an hour before, Jennifer had been having convulsions. During the next couple of hours, the staff performed various tests to try to determine what might have caused her strange behavior. Her symptoms were puzzling because, in addition to me, no one at Huntington had ever seen them before. I was baffled. Obviously, something had been very wrong. Yet Jenny had shown no pain and appeared to return to normal quickly. My air bubble theory was not plausible. Besides, I had gotten up an hour or two before she awakened and turned her pumps off when the bells sounded to indicate that they were finished operating.

Finally, the pediatrician came and talked to me. Everything had checked out to be normal—except Jennifer's blood sugar, which had been fairly low initially, but had returned to normal. However, her records showed that when Jenny had lived at the hospital, her blood sugar had often been low in the mornings right after her feedings, but quickly became normal. I mentioned that since tests were not made until forty-five minutes after her convulsions, Jenny's blood sugar could have been much lower around 8:00 A.M. when she awakened. I wondered aloud if this could have caused the convulsions.

The bottom line was that it could not be determined why Jenny had shown such unprecedented symptoms. The pediatrician's observation was that it was probably a fluke that would never happen again. Of course, I was far from completely satisfied. I felt uncomfortable about going home with the matter so unresolved, but I did not see any choice. The pediatrician seemed cheerful and confident in her assertion, so Jenny and I left the hospital, returned home, and had a normal day.

It was, of course, ironic and upsetting to me that the very first morning after Suzanne's departure brought such troubling events. I called Suzanne at the Abbey of Our Lady of Gethsemani and told her what had happened. Suzanne raised her concern about a possible brain hemorrhage, but it did not seem to make sense, given Jennifer's apparent quick recovery. Thus, at that time, it seemed like little more could be done, so I told Suzanne that I would of course contact her immediately if anything else happened and left it at that. Meanwhile, as I said, Jenny and I passed the rest of the day together without further incident, and I put her to bed that evening as usual.

The next morning, Sunday, I awoke a little before 8:00 A.M. and lay quietly in bed, waiting. I had risen earlier, as usual, turned off Jenny's pumps, and gone back to sleep. Although everything was now quiet, I felt apprehensive. I had an uncomfortable feeling I could not explain. A few minutes passed. Suddenly, Jenny cried out. Locking on immediately to the fear in that short yell, I jumped out of bed, knowing without any doubt what I would find. Jenny was lying in her crib, her body jerking with the same frightening spasms that she had had the previous morning.

My heart was pounding. I felt sick with fear, panicked perhaps even more than the day before, since I now knew, agonizingly, that this was no fluke. I tried to reassure Jenny by telling her that everything would be all right and then rushed to the telephone long enough to dial 911 and ask for an ambulance. I was not going to fool around. Shortly thereafter, just like the previous morning, Jenny's convulsions stopped, she returned to normal, and I got her disconnected from her lines. Therefore, when the paramedics arrived a few minutes later, there was little for them to do. Nevertheless, after I explained the situation, they gladly provided transportation to the Huntington ER. I had already called the pediatrician to let her know that Jenny would be going to the ER again.

As the ambulance drove us up the freeway toward Pasadena, I held Jenny, in her diaper and T-shirt, close to me. She seemed fine and was very calm, but I felt the need to hold her next to me. Although she had no fever, we were both sweating, particularly me. It was a warm day, I was nervous and agitated, and since both Jenny and I always seemed to radiate a lot of body heat, our body chemistries often interacted to create the effect of a miniature furnace when she got close to me. As I held her, I looked out the rear window of the ambulance and noticed how fast the cars going in the opposite direction seemed to shoot past us. I commented on this to one of the paramedics, and he said that people often noticed that from my vantage point, since they were unaccustomed to looking out the rear windows of moving vehicles, and that the resulting sensation of high speed was quite pronounced.

When the ambulance arrived at the entrance to the ER, I disembarked and carried Jenny inside. By that time, she was even more bubbly than usual. She was having a great time and made a game of chasing me around a tall chair I had been sitting on. As on the previous day, more testing was done, and no conclusive results were forthcoming. This time the pediatrician opted to admit Jenny to the hospital for observation, and I agreed with her. I got Jenny checked in and transferred to the pediatric ward. She got a room all to herself which, as I remember, was right next to the one she had lived in. She knew a number of the nurses and did not seem to mind being there. I stayed with her for a while, then called a cab in order to go home, get cleaned up, and come back later in the afternoon. I promised Jennifer that I would be back in a couple of hours.

Sometime late that morning or early afternoon, I talked to Suzanne again. Later that day or the next, she had a telephone conversation with the pediatrician and asked her if it was appropriate for her to return to Los Angeles. Based on what was known at that time, the pediatrician did not feel that it was necessary, so Suzanne remained in Kentucky. My own dialogues with Jenny's pediatrician gave her some additional background on Jenny based on my own experiences and insights, and she in turn conveyed her strategy for the next couple of days.

One thing I explained to her was that, with Dr. Laurance's blessing (and possibly even at his suggestion), Suzanne and I had recently cut back the time on Jenny's feedings by about an hour. This meant that, although she was receiving the same amount of nutrition every night, the time over which it was being delivered into her system was compressed. Although having Jenny hooked up to her pumps for less time each night gave her more freedom and was advantageous for Suzanne and me, I was beginning to wonder, again, if the new arrangement was putting too much stress on her system. When I had raised the issue with Dr. Laurance previously, he had not thought that it would be a problem, and the new pediatrician seemed to concur when I brought it up again with her.

However, she did point out something to me I had not known; namely, that the pumps in the hospital were designed so as to taper automatically the rate of Jennifer's feedings at the beginning and end of each cycle. In other words, when the feeding began, the rate of delivery started slowly, then increased to a steady level. Near the end of the cycle, the rate automatically slowed down again, decreasingly gradually until the feeding was completed. Since the pumps at home did not have this feature, the rate of delivery of Jenny's feedings was constant throughout the cycle; there was no gradual increase at the beginning or decrease at the end. At home, the probable result of using pumps whose cycles could not be tapered was that Jennifer's system experienced more of a shock at the start and close of each feeding. This was perhaps causing a sudden drop in her blood sugar at the end of the feeding, maybe even enough to have initiated hypoglycemic shock and the resulting convulsions.

This made sense. Even though I was not a doctor and my point did not appear to find its mark, I suspected that the recently instigated shortened feeding cycle was also a factor. After all, if Jenny had a history of low blood sugar at the end of her feedings even when she lived at the hospital, and if her system had been stressed additionally by untapered feedings at home, why would the negative effect not be even further compounded by a compressed cycle?

At any rate, the pediatrician's strategy was to keep Jenny at Huntington for two or three days, monitor her closely, and see what happened. Thus, on Sunday afternoon, after I had taken a cab home to get cleaned up and straighten the house, I drove back to Huntington to visit Jenny and stayed with her until she went to bed and fell asleep that night. The next day, Monday, I telephoned All Saints Children's Center early in the morning to inform them that Jenny would be out for a while and then went to work. I planned to go back to the hospital in the evening.

Something extremely unfortunate happened very early on during Jennifer's stay on the pediatric ward. One of the children had contracted measles and Jenny had been exposed. Although the child with the disease had been released to go home, Jenny, who had never had measles, had to be quarantined in her room until it could be determined if she had contracted them herself. In addition, since the nurses on the unit were fairly busy for most of their shift, they did not have a lot of time to spend with Jenny in her room. Because there was some concern about Jenny's welfare if she were left to play in her room unattended, she was confined to her crib whenever she had to be alone. Although, of course, I understood the quarantine, I never saw the point of the crib business, and I objected to it strongly as unnecessary and cruel. Jenny was virtually incarcerated for the largest portion of the day, imprisoned behind the closed steel bars of her crib. My appeals, however, were overruled, and under protest, I submitted to the arrangement. There was nothing I could do.

I felt deeply sorry for Jenny. She had a hard enough time just with the idea of not being able to go out in the hallway and staying in her room with the door closed. Confining her to her crib was ridiculous and inhumane, and she utterly failed to comprehend why she was being subjected to that. When I rushed over to the hospital after work late Monday afternoon to see her, I looked through the large window in the door to her room to see her sitting miserably in her crib. I immediately freed her and hugged her. We played in her room all evening. Jenny became upset several times and sometimes cried when I had to prevent her from going out into the hall. I tried to placate her by saying that she was being kept in her room to protect her from catching something from another sick child, which was not really true, but it was the best story that I could come up with that she might be able to understand.

Jenny's physiology was monitored by her pediatrician and the hospital staff. Nothing unusual turned up, and I was not surprised when no more convulsions occurred. The period of time over which Jenny received her feedings each night at the hospital was a bit longer than at home, and this, in my personal opinion, in addition to the fact that the cycles on the hospital pumps were tapered, lessened the strain on Jenny's system enough so that no severe glucose imbalances or other physiological abnormalities occurred.

Her pediatrician informed me that pumps for home use could be obtained which had the tapering feature. This was good news, although she told me also that it would take a little time to get these new pumps and exchange them with the ones currently in the house. She suggested that in the meantime, after Jenny went home, I could manually taper Jenny's feedings toward the end of each cycle by adjusting their programs every half hour, starting two hours before the end of the feedings. For me, this would mean setting my alarm several times and getting up every half hour from 5:00 A.M. on, but I was willing to do this if it would help Jennifer.

Also, during Jenny's few days at Huntington, her pediatrician had another idea which, although I was virtually certain was doomed to failure, I agreed to try. The pediatrician reasoned that clamping off Jenny's gastrostomy tube might force any water or bile in her stomach through her gut and make it work. I was convinced that Jenny's medical problems were much too complex to be amenable to such a simple solution, and I told the pediatrician that, in all likelihood, all that would happen would be that, as soon as enough bile had collected in Jenny's stomach, it would force its way out around the tube, out through the gastrostomy site, and burn her skin, and that she would start throwing up. Nevertheless, I felt that Jenny deserved the chance.

We clamped off Jenny's tube, and in only a few hours she started to vomit and to leak a great deal of bile around her gastrostomy site, which soaked her dressings and made them useless and blistered her skin. I called the experiment off. It was not going to work, and it was absurd to make Jenny suffer for nothing. The pediatrician asked, "Don't you want her to get better?"

"Of course I do," I replied, "but this isn't working and it's only making her miserable." That was the end of the experiment.

I went to visit Jenny Monday afternoon after work. While I was with her, something very beautiful happened, something that touched me deeply which I will never forget. I was sitting with Jenny on the floor of her hospital room while we played with crayons and paper. The door was closed and we were alone. It was late in the afternoon, but the room was still pleasantly lit with sunshine. Jenny was in a very good mood and happy that I had come.

I took a crayon and a piece of paper and slowly printed out her name, saying each letter aloud as I wrote it: "J-E-N-N-Y."

When I finished, Jenny then took a piece of paper and, with her own crayon, made three marks. As she made each mark, she said something. The words that came out were, "I-love-Daddy." She beamed up at me. Tears filled my eyes. I knew that Jenny loved me; she had shown it in a thousand ways. But this was the first time she had ever said it, and she had done so without prompting. It had come to her of her own accord to tell me how she felt. I thanked her and hugged her, and she knew how deeply happy she had made me.

Those three words Jenny said to me that afternoon mean more to me than anything else anyone has ever said to me during my whole life. Hearing her say that was a gift of immeasurable value, especially given the things that were to come, but which I could not possibly envision that afternoon.

To my great relief, the pediatrician saw no reason to keep Jennifer in the hospital beyond Tuesday. No specific problems had been identified, but at least Jenny had experienced no more convulsions and the prospect of the new pumps with tapering capabilities offered hope for the future. On Tuesday afternoon after work, I retrieved Jenny from Huntington and took her home. I had never been so happy to get her back home from the hospital as I was that day, especially because she had been virtually a prisoner there.

After Jenny and I arrived home and were walking up the driveway at Vallejo Villas, a jetliner happened to pass high overhead, just as one had done a few days earlier when I had tried to explain where Suzanne had gone. This time, Jenny pointed up at the airplane, looked at me and smiled, and said, "Mommy!" I realized that she thought it was the same plane which had been up there several days earlier, and that Suzanne was still in it. How logical children are, within the limitations of their knowledge of things! It was perfectly logical for Jenny to infer that the plane was the same one, and that Suzanne was still up there flying around, doing whatever it was that she was doing. I saw no reason to alter her concept of aviation, so I let it pass as we walked to our unit.

Everything went smoothly. Tuesday night was uneventful, and I arose at around 5:00 A.M. and every half hour thereafter until 7:00 to taper down Jenny's feedings manually. On Wednesday morning, Jenny returned to day care. The following morning, I also arose early at half-hour intervals to adjust Jenny's pumps and later took her to day care. In my mind, I clearly see myself arriving at All Saints Children's Center after work on Thursday to pick her up. I can still see the dress that she was wearing as she sat playing in the sand. I can see her turning to see me, dropping her toys, running to me and hugging me, and saying happily and proudly to her teachers, "My daddy!"

I carried Jenny to the car and we left. On the way home, she fell asleep, or seemed to. By the time we pulled into the driveway at Vallejo Villas, she looked dead to the world. It had only been her second day back at day care and the weather had been hot, so I figured that she was probably worn out. When we pulled up in front of the garage, I said her name. She did not respond, so I repeated it, louder. Nothing happened. I spoke to her several times, each time more loudly, until I was practically yelling. I even tapped her cheek gently with the palm of my hand, but she showed no signs of life. Frightened, I was on the verge of making a U-turn and beating it back to the hospital when Jenny suddenly came around. Her head jerked a bit and her eyes snapped open. She looked a little disoriented, but glanced around and quickly got her bearings. It was just as if she had suddenly stirred out of a sound sleep and then everything seemed fine. She was herself again.

After that, and until bedtime, Jenny appeared to be all right. Somehow, though, I was a little troubled, because nothing quite like that had ever happened before with Jenny. I think it was before Jenny went to bed that I telephoned Zippy, Suzanne's nursing colleague and close friend. I told her what had happened with Jenny in the car, and she reminded me that it was quite normal for children to fall into deep sleeps like a sack of potatoes in the car, in strollers, and so on. They were very hard to wake up. I had, in fact, seen this happen in public with other people's children many times, so Zippy's assurances that everything was all right pretty much put my mind to rest and I did not think too much more about it.

Later, Jenny and I bathed in Mommie's shower. Jenny and I talked a lot and read some story books. Finally, I hooked her up to her pumps and put her to bed. She was sound asleep by around 8:00 P.M.

Our Last Night

Around 8:30, I went into Jenny's room. She seemed to be sound asleep. I tiptoed around on the carpeting without making a sound. However, as I was about to leave, I opened one of her closet doors to check something, and when I started to close it again, it made a small squeak, but loud enough, apparently, to awaken Jenny. She lifted her ahead unhappily and started to cry.

From then on, until around midnight, I had a terrible time with her. She had never been like that at home. At best she was fussy, and at times she grew extremely fretful and had spells during which she acted almost wildly. If she slept at all, it was very little. She often thrashed about and repeatedly entangled herself in her lines. It was an effort for me to hold her arms and legs still long enough to extricate her. I was very concerned about the damage she might do to herself.

Whatever was going on, I knew Jenny was not in physical pain. If she had been, she would have told me. I also checked carefully several times to make certain that she had no temperature. She did not seem ill, but something was not right.

Several times, I tried leaving her alone, thinking that she would be better off, since I could do little to calm her, but this did not help things at all, so I decided I had better stay in the room with her. I tried everything I could think of to soothe her. I played tapes. I talked to her. At one point, I took her out of the crib and held her in the rocking chair, but she only thrashed against me and continued to vent her frustration and unhappiness by crying or complaining. I spread blankets on the floor and laid her down next to me, but this did nothing. She crawled about like a restless animal, so finally I put her back in her crib.

As time passed and her behavior showed no signs of abating, I got more and more worried, frustrated, and upset. I am very sorry to say that once, while she was lying in her crib and fussing and thrashing about so much in her lines that I thought she would hurt herself or pull them apart, I even yelled at her, out of frustration and deep anxiety, to try to make her quiet down, which I had never done before. But I honestly do not think that she even really noticed or heard me. She seemed completely oblivious to my voice, as if she were totally withdrawn into her own inner world.

Once, during all the chaos, during one of the periods when Jenny was in her crib and churning around, I thought or imagined that I heard a soft but urgent voice inside myself, a kind of intuition or prompting that seemed to say, "Turn off the pumps!" It arrested my attention completely for a moment, but I was puzzled.

I was confused, frustrated, and almost desperate. I could not tell if the voice was real or not, if it was just my own imagination or a manifestation of my growing sense of helplessness. Perhaps it was just my mind frantically searching for an explanation or a course of action.

I chose to dismiss the voice. Rather than interpreting it as a genuine intuition, I decided that it was just my own mind groping for some strategy or solution. Turning off the pumps did not make sense. What harm could they be doing? There were no air bubbles or alarms going off. And Jenny had to "eat." I could not deprive her of her nutrition just because she was fretful.

Now, I will never know if I did the wrong thing. I will never know, for certain, whether or not shutting down the pumps might have led to an entirely different outcome for Jenny. I will never know if that voice was real or just part of the growing desperation and concern that I felt.

Finally, at 10:30, I called Dr. Laurance. I was torn. I did not want to disturb a hard-working doctor unnecessarily, but Jenny's wildness, which showed no signs of diminishing, her sporadic bouts of fretting and crying, and the strangeness of it all compelled me to make the call. After reaching him and describing what had been going on, I got the feeling that, under his essentially polite demeanor, he might have been wondering why I had called him, since, in my own words and in his judgment, Jenny did not actually seem sick and was not running any fever. Frankly, there was something in Dr. Laurance's voice that made me feel foolish. I accepted his presumption that Jenny was just "having a bad night," as all children sometimes do. I tried to be encouraged and thanked him and hung up.

Many times since that night, I have thought to myself that Suzanne's presence then—her medical knowledge and experience, and her personal support—might have been of great, if not critical, importance. But I was alone, and I had to make the best decisions that I could. I may have called Zippy again that evening. Parts of my memory are blurred. I felt something was wrong, but I was at a loss, especially after the phone call to Dr. Laurance, about what to do.

Jenny finally quieted down around midnight. Once after that, I went quietly back into her room. She lay there silently; and without moving, she looked directly into my eyes with her own wide, deep, unblinking eyes, without saying a word—something very unique and especially arresting because she had been so agitated earlier. When she looked at me, the thought went through my mind that the poor child was just too tired to say anything at all.

Jenny fell asleep, although she remained restless, dreamed a great deal, and talked in her sleep for the next couple of hours. I returned to my room unable to sleep and lay or sat in bed, listening. I heard her say "Daddy" two or three times, but not as if she was calling to me. Rather, I had the distinct sense that, in her dreams, she was talking about me to someone. And, several times, very distinctly, I heard her say "all done, all done," something she would almost always say when Suzanne or I had finished changing her dressings or completed cleaning the site of her Broviac catheter, or were done reinserting her gastrostomy tube. I lay in my bed wondering what Jenny was dreaming about, and what was "all done."

At one point, I found myself experiencing the oddest feeling that Jenny and I were the only two people in the whole creation. As I looked out the window from my bed at the darkness and the quiet night sky, it was as if she and I were alone someplace on a tiny island in an otherwise empty universe.

From time to time, she coughed a little—odd, single, quiet, dry little coughs that I had never heard before. And occasionally, I heard her make a very quiet, expressive little sigh.

Despite Jenny's relative quietness, I felt strange and apprehensive. Deep inside, I knew something was wrong, but I could not define it. I sensed that, in her own way, Jenny also knew that something was different that night. Around 1:00 A.M., I telephoned Sue Collins, Jenny's former child life therapist at Huntington, in Las Vegas where she now lived. I had to talk to someone, and Sue, who had last been to see us on the Fourth of July and who knew Jenny and loved her so much, seemed like the person to call.

She was very understanding when I apologized for telephoning at that time of night. I talked with her for nearly an hour, filling her in on everything that had been going on in our lives, especially with regard to what had taken place over the last week, and that night in particular. During our conversation, Jenny continued to dream and talk in her sleep. For some reason I could not explain, I brought up the subject of death and talked about it quite a bit—not just with respect to the possibility of a short life for Jenny, but about death in general. As the hour passed, the indefinable, agonizing apprehension I had been feeling was somewhat alleviated. At last, I thanked her for listening and for her support and ended our conversation.

It was about 2:00 A.M. Although Jenny was quiet, I lay awake until around 3:30, then fell asleep. I got up at 4:00 A.M. and every half hour thereafter until 5:30 to check Jenny's pumps and manually taper her feedings. Jenny's room was dark and she was very still. I sensed nothing wrong, and after shutting the pumps off at 5:30, I went back to bed and fell asleep again.

Jenny Is Gone

I awoke around 8:00 A.M.. From my bed, I looked out the window across the bedroom. It was sunny and quiet outside, and things seemed peaceful. I even felt rested. There was no sound from Jenny's room, and I was certain she was still sleeping. I remember thinking that, since it was Friday, a work day for me, I would not awaken her. She'd had a very difficult night and needed a lot of rest. I decided to let her sleep and that, when she awoke, I would take her to day care if she felt like going. Otherwise, I would take the day off from work and stay home with her.

I decided to check on her, so I got out of bed and quietly went into her room. I approached her crib cautiously, in order not to awaken her. She was on her stomach, with her head turned toward the center of the room. As I watched her, I noticed how very, very still she was, and I could not see her back rising and falling. Since a child's breathing is not always apparent when it is asleep, I did not feel alarm, but I found myself leaning over the crib and looking at her more closely. Seeing no movement, I reached out instinctively and slowly placed my hand on the middle of her back. It was as hard as a rock and ice-cold. I drew back in horror, and even before my mind could form the thought I knew absolutely, in my soul and in every cell of my body, that she was dead, and that she had been dead for several hours.

Knowing, yet not able to believe, without thinking, I took hold of her little arm and lifted it. It, too, was cold and hard, and I let go of it. In an instant I saw that her eyes were half open and clear, yet oddly and terribly empty. There was no life in them. Her soul had departed. Jenny was gone.

I remember uttering, "Oh, Jenny!" I gasped and felt my heart pounding in my chest. I could feel the adrenaline pouring into me. Just in the few seconds since I had first touched her, I knew fully the agony of realization that those past months, so full of loving, sharing, worrying, working, and hoping, were irretrievably gone. Jennifer had been taken from me. My whole life and my motivation for living, the child whom I had loved with immeasurable depth and passion, was gone—forever. And I felt utterly abandoned.

The next several hours were a blur. I remember many things I did, but even now the sequence is a jumble in my mind. Shaking, in shock, overcome with panic and engulfed in an emotional whirlwind, I made my way blindly out of Jenny's room and back into the bedroom. Mechanically, I picked up the telephone and dialed 911. Breathing rapidly, I told the dispatcher that my daughter was dead. She asked me if I was certain. I did something utterly illogical. Although I knew she had been dead for hours, I numbly went to her crib and touched her again to convince myself that it was really so, hoping some desperate, insane hope that she was not really gone. I returned to the phone.

Over the next few hours, mechanically, resolutely, I made call after call. It seemed to be the only thing my mind and body could do. It was the only thing I could hold on to. I went to my neighbors, Lee and Lillian, right away and told them Jenny was dead. Lee came back with me and stayed for most of the morning while I did the things I had to do. Dr. Laurance was not in his office, so I left a message. I called Huntington, the Los Angeles County Department of Children's Services, and All Saints Children's Center. I called my office, my mother, and my close friends—I lost track.

Then, I had to tell Suzanne. I telephoned the Abbey of Our Lady of Gethsemani and spoke with the brother at the switchboard. Telling him what had happened, I urgently requested him to find Suzanne and have her call me back immediately, cautioning him not to break the news of Jenny's death to her. Then I called Dale Roggenkamp, our dear friend in Louisville who, with her husband, Jim, had been visiting in Los Angeles a few weeks earlier and had come to Jenny's third birthday party. Dale was stunned and promised to do her best to locate Suzanne's brother, Charlie, who was in Los Angeles. Then she would drive down to the Abbey to get Suzanne, while I was waiting for Suzanne to call me back.

After people started arriving at my home, Suzanne called. Her voice betrayed concern and a note of apprehension.

"Suzanne," I said, "I don't know how to tell you this—but Jenny is dead."

At first she could not process what I had just told her.

"You're kidding," she said, numbly.

I told her that I had found Jenny dead that morning. My words sank in, and Suzanne cried out, "Oh, my baby," and burst into tears. I cannot remember the rest of the conversation, except that, since Suzanne had driven her sister's car to the Abbey, she would leave it there. She would wait for Dale to arrive and go back with her to Louisville and fly to Los Angeles immediately.

The sequence of things that morning is still a jumble in my memory. A team of paramedics had quickly arrived, realizing right away there was nothing they could do. I heard one paramedic mention to another one that he had also been to the house the previous Sunday, when their ambulance had taken Jenny and me to the Huntington ER. Other people began arriving. Derrick, my friend from the office, got there first. Upon hearing the news at work, he had been kind enough to drop everything and come over immediately, anticipating that I would be alone. I hugged him and cried. I cannot remember who came next, but within an hour or two, many people appeared. Dale had somehow been able to locate Suzanne's brother, Charlie, who came right away. Dr. Laurance came. Fran, the social worker from Huntington, and others from the hospital appeared, and also a lady who represented the company that provided much of Jenny's medical equipment. Sometime, two police officers had also come, probably having been notified by the 911 operator. The house was full of people. They were all over the place. I was all over the place.

I had gently placed a blanket over Jenny. I could not bear to look again at the emptiness in her half-opened eyes. Several times I felt the need to touch her body. It seemed to grow colder and colder, like ice, and her feet were turning blue. Her diaper was soaked, as it always was in the mornings because her body processed so much liquid nourishment during the night. I wanted to change it, but it would have been extremely difficult because she was very stiff.

Once when I entered Jenny's room, I noticed that the blanket covering her head and face had been removed. Dr. Laurance, along with two other people, was sitting on the sofa bed, looking at Jenny through the red vertical railing of her crib. He told me that somehow he needed to see her face, and I did not wish to deny him, even though it was painful for me.

Finally, a man from the Los Angeles County Coroner's office arrived. I am not sure, but, since Jenny was a ward of the county and state, I think the coroner needed to be involved. Jenny had to be taken to the county morgue. I took the man downstairs to Jenny's room. Several people were still there, including Dr.

Laurance, Fran, and Derrick. The man lifted Jenny's body from her crib and placed it on a plastic sheet he had spread out on the carpet. She was still attached to all of her tubes from the previous night's feeding.

It was his intention to cut the tubes in order to free her body from them, but I stopped him, saying quietly but resolutely, "No, I'll do it myself. I've been taking care of her all this time. There's no reason for me to stop now."

Everyone was standing around me. Taking a pair of scissors, I knelt down beside Jenny and grimly cut the tubes. The man from the coroner's office then carefully wrapped Jenny's body with the edges of the plastic sheet and taped it securely. He was going to carry her body out of the house, but I could not think of anyone else doing that but me. I did not want to let her go.

The time had come. With indescribable sadness, I lifted Jenny from the floor. She felt oddly heavy to me. I could not remember her weighing so much. Her little body was hard and absolutely stiff, like a mannequin, but very heavy. Holding her against my right hip with my arms around her, much as I would if I were carrying her in the grocery store or the park, I turned, walked out of her room, and slowly climbed the stairs. Outside, a white panel van was parked in front of my garage. The man from the county opened its rear doors. The back of the van had no seats or equipment; it was completely empty. I gently laid Jenny on the floor of the van near the wall, and the man shut the doors. I must have watched him turn the van around and drive away, but I do not remember. I cannot remember the people who went outside with me, nor do I recollect going back into the house.

At some point I noticed Fran and the lady from the firm who supplied the medical equipment carrying much of the apparatus up the stairs and out of the house. This took me aback, somehow. I felt that they were being very premature, and I clearly remember thinking, however illogically, that Jenny might still need this equipment. Part of me had not accepted that she was gone forever. Fran tried to tell me that it would be easier on me if they took it away as soon as possible. Numbly, but still troubled, I acquiesced—by my silence, if nothing else. Later, I think after almost everyone had gone, I noticed that, in addition to the three pumps and their stand and the small refrigerator with the liquid feedings it contained, almost all of the other disposable medical supplies had been removed. This was too much for me, and too sudden. Despite what I assume were good intentions on their part, I strongly regretted, then and many times since, that I did not make them wait a day or so before removing anything, because I very much wanted to keep some of those things. Fortunately, they did not find the cloth handbag that I kept for outings with Jenny, which contained things like spare colostomy bags, medical tape, gauze, scissors, and the like. That, at least, I still have.

Eventually, as time passed, people began to leave singly or in small groups. Fran was one of the last to go. We stood outside by the garage for a few moments. Fran offered to me her conviction that Jenny's dying at home, alone with me, was somehow appropriate, even ironic; and that, in her mind, the primary destiny in all of this was that Jenny and I should find each other. I also felt that this was so.

Charlie and Derrick remained with me. By the time everyone else had gone, it must have been late morning or early afternoon. Most of that afternoon is a blank to me. However, one of the first things I did—something I felt a real need to do—was to remove all of the linens and blankets from Jenny's bed and wash them. It was almost an automatic action, since I did this daily. Typically, Jenny wet so much during the night, because of her liquid feedings, that her bed, as well as her diaper, usually a double one, was soaked by morning. After laundering everything, I carefully, lovingly remade her bed and draped her little folded blankets over the railing of her crib. My heart could not understand that she would not sleep there again.

The agony, sadness, and loss I felt that day and continuously for weeks and months to come is indescribable. Words cannot possibly convey, except perhaps to those who themselves have experienced the death of their child, the unimaginable pain and desolation. Suicide was not, at that very early stage, a thought that entered my mind. Nevertheless, had I been able to join Jenny that day, wherever she was, by turning my back forever on the world and everything in it and walking out, I would have done so without a second's hesitation.

Sometime during the day, after people had gone and the house had quieted down, I made one more phone call—to Shupshe Wahnah in Fort Wayne, Indiana. Shupshe was a Potawatomi Indian chief and a medicine man, and much more. Although I had not had any contact with him for quite a while, I still considered him a real friend. I had met him in September 1981, while I was doing research on certain Indian tribes and terminology for a book I was writing. Shupshe had befriended me and provided me with critical information and insight into certain aspects of my own psychic experiences, and had remained my friend and counselor. His metaphysical ideas and spiritual outlook were very much in harmony with my own, and I felt the need to talk to him.

He had not known Jenny, so I told him about her and that she had just died that day. Shupshe was very kind, and I found reassurance just in hearing his gentle voice. He mentioned something that I have never forgotten, namely, that Jenny's medical problems in this life might have been an indication that, in a past incarnation, she was some kind of martyr. He explained that sometimes physical problems in a present life are repercussions from injuries or wounds from a former existence. I was familiar with this idea and open to it. He also suggested that Jenny might have deliberately taken on some of the karma of her Siamese twin, as advanced spiritual teachers are believed to do sometimes, in helping a follower or a friend.

Neither Shupshe nor I could say for certain what the truth was, but it was something to reflect upon. In the coming months, I would try to discover the causes hidden beneath all that had happened. But for the time being, there was only the shock and sadness and no room for anything else. We said goodbye, but I called him the following day and we talked a little more. I knew his special prayers were with me.

The afternoon wore on, and near dinnertime a dear colleague of Suzanne's from Huntington who had come to the house that morning returned with food and prepared something for Charlie, Derrick, and me to eat. Her thoughtful gesture was deeply appreciated, but I was able to eat little. After dinner, we talked awhile until Charlie suggested that we should leave for the airport to pick up Suzanne.

I do not remember the trip to the airport with Charlie and Derrick. The only thing that comes to mind is seeing Suzanne coming through the gate from the airplane, our eyes meeting, and her walking toward me. We embraced each other, said something I cannot remember, and walked out with Charlie and Derrick. The drive home and any conversation in the car is missing from my memory. After we got home, Derrick stayed for a bit and then went on. Finally, Charlie also said good night and left.

Suzanne and I were alone in the empty house. We were in shock and exhausted. We talked awhile, and I told her what had happened that day. Finally, late in the evening, we went to bed. As I lay still in the darkness, facing a large, open window and the night sky, my heart and my whole being, the house, the whole world, my awareness and everything in it were known to me only as they existed in a terrible, indescribable void—an empty silence—the numbing, agonizing reality that our sweet Jenny was gone. There was no fantasy or dream which could keep at bay the realization that pierced my heart like a knife, which pushed against me every second, relentlessly, mercilessly, from every side. I lay there without thought, existing only in a state of feeling, identified totally with Jenny—her overwhelming presence, and her overwhelming absence. Then I fell asleep.

Jenny's Message

I awoke and opened my eyes instantly to the darkness. The reality was still there. It had been with me, up against me, every second that I slept, waiting, patient and unflagging in its vigilance, a predatory animal silently watching its prey, intent upon pouncing at the right moment. And with it, the strangest, most indescribable feeling! My body had not shifted positions. I put on my glasses. The digital clock on the dresser said 3:35 A.M. Softly, a melody was going through my head, so hauntingly familiar, yet evading me! What was it? I had awakened in the middle of it, and also with the overwhelming, absolute conviction—beautiful, yet painful and deeply haunting—that Jenny had been there with me!

The song. It was one of the tunes from Jenny's bedtime tapes, but which one? I had heard it God knows how many times, and yet consciously I had never paid particularly close attention to the words or the title. But again and again the melody went around in my mind like a loop, and yet the words escaped me. Suddenly, stunningly, three words of the refrain came to me: "Sleep, Daddy, sleep!" Yes! Oh, God, I knew beyond any doubt, with my whole heart, that Jenny had been there with me! She was watching over me, caring for me, wanting me to rest, to sleep. With a conviction that comes only from the depths of the soul, I knew that she had been there. I awoke Suzanne. I had to tell her.

In the morning, I felt strongly compelled to find out about the song. Going into Jenny's room, I looked through the collection of cassette tapes on her shelves. To my amazement, on one of her tapes of bedtime lullabies, a Disney tape entitled "Disney Babies Lullaby Favorites," was a song entitled "Sleep, Daddy, Sleep," by Baer. In the past, I had never really read many of the titles of songs on Jenny's tapes, and although, as I said, I am sure I had played that tape for Jenny uncounted times after putting her into her crib at night, I was not consciously aware of this piece of music. Nevertheless, the phrase, "Sleep, Daddy, sleep," had filled my awareness during the early morning hours. Deeply curious, I played the selection, listening closely to the words.

The song conjured up charming images: a child's love for its father, who has fallen asleep in front of the television; the child's sense of love and security as he watches his mother rock his little brother; and the pleasure of being tucked in bed at night; and the refrain, "Sleep, Daddy, sleep."

It is now August 1995, four years later. Two days ago, I went through Jenny's things, got out the tape, and played the song again and again. I had forgotten all of the words except "Sleep, Daddy, sleep." Saturday, August 10, 1991, when I played the tape the morning after Jenny's death, I do not think that I absorbed much of the song, except that I was profoundly struck by the phrase, "Sleep, Daddy, sleep." Two nights ago, as I listened to the entire song again, I was deeply affected by its sweetness and beauty; it touchingly conveyed the warmth, innocence, love, and trust a young child feels in the nurturing surroundings provided by its parents. The words and melody aroused in me the powerful love and fatherly instinct that I felt, and still feel, for Jenny; and although the song made me feel good and warm, it also made me very sad. That sweet little song made me ache to have Jenny back downstairs sleeping securely in her bed, with me watching over her.

And today, as four years ago, I know with all my being that Jenny was there with me in those early morning hours of August 10, 1991—looking after me, caring for me. I cannot prove it, and I cannot prove that the experience was more than just wishful thinking. I shall not try. But Jenny's spirit was in that room with me. I felt her there. I felt her love.

Beginning that morning and nearly every morning after that for many days and perhaps weeks, I awoke at 3:35 A.M., or within three or four minutes either way. Again, I cannot prove it, but I feel very deeply that Jenny died at that time. From midnight to 2:00 A.M., Friday morning, August 9, Jenny had slept restlessly, dreaming, talking in her sleep, and so on. Then she quieted down. I fell asleep around 3:30 A.M., then got up again at 4:00 A.M. and periodically thereafter until 5:30 A.M. Then I slept until 8:00 in the morning. I am convinced that Jenny actually died right after I fell asleep at 3:30 A.M. The state of her body when I found her in the morning supports this. My deep intuition also tells me this is true. That's why I began to awaken at 3:35 every morning for a long time after that.

I would awaken suddenly and totally, but quietly, and look at the clock, as I had on August 10. I would have that same strange, inexplicably overwhelming feeling of Jenny's spiritual presence in the room, and I would experience that inexpressible ache in my heart, like a fresh wound, each morning—the crushing reality that, physically, Jenny was gone forever.

I believe that some plan known only to the soul—a knowledge, and the harmony of timing shared between Jenny's soul and mine—some design called her from the earth early that Friday morning only after I had finally gone to asleep. Perhaps the bond between us was so strong that only after both of us had fallen asleep could we be separated. Only then could Death slip into her room and quietly take her from me without a struggle. Otherwise, I would not have let her go.

Was I to regard this as merciful for both of us? Sometimes I have felt that this was so. At other times, in despair, I have felt as if Jenny was stolen from me, that Death came like a "thief in the night," robbed me, when my back was turned—even though only for a moment—of the one who was most precious to me. At such times, I felt cheated, even tricked. Yet often, I would come to see in the circumstances of Jenny's death a fitness that could even be regarded as a gesture of love from the Power that had entwined our lives. Looked at in this way, the unavoidable brutalization that I would feel from Jenny's death was mitigated as much as possible by the gentle way in which she left me. And for this I am truly grateful.

Funeral Preparations

The next few days which followed were strange, confused, and filled with inexpressible sadness. Still in shock, as we would be for some time, Suzanne and I faced the immediate responsibility of getting Jenny buried and dealing with all the details that came with her death. So much happened between Saturday and Wednesday, and there were so many problems, that it is difficult to sort everything out four years later.

On Saturday, August 10, Suzanne and I, accompanied by her friends, Zippy and Julie, who had come to offer emotional and practical support, met with the funeral director from Cabot and Sons, who had been recommended to us by the priest from Suzanne's church. Suzanne and I sat in his office in a daze, trying to focus on making decisions that had to be addressed without delay. One of the most difficult issues was the coffin. Suzanne was more emotional than I was. I felt numb and empty. There was no energy within me for any upheaval of feeling.

Given the condition I was in, it was good that, with my blessing, Suzanne was willing to take the lead in resolving various details, starting that day, asking for my input whenever appropriate. Although I made notes about various costs, she looked after many things, including the organization of the funeral mass to be held on Wednesday, August 14, at Holy Family Church, the speakers, the music, and the pallbearers, who would be Charlie, Derrick, Roger (the film director who had played a role in our initial interest in Jenny), and Dr. Laurance.

Suzanne chose the flowers for Jenny's coffin—a spray of four dozen pink sweetheart roses with baby's-breath—and a ribbon with the inscription, "Jenny, Our Precious Baby." She and I also specified that certain mementos of personal and spiritual significance were to be placed in Jenny's coffin and buried with her. Suzanne also selected Jenny's burial clothing—her best underwear, her black, patent leather shoes, and the lovely dress that she had last worn to her little friend's birthday party on June 8. The dress still had traces of candle wax on it from the party, and Suzanne asked that it be left as it was to commemorate Jenny's going to that event. Finally, Suzanne instructed the funeral director to get some clippings of Jenny's hair and fingernails for us to keep.

Suzanne would help make arrangements for a brunch at Charlie's condominium in Glendale after the funeral mass. I would work with the funeral director in resolving other matters, including the autopsy to be performed by the Los Angeles County Coroner's Office (at my request), the autopsy report, the listed cause of death, and the death certificate. Although it would turn out that I would not talk with the pathologist who did Jenny's autopsy until mid-December, I received at least one telephone call from an investigator (who was very kind) from the county coroner's office, during which I gave him a lot of background on Jenny's medical condition.

One very large question that faced Suzanne and me almost immediately, and which we talked about over the weekend, was where to bury Jenny. I did not know where to start. My mother had the deed to a family plot of four graves in a cemetery in Pomona, an hour or so west of Los Angeles. Two of these graves were still empty, so that was a possibility, but I had never known the other people buried there, who were my mother's adoptive parents. I did not have a good feeling about burying Jenny anywhere. I had no emotional ties to any cemetery in the L.A. area, since no one I knew was buried there, and the thought of Jenny lying somewhere among strangers, with her grave run over once a month or so by a lawn mower driven by someone who cared nothing about her, left me feeling empty and unsatisfied.

Another factor was Suzanne's wish that Jenny be laid to rest in consecrated ground. And, although a couple of local cemeteries had been recommended, they were unknown to us, and therefore our reaction was lukewarm. But what were the alternatives? Burying Jenny with Suzanne's family in Kentucky was a possibility, but it would not have much emotional significance for me. On the other hand, if my mother were to let me bury her in Bloomington, Illinois, in our family plot, it would not have a lot of meaning for Suzanne. A decision had to be made and I was emotionally and mentally blocked.

Then, on Saturday or Sunday, Suzanne shared with me with the possibility of burying Jenny at the Abbey of Our Lady of Gethsemani in Trappist, Kentucky, where she had made her retreat. Before flying back to Los Angeles on Friday, and on a sudden impulse, Suzanne had approached one of the brothers at the Abbey to whom she was close and asked if he thought that the abbot might consider her wish. In a kind and tactful manner, the brother had replied that the abbot was not wont to grant such requests, understandably, given the very small size of the private cemetery on the grounds, the reclusive setting, and the nature of the religious community there. He did, however, assure Suzanne that he would carry her request to the abbot. There the matter rested for the time being, and Suzanne had returned to Los Angeles.

When Suzanne introduced the idea to me, I was immediately receptive. Although I did not say yes right away, and although, naturally, such a possibility had never occurred to me, I had no negative feelings about it. I told her to call the Abbey without delay and pursue the issue. Suzanne telephoned her friend there and told him that we definitely wished to have our request considered. Then, we waited.

It took only a day, or two at most, to receive a reply. Not only did I remain open to the idea of burying Jenny at Gethsemani, but I became convinced that it was entirely fitting and appropriate to bury her there. On a deep, intuitive level, I regarded the opportunity as a divine gesture, as if God were graciously extending His hand to us. Thus, even before we had heard from Gethsemani, I had made up my mind, through faith, I suppose, that our wish would be granted, and that taking Jenny to Gethsemani was the only choice. After that, I never had a second of doubt. It just seemed right. And even though time was limited and we still awaited an answer, I completely halted my investigations into any other alternatives. I just knew.

Suzanne and I were deeply happy and relieved when the brother called us from Gethsemani and told us that the abbot had graciously granted our wish. The abbot, I am sure, had taken into consideration the uniqueness of the circumstances—a little child dying unexpectedly while its mother was away on a religious retreat. And in addition to all the fine personal qualities which I know, now, that the abbot possesses, I feel that he must have considered the matter in prayer or that he had at least been guided by a voice that prompted his decision.

Suzanne and I were profoundly gratified and could move forward with other plans. Some people who knew me were surprised by my attitude about burying Jenny at Gethsemani. After all, I was not Catholic, nor even a Christian by traditional definition. And Kentucky was a long way from Los Angeles. Even before Jenny had come into our lives, I went to Louisville very infrequently due to financial and scheduling constraints. I knew that my opportunities to visit Jenny's grave would be few and far between. Finally, given the conflicts between Suzanne and me, especially recently, who knew what the future held for our relationship?

Nevertheless, I had wholeheartedly agreed to the idea of Gethsemani, and had done so, contrary to what others may have thought, completely of my own accord and without pressure from Suzanne. When Suzanne brought up the possibility of taking Jenny back to the Abbey, she told me clearly that she felt that it should be my choice and that, wherever I decided that Jenny should be buried, she would support me. I believed her. She seemed absolutely sincere, and I felt no pressure from her.

Something within me recognized that Jenny belonged at Gethsemani. She was a very special being. Her soul was very old. She was wise, not only beyond her own years, but far beyond the average capacity of most adults. Whatever forces had complicated her life so much were neither understood nor known by me, but I did know clearly that Jenny was a very advanced spiritual being. What could be more fitting than to lay her to rest in a place that even I, a non-Catholic and a non-Christian, recognized as holy?

At Gethsemani, Jenny would lie within ground that had been set aside for the pursuit of God, near to saints both living and dead who had chosen, as their life's goal, the highest calling—taking up the difficult and often lonely quest for spiritual realization. In my mind, any denominational or other traditional religious boundaries did not matter in light of the real significance of Gethsemani. I knew for certain that her grave would be tended carefully and lovingly by the brothers who had chosen the Abbey as their home.

I had no idea where Suzanne and I would be living, either together or separately, in the coming years. But I would always know that Jenny was where she belonged.

Meantime, during the week following Jenny's death, I found it deeply distressing, physically, to leave the house. All of my senses seemed acutely and painfully sensitive, and even when I would go somewhere for a short time in the car to run necessary errands, I was overwhelmed by sensory stimuli. The sunlight seemed blindingly harsh and bright and the heat, brutal. Average noises, such as passing cars, horns, and radios, were almost unbearable. Any aspect of the physical world beyond the protective walls of my home seemed abrasive and cruel.

On Monday, August 12, Nancy and Erica Nemeth, Suzanne's sister and niece, and Dale Roggenkamp, our close friend, flew to Los Angeles from Kentucky to help us get through the coming week. They would remain with us until the following Saturday, when we would all fly back to Kentucky together. On the day they arrived or the day after, I had another psychic experience that clearly indicated Jenny's presence. It was early in the afternoon, and we were about to leave the house. Everyone was upstairs waiting for me. I had just come out of our bedroom in somewhat of a hurry, had passed by Jenny's room on my right, and had started up the stairs. For some reason I cannot explain, I suddenly stopped, turned around, went back down the stairs, and looked into Jenny's room. I looked toward the ceiling and immediately saw some very tiny, subtle, and beautiful lights floating about in a cluster, perhaps light blue or pink, almost like fireflies, except that the perception was much more refined and exquisite. I had no thought, except a kind of purity of awareness in which I sensed that Jenny's spirit was there. After a few seconds, the experienced passed, and I turned and went upstairs and left with everyone else, saying nothing of what I had seen.

I had no way of knowing it then, but I would have this experience repeatedly as the years passed. As I write these words more than four years after Jenny's death, it still happens, sometimes fairly often, sometimes with weeks between each manifestation. The experience usually takes place at home, but not always, and there is usually just one small, very subtle light, which I see at first almost out of the corner of my eye, and which then soon disappears as I am watching it. With the light always comes the feeling that Jennifer has shown up to look in on me.

Some other odd things happened soon after Jenny's death, mostly during the following week. Several times, I would awaken during the night to realize that I had stopped breathing. My body would feel strangely cool and still. The experience was not frightening, and I did not feel out of breath or panicked. However, lying there in a strange state of utter calm, I sensed that I was feeling what it was like to die, to let go of the body. I wondered if this was Jenny's way of telling me that death was all right, that there was nothing to fear in it, and that death did not have to be traumatic or painful, but only a letting go. I had never had such an experience before, nor have I ever again since the first few days after Jenny's passing.

Often, during the first few days following August 9, I would sense a kind of presence in the house, but not necessarily Jenny's. It was more general in nature, and a little ominous, although not in any way frightening or intimidating. It was almost like Death itself was there, but unobtrusively, and very quietly, or perhaps some kind of shadow of Death that lingered behind for a while after it had departed and taken my daughter. It was eerie and almost impersonal. Was it perhaps merely the fact of Jenny's passing?

Early during the night that Jenny died, after it was dark, I thought that one time I sensed a presence in Jenny's room near her crib. The impression actually did not surface until a couple of days afterward. It was as if my mind photographed something that night but did not process it for me to see until later. Yet afterward, there was a fleeting image of someone or something standing near Jenny's crib. Was this some kind of escort, sent to accompany her when she left?

Not long after Jenny's death, even Dr. Laurance and my friend, Derrick, mentioned experiencing odd things. In Dr. Laurance's case, it was the hearing of a mysterious heartbeat; in Derrick's, the feeling of a presence near him.

Suzanne and I quickly became aware of three more critical issues that needed to be resolved. The first was getting Jenny's autopsy performed. The second was that, according to the authorities at the Los Angeles County Department of Children's Services, Jenny's body could not be released from the coroner's office and picked up by the funeral director until someone in her immediate family—that is, her mother or father—had signed the appropriate documents. The third was that permission would have to be obtained from the court in order to bury Jenny outside of California.

Unless all of these things happened, quickly, Suzanne and I would be held against our wills in an agonizing limbo. All of the plans and complex arrangements that we were trying to finalize would be overturned and indefinitely delayed.

Jenny's funeral mass at Holy Family Church was scheduled for Wednesday, and all the strategies necessary to make that come about needed to get under way. And, Suzanne and I were anticipating that Jenny would be buried at Gethsemani the following Monday, which meant working closely with the brothers there and with the undertaker in a nearby town who had been recommended by them. He would have to pick up Jenny's body at Standiford Field in Louisville, take care of her until we arrived, prepare the grave site, and so on. Finally, all of these plans needed to be finalized before we could make airline reservations for the trip to Kentucky.

I had requested that an autopsy be performed on Jenny. I needed to know why she had died. Had I not done this, I am not sure if the county would have required it or not, but I do not think so. Although my memory is unclear about why Jenny's body was picked up and held at the county coroner's office, I believe it was because she was legally a ward of the county. Had I not told the paramedics or the police this, perhaps it would have been possible to have had her body taken directly to a funeral director. But then I do not know how the autopsy would have gotten done.

The day Jenny died, her body was taken from our home to the county morgue. Suzanne and I then learned that, as always, there were a great number of autopsies to be performed by the coroner's office, and it was uncertain when Jenny's could be done. I am uncertain as to how, exactly, this issue was resolved, but fortunately, and to our great relief, Jenny's autopsy was performed in a fairly expedient manner, removing one obstacle.

However, Suzanne and I were now faced with another critical problem that would prove to be far more frustrating and vexing than the issue of the autopsy. We learned that the coroner's office could not release Jenny's body to Cabot and Sons for embalming until a release form had been signed by someone in her immediate family. Since Jenny's next living relatives were her mother and father, a difficulty immediately surfaced. Given that Rosa, Jenny's mother, had been declared legally in contempt of court, long ago, for repeated failures to appear at court hearings regarding Jenny's custody, her parental rights had been terminated. And, in fact, at the time of Jenny's death, she was in jail again for drug offenses. This meant that all attempts had to be made to find Jenny's biological father and obtain his signature on a consent form.

Jenny's biological father, an individual whom I have never regarded as her father in any sense, was a member of a violent, satanic L.A. gang. Immediately after Rosa had given birth to Jennifer and her dead twin, Wendy, he had conveniently distanced himself from any and all involvement, and had absolved himself of all future parental responsibility — thank God. Thereafter, as far as I know, his only presence in Jenny's life had been to shoot off his mouth a couple of times to Rosa's family during the time that Suzanne and I were applying to become Jennifer's foster parents, boasting that he would never allow his daughter to be raised by white people. His meaningless words never came to anything.

Now, after Jenny's death, this character, whose only known address was his grandmother's house, had to be located. Suddenly, when he learned that the county was trying to get in touch with him, he became impossible to find. The staff at the L. A. County Department of Children's Services made numerous attempts to make contact with him through his grandmother, but he evaded them and was never found.

As I write about this period in our lives, I am amazed that it was only ten days between Jenny's death and her burial at Gethsemani on Monday, August 19. It seems much longer because of the suspense and frustration that Suzanne and I experienced, and which, in an odd way, postponed the full emotional impact of Jennifer's death. As time drew closer to Jennifer's funeral mass on Wednesday, her body remained at the county because her "father" could not be located. Suzanne and I were incredulous and outraged by the fact that Jenny's service and burial, and our whole lives, were being held hostage by some slimy gang member who had gone into hiding.

Some of the people at the Department of Children's Services made a very credible effort to find Jenny's father and get the matter resolved. However, others at the department, and one woman in particular, failed miserably in the manner in which they dealt with Suzanne and me. The insensitivity which we experienced, and which especially upset Suzanne, is not to be forgotten. Of course, Suzanne and I both were deeply concerned. However, whereas most of my frustration was expressed somewhat aggressively, hers began to take on more and more a note of desperation.

As the days and hours began to run out and it started to look as if we might not even have Jenny's body in time for the funeral mass, Suzanne called the county once or twice in a deeply emotional state and implored them to get something done. The problem was that, if one went by the impression created by the people on the other end of the phone, they did not give a damn. The lady in question actually said to us that the problems with Jennifer had inconvenienced her more than once by interrupting her lunch hour, and that the whole affair was, in her eyes, like a kind of soap opera with amusing overtones. Whereas this kind of crassness cut Suzanne deeply, I, typically, simply ascribed it to the general level of human stupidity.

Time became so critical that it looked like we might either have to postpone and reorganize the funeral mass, which would be a nightmare for us and disrupt all of our other plans as well, or have the mass without Jennifer's body. The way things were going, even if the funeral director, whose hands were presently tied because of the legalities, were able to pick up Jenny's body, there might not be time to embalm it before the service. Suzanne even began to wonder if, in such a case, Jenny's body could be put inside a bag and placed inside the coffin for the service and then embalmed afterwards.

Finally, in the nick of time, after our emotions had been pushed to the limit, and with the application of pressure on the Department of Children's Services from several sides (including, I believe, help from Fran, my friend and medical social worker at Huntington), a breakthrough was made. People with decision-making ability at the Department of Children's Services concluded that, given the critical time factor and the persistent unavailability of Jenny's biological father, it would be acceptable for Graciela, Jennifer's maternal grandmother, to sign the necessary papers. Thus, in the end, a representative from the department, accompanied by an English-Spanish translator (since Graciela's English was far from fluent) drove to Malibu where Graciela and her family were living and obtained her consent and signature.

With barely enough time left, Cabot and Sons was then able to pick up Jenny's body from the county, and by having an embalmer work overtime well into the evening on Tuesday, have it ready for the funeral mass the following morning.

After Jenny died, any information concerning her death and the date and location of her funeral mass was conveyed, I assume, to Graciela and her family by county staff. Neither Suzanne nor I had told them anything—not even that Jenny had died—since we naturally associated them in our minds with Jenny's father, a person whom we wanted to keep totally out of our lives. In accordance with our wishes, we had had no contact whatever with Graciela or any of her family since Jenny had come home to live with us. This was due again, primarily, to the threats Jenny's father had made.

A couple of days after Jenny's death, I was quite surprised and a little uncomfortable to receive a telephone call from Nancy, one of Graciela's daughters (and Rosa's sister), asking me where and when the funeral mass would be held. I had given her the details, but with some reluctance, mostly because of Jenny's father. In fact, Nancy had intimated to me that Jenny's father was making noises again, this time about showing up, possibly with other gang members, at the service. The last thing Suzanne and I needed was to have to be worried about some kind of trouble from a person like that at the church.

A day or two before the service, Suzanne spoke at length about the issue with a friend of hers who was an experienced police officer and who had dealt a lot with L.A. gangs. His opinion was that, although Jennifer's father was a member of a particularly notorious gang, and although they were certainly capable of violence, neither he nor any of his fellow gang members would be interested in actually making a presence at the church, since, according to him, they and others like them were all mouth and little substance. Suzanne and I hoped that his assessment was correct, but we remained somewhat apprehensive.

The issue of obtaining permission from the court to have Jenny buried outside of California, and indeed the whole question of whether or not such a thing would be granted, remained unresolved. For the moment, Jennifer's service was the most important issue, and Suzanne and I needed to focus on preparing ourselves emotionally for that.

Holy Family Church

Jenny's funeral mass took place at 9:30 in the morning on Wednesday, August 14, 1991, at Holy Family Church in South Pasadena. As with other episodes from this period, my memory has significant blanks interspersed with vivid images of various scenes. This is due to my emotional state at the time. Suzanne's experience has been similar to mine, although in several instances her memory seems more intact than mine. Without her input, it would have been difficult, if not impossible, for me to reconstruct some of the details of the day of the mass and even of the mass itself.

That pretty summer morning, Charlie came by our condo and picked up Suzanne and me, along with Nancy, Erica, and Dale, and we all rode to the church together. We arrived early so Suzanne and I could attend to any necessary details. My first vivid recollection from that morning—an image I still see clearly in my mind after four years—is the first time I saw Jenny's coffin. The large, black hearse arrived from Cabot and Sons, the funeral directors, and stopped in the parking lot near the front entrance of the church. I walked to the back of the hearse and looked through the glass of the rear window. In striking contrast to the imposing, powerful dimensions of the vehicle, a small, beautiful coffin lay in the middle of the compartment. I had never seen a child's coffin except for the photos I had been shown a few days earlier at Cabot and Sons, and although it was just the right size for Jenny, I was unprepared. It looked so small! Without the conscious thought, something inside of me was saying that coffins should be large—for adults. They should not be small, the size of a doll box. Children should not die! How could Jenny be inside? How could that little box now hold the lifeless mannequin that, only a few days ago, was my laughing, radiant, beautiful daughter?

Jenny's coffin was taken inside the church; it was not opened for the service. The rest of us sat down while others began to arrive. There were many people from Huntington, including nurses from the pediatric ward, the medical social workers and child life therapists, and other staff members; Dr. Laurance, Sue Collins, Jenny's former child life therapist from Huntington Memorial Hospital, whom I had called the night she died, many of the staff from All Saints Children's Center; someone from the Department of Children's Services, two friends from my office, and other friends of mine and Suzanne's, including some of her family who lived in southern California. I was glad to see the church filling up.

My blurred memories of the liturgy and mass include a short, moving talk that Charlie gave, and the homily by Father Michael. I was struck by the beauty, sensitivity, and eloquence of his words, which, as everyone saw unmistakably, came from his heart. I wish I had a record of what he said that morning; I probably would have included it here in its entirety. In comparison to the hollow words I have heard at funerals, spoken by pastors who barely knew the deceased, Father Michael held my total attention with his deep insights into Jenny's life and the impact it had made on so many people. In time to come, both Suzanne and others who knew Father Michael would say that they had never heard him speak as eloquently as he did at Jenny's funeral mass.

The music for Jenny's service included many beautiful pieces: the processional, a compline from Gethsemani, sung a cappella by the soprano; "Panis Angelicus" by Franck; Schubert's "Ave Maria"; another piece of extraordinary beauty, which I did not know and do not remember, sung with accompaniment by the soprano; and the recessional, Ravel's "Pavanne for a Deceased Infanta." If some of this music had not already been very well known to me, I would not have remembered it later. I had not selected it; the decisions had been made between Suzanne and the musicians. Wherever my mind was during the service, it was far from the music most of the time. Circumstances notwithstanding, this is surprising, especially given my training and experience as a professional musician. I had performed the "Pavanne" (a favorite piece of mine) myself as piano soloist during a concert at the Interlochen Arts Academy summer music camp in 1978. It was an odd coincidence to hear it at Jenny's service.

Suzanne and I were sitting on the right at the front of the church next to the center aisle where Jenny's coffin and stand had been placed. At some point during the mass, a movement in the aisle at my left shoulder caught my attention and I turned my head to look. It was Graciela, Jenny's maternal grandmother, who had arrived late with her daughters, Maria and Nancy, and her sons. She had come forward to place a plant near the coffin. Fortunately, our concerns about possible gang activity were unfounded. No one else in their family or circle of people came, and Jenny's father—again, a title with which I hate to dignify him—was nowhere to be seen.

At the appropriate time, I arose and went up to the pulpit. It was a long mass, and I spoke at some length myself. To my surprise, I was not nervous or shaky. The detailed outline I had prepared beforehand, and which I still have, helped me greatly. But I knew then, as I do today, that what enabled me to hold myself together during that talk was the love that I felt for Jenny. Because of that, and because of the power that I felt in her love for me, I was carried up and supported, so that I could say clearly, with control and perhaps even with joy, the things that I wanted everyone in that church to know about my precious and wonderful child.

As I spoke, my eyes fell upon many familiar faces who had been part of Jenny's life, and who had also been a very meaningful part of mine. I talked about Jenny's beauty and pointed out that it was in large part due to the love and commitment of her first family—the hospital staff, the doctors, and others. While welcoming everyone, I recognized three circles of people—the outer circle, made up of those who had come simply to offer their support; the middle circle, comprised of those who knew Jenny and had participated in her life, such as the nurses, doctors, therapists, and so on, who cared for her and supported her and some of whom Jennifer had loved deeply; and the innermost circle, the few who, in my eyes, understood the full spiritual dimension of who and what Jennifer really was to some of the people there, and to me.

I spoke of the fullness of my life over the past months, of how it all began and developed with Jenny, and about the knock of destiny in November 1990 that inspired my commitment to take her sight unseen, which led to that first time I had seen her in her wagon at Huntington. I talked about the months I had visited her at the hospital prior to her move to our home on February 22, 1991; the early wagon rides, our ritual of putting coins in the vending machines, of the orders that she would give me and which I was so happy to follow. I described that first time I rocked her to sleep in her hospital room, how she fashioned herself a pillow from the towel, and how at peace I felt that night when time stopped.

Then I recounted Jenny's first trip "home" in December 1990, how natural it seemed for her, and how thereafter she seemed to blossom and grow almost instantaneously. I reminded those present of her astonishing and wonderful physical, emotional, and intellectual development—of her brilliance, how she absorbed new words, concepts, and behaviors. I described what it was like to pick her up at All Saints Children's Center at the end of the day, the joy I felt, and how she would drop her toys and run to me and embrace me, saying "My daddy" to her teachers, as she did her last day there. And I thanked the people from the center for what they had done for Jenny.

I talked about the pictures that Jenny would make me for my office, about our long "talks" and reading books together, and about the way we would joke with each other. I described how I held her hand every night through the bars of her crib until she fell asleep. I shared how she came to love the swimming pool. There was still so much I had wanted to teach her.

As many people in the church knew, Jennifer ate almost nothing, and I suggested that this perhaps enhanced what I perceived as a kind of "purity" that she radiated. I told them that she loved water, grains of rice, small bits of pasta, and, to the amusement of everyone in the church, pieces of raw potato and even kitty food, if I did not prevent her from sampling it.

Jenny loved her Legos, her Raggedy Anne doll, and her two Minnie Mouse T-shirts, an old one and a newer one, which Suzanne and I would wash and rotate so that she always had one or the other available.

Standing in front of those people, I reflected how terribly short our time with her was.

I recalled how I winced the first time I saw Jenny's abdomen, with its scars and tubing, but added that I *never* again viewed her as disfigured, but as perfect, simply as Jenny, as she saw herself.

I assured everyone present that having Jennifer and taking care of her was *never* in *any* way a sacrifice, at least in my mind, in contrast to how I think some people saw it. I said that Suzanne and I had given up *nothing;* that we had gained *everything.* I stressed that if anyone had any doubts about Jenny's care in our home, they could rest assured that Suzanne and I saw to her every need with joy, and that the smallest details were not overlooked. Our aim was for perfection in her physical care. She lacked nothing; and we surrounded her with encouragement, protection, nurturing, and love. I made it clear that I loved Jenny fiercely and totally, with my whole being, that her love for Suzanne and me and her trust in us was total, and that she had felt utterly secure in our care.

Because most people there, including many who had been close to her at the hospital, knew little about the circumstances surrounding Jenny's death, I spoke at length about what had taken place on Thursday, August 8, and Friday, August 9, the day she died. I started by saying how happy and relieved I was when I got her out of the hospital and took her home on Tuesday, August 6. After getting her from day care on Thursday, we showered in Mommie's shower, talked a lot, and read storybooks. I hooked her up to her feedings and put her to bed.

I described the ominousness of Thursday night, how disturbing it was for both of us, and I said that Suzanne was away on a retreat at that time. I recounted how fitful Jenny was from 8:30 P.M. to around midnight, and how I tried to calm her. Around 10:30 P.M., I had called Dr. Laurance, but he saw nothing that would indicate any medical difficulties. And yet, part of me "knew" that something was wrong. From about midnight to 2:00 A.M., Jenny slept restlessly, dreamed, talked in her sleep, saying my name ("Daddy") and "all done" many times. She coughed—odd, dry little coughs, and from time to time she made expressive sighs. Once I entered her room (earlier, I think), and she looked at me without saying a single word—something utterly unique.

I said that, on some level, I thought that Jenny and I both sensed something foreboding. I felt alone with her, like we were on a tiny island someplace, in an otherwise empty universe. I recounted my phone call to Sue Collins in Las Vegas around 1:00 A.M., and that we talked for almost an hour in order for me to alleviate an indefinable, agonizing apprehension.

Things grew quiet, and I finally fell asleep around 3:30 in the morning. I went into Jenny's room to check the pumps at 4:00, 4:30, 5:00, and 5:30. It was dark. I sensed nothing. But afterward, as I told the people in the church, I thought that she was already gone.

I told how I had awakened Friday morning, at almost 8:00, how I had decided to let Jenny sleep, and that I thought I would perhaps take her to All Saints Children's Center later, if she felt like going. I described entering her room, and how still she was, lying on her stomach. I bent over her bed to look for the rise and fall of breathing in her back. She was so still! I reached out to touch her back, and it was hard and cold. In horror and with instantaneous realization, I drew back. I lifted Jenny's little arm, but it was cold and stiff. Then the utter, indescribable shock, horror, realization—and denial: "Oh no, no—my poor baby!" Again and again.

I was almost certain that Jenny had died about the time I finally went to sleep around 3:30 A.M. Phone calls followed; paramedics, people from the hospital, and friends arrived. I recalled going in to look at Jenny and touch her many times during the morning. Then, a little after 11:30 A.M., they finally removed her. I cut her tubes, saying, "I've taken care of her all this time. There's no reason to stop now." I carried her precious little body out of the house.

I talked about how brutal that experience was and said it did not fit any scenario that had gone through my mind, although never a day had passed but that I wondered how long Jennifer would be with us. I said also how deeply grateful I was that Jenny had left this world in *her* home, in *her* bed, with *her* daddy. Suzanne had seen Jenny *really* sick before I ever knew her, and I was thankful that she was spared all of that, and death in a hospital. And I expressed how deeply happy I was that Jenny's last six months were full of happiness and security.

For a moment, I pondered the direction that my life would take from then on; I related that I had seen a plan in everything that had happened and in the way that Jennifer had found us.

Then I spoke about the Abbey of Our Lady of Gethsemani in Trappist, Kentucky, about the monks who lived there, and about the significance of Jenny being buried on those beautiful grounds; and I touched upon Suzanne's retreat there at the time of Jenny's death. I expressed my deep conviction that Jenny was an old soul, a great soul, before this life, during it, and forever after. Jenny's burial at Gethsemani was, in my eyes, both a magnificent and fitting gesture from the brothers there, and a sign from the Deity. The dignity and holiness of Gethsemani befitted Jenny and gave Suzanne and me deep peace. She would receive prayer and loving care there. Her burial represented an opportunity for Suzanne and me to do one more thing for her. And, I reflected that, although Jenny's body would for now be far away, it would have the sanctity and honor she richly merited.

I closed by saying that Jenny was our little saint, that it was fitting for her to rest with those who loved God and that she deserved this. It was fate. Finally, I vowed that just as I had cared for Jenny over the past months, I would be her protector for all time to come, until our final goal was reached, whatever it might be, and that I would seek her love, her presence, and her guidance.

After the funeral mass ended, Suzanne and I were the first to make our way to the back of the church, following Jenny's coffin as it was wheeled out. For a while, we stood outside and talked with many of the people who had come. Although Suzanne and I were given the opportunity to view Jenny's body, neither of us did so. Suzanne wanted to remember her as she was while she was alive. For myself, given my knowledge of the extent of the autopsy, I also felt that I did not wish to see her inside her coffin. I, too, wished to remember Jenny as a living, vibrant child; and besides, after the shock of discovering her dead in her crib, I did not see what could be gained by exposing myself to the pain of such a viewing. However, Fran, the medical social worker from Huntington, and Sue Collins very much desired to look at Jenny, which Suzanne and I permitted without hesitation; and, along with the other personal mementos already in Jenny's coffin, Sue placed a key chain that had been a favorite of Jenny's. At our request, Charlie also went to look at Jenny and returned to assure us that she had been very properly treated and that she looked very good. That was all that Suzanne and I wanted to know.

Afterward, many people who had attended the mass drove to Glendale and Charlie's condominium to get together, talk, and have refreshments. Later, Charlie drove Suzanne, Nancy, Erica, Dale, and me back to Vallejo Villas. With little time for rest, Suzanne and I began to focus on the next step to be taken; that is, having Jenny's body flown to Kentucky and getting her buried at Gethsemani.

We still had received no word on Wednesday as to whether or not the court would give its permission to have Jenny buried out of state. Either right after the funeral mass at Holy Family Church or the very next day, I had a conversation with the funeral director. He had really been quite helpful and cooperative in getting everything done that week, and now his question to me was what he was to do with Jennifer's body. He was familiar with the situation with the court, and I reminded him of the dilemma.

Frankly, by that time I had had about all I was going to take of regulations, bureaucracies, and other people who personally did not give a damn about Jennifer or our feelings making the decisions, and I said this to the funeral director. He was very empathetic, and in a way which touched and impressed me so that I still clearly remember it, he said something like, "Well, you're the one retaining my services and guaranteeing payment, so, as far as I'm concerned, your directions are the ones that I'm going to act on."

In others words, he was making his position clear to me; namely, that as far as he was concerned I was in charge, and if I were to direct him to have Jennifer's body flown to Kentucky and delivered into the care of an undertaker there, such a request was perfectly appropriate and as far as he knew (and no one could prove otherwise) within the bounds of the law.

We looked at each other and understood. I even smiled a little. Without a moment's hesitation, I said simply, "Do it!" Although apologizing for what might seem like disrespect for the law does not alter the questionable character of my decision, I offer it anyway and hasten to add, again, that I simply could not bear any more delay, confusion, apprehension, or interference. The question that crossed my mind then and afterward was how I would defend myself if it came to light that I had made my decision without the court's approval, or, even worse, if the court withheld approval for some reason and it was learned that Jennifer was already buried in Kentucky.

At the time, I had no more patience; and my feeling, which was tinged with defiance, was something like, "So, if they find out, what are they going to do? Go over there, dig her up, and bring her back? Are they going to put me in jail over it?" Actually, I was not as clear as I would have liked to be about the answers to those questions, but I had made my decision and I would face the consequences, if any, later. I did worry about it some, but what was done was done.

Several people, whom I shall not name because their positions required that they not know officially about my course of action or sanction it, did in fact suspect or in some cases know of my plan and offer no interference. For this, they have earned my sincere appreciation and respect. As it turned out, Suzanne received a telephone call from the Department of Children's Services on Friday, the day before we left for Kentucky, saying that a judge had granted us permission to bury Jenny at Gethsemani. Of course, by the time we got the phone call Jennifer's body was long gone and had arrived at its destination.

Gethsemani

Airline reservations had been made, and on Saturday, August 17, 1991, Suzanne and I flew to Louisville, Kentucky, for Jenny's burial. Dale Roggenkamp, our friend from Louisville, Charlie, and Nancy and Erica Nemeth, Suzanne's sister and niece, traveled with us. We stayed with the Roggenkamps in Anchorage, which was on the outskirts of Louisville. Jenny's graveside service and burial at the Abbey of our Lady of Gethsemani was scheduled for the morning of Monday, August 19. Brother Rafael and Father Matthew were to conduct the service.

Most all of the preparations for Jenny's service and burial had already been made. After our arrival in Louisville on Saturday, there was not a great deal for Suzanne and me to do until the service on Monday. We passed most of the time in a fog.

Since Jim Roggenkamp, Dale's husband, had some loose ends to catch up on over the weekend in his engineering office in downtown Louisville, I tagged along. While I was in Jim's office, I lay down on the large, comfortable sofa near his desk, fell asleep, and began to dream. I was on a beach by the ocean. Sitting on a large wooden chair (which I know symbolized my own little baby chair I gave Jenny, but which was unpainted in the dream), I watched the waves come in and go out. I looked down at the gentle, white froth surrounding the legs of the chair, and I saw that Jenny was floating on its surface, smiling up at me. But she was tiny, like a little doll or a starfish; nevertheless, her features were very clear to me as she was carried in and out, under my chair, by the gentle ebb and flow. Finally, one time, Jenny floated out and returned no more.

I awakened, still deeply immersed in the emotions of the dream, and realized immediately how clearly it had symbolized Jenny's passing. One vivid detail of the dream was the plaid dress that Jenny was wearing, the one that she had worn when Suzanne and I took her to Rancho Calamigos. In my mind, this dress was powerfully connected to the idea of water, since during that afternoon at Rancho Calamigos I had seen how attracted Jenny was to the swimming pool and how much she had wanted to go in. I had taken a haunting, lovely photo of her sitting by the side of the pool in that plaid dress. Two or three days later, I bought Jenny a swimsuit and began to take her to the pool at our complex.

On Monday morning, August 19, Suzanne and I rode with Dale, Jim, and others from Louisville south through Bardstown, to Trappist and the Abbey of our Lady of Gethsemani. It was a beautiful summer day. We approached the Abbey by way of lovely, winding country roads flanked by farmlands and sunny woods. As we turned into the grounds of the Abbey, I realized how beautiful and peaceful it was, and how utterly fitting for Jenny. Within a hundred feet or so of the Abbey, in front and to the left as one approached the entrance to the church, was a small cemetery. The first thing I saw was an awning and some chairs, in front of which was a small coffin on a stand.

My memories of this day, as with the day Jenny died, the day of her funeral mass at Holy Family Church in South Pasadena, and other such times of over-whelming emotion, are a collage of vividly etched scenes suffused in a bath of more nebulous images, impressions, and feelings, often sketchy and in some cases even leaving complete voids in my recollection. But that first sight of Jenny's cof-fin at the grave site is indelible. After we had disembarked from the car and began walking toward the Abbey and the little cemetery, my eyes suddenly filled with tears. With a rush of emotion, I took Jim's arm, saying, "I just can't believe she's in that little box!"

From then until the service began, I have fragmentary memories of walking around with Suzanne, Dale, Nancy, and Erica. We went into the church, which was very beautiful, looked around, and sat quietly for a while in the pews in the rear. We covered some of the grounds immediately surrounding the Abbey, including the cemetery toward the back of the edifice wherein were buried many of the brothers, including Thomas Merton, who had lived at Gethsemani.

I recall speaking with Joseph Greenwell, Jr., the undertaker from nearby New Haven, who had been recommended to Suzanne and me by the abbey and who had provided for the burial of many of the brothers there. He told me how nice Jenny looked and that the various offerings which had been placed in Jenny's cof-fin in California were there. These included my meditation beads, which Swami Nirmalananda Giri, a former spiritual teacher of mine, had given to me when I was eighteen years old; Suzanne's first holy communion rosary; a key chain with a little figure attached to it that had belonged to Sue Collins, Jenny's favorite child life therapist; a small, white, folded liturgical cloth which had been my best friend Jerry Alber's; and, pinned to Jenny's burial dress, a medal of the Blessed Mother that Suzanne had tied to a pink ribbon taken from the braid of a doll given to Jenny on her third birthday by a friend and doctor from Huntington.

As the hour of the service drew near, we began to gather near the grave. None of my family were present. The drive was too far for my mother, and I was in no way fit to go to Bloomington, Illinois, my home town, to get her and then take her back. Many of my other relatives, all of whom lived even further away than my mother, had not even known about Jenny, since at that time I was not in very close contact with most of them. I had no brothers or sisters, and my father had died in 1969. Charlie, Suzanne's brother, was not able to attend, but Nancy and Erica, her sister and niece, and a number of Suzanne's other relatives who lived in or near Louisville and who were invited to attend were present for the service. Suzanne's father, like mine, was dead, and her mother, who was not in good health and living in a nursing home, was not up to such an event.

This intimate circle of family and friends who had come to pay their respects to Jenny as one of their own collected under the awning. What I can recall of the service, which was touchingly and lovingly conducted by Brother Rafael and Father Matthew, included the reading of scripture, incense, prayer, a beautiful talk, the blessing of Jenny's body and soul, and the commending of her spirit into God's hands. Oddly juxtaposed to these images, I distinctly remember part of my mind being split off and preoccupied with the perception that Jenny's coffin, which was on a small stand atop a platform covering the open grave, was not especially stable. I could not stop worrying that it might fall if it were bumped, and wondered what in God's name I would do if it should topple over.

After the service, people moved away a bit in small groups, to stand or walk about and talk quietly. At one point, I found myself alone at the foot of the grave, the only others present being the undertaker his two assistants. I had no desire whatsoever to move away, so as I watched, they moved Jenny's coffin and stand to one side and uncovered the open grave. I looked down at the small, reinforced concrete vault which was already positioned in the bottom of the hole. Cradling Jenny's coffin with long canvas belts that had been slipped through the handles, they carefully lowered her into the vault. After retracting the canvas belting, they used it once again to lower the lid of the vault into place. Finally, all that was left to do was to fill in the grave, so the two assistants began to shovel in the nearby mound of dirt. I watched as the vault was covered and the hole slowly filled. When the dirt in the grave was nearly at ground level, the two men tamped down the soil with their boots as much as they could and filled in the remaining dirt.

I watched all of this in a very odd state of mind, in which I paid the closest attention possible to every detail while at the same time being strangely numb and almost unthinking. In a way I cannot explain, and which was understandable only in terms of the irrational "rationality" of the independent rivers of emotion deep within me, it was as if for a few brief moments Jenny was somehow still "alive," because I was still there taking care of her, overseeing her welfare, observing everything with a watchful eye just as I would have if she had been in Huntington and I were watching a nurse change her dressings. It was habit for me, automatic; and the blind, unreasoning part of my emotional nature that lived separately from my mind in its own world regarded Jenny as still alive, as still needing my care. When I think of what I experienced that morning, I come face to face with the frailty of human nature, at least in its chaotic, emotional dimension. And, although this may sound odd, I now understand fully the sadness of that image everyone has heard about—of dogs lying by the graves of their masters, unable to understand that they are not going to come back, unwilling to leave even for food or water.

Finally, reluctantly, I turned away. Perhaps someone called to me or approached me; I cannot remember. And I do not remember what happened next, except that a little after that all of us began to get into our cars. Everyone in our party drove back as a group through the countryside to Bardstown, where we all stopped and had lunch together, since it must have been around noon. I seem to remember being very hungry, and, along with some of the others, I think I had some kind of mixed drink, probably a Bloody Mary. I do not remember anything that happened the rest of that day.

The following evening, Tuesday, August 20, Nancy, Suzanne's sister, had a dinner for the family and relatives and a few close friends at her home in Pewee Valley, a small town just outside of Louisville. Nancy lived just a few doors down the road from the house where she, Suzanne, and Charlie had grown up, and in which Charlie still lived. The get-together at Nancy's was appropriate, and I am grateful to her for organizing it, but I did not look forward to it. I felt numb and completely hollow, and the responses that I heard myself give to the standard comments and questions that one hears on such occasions sounded empty and mechanical to me.

The next thing that happened was that Suzanne's mother, Helen, became gravely ill. After vomiting fecal material, she was rushed from her nursing home to a hospital in Louisville, where it was determined that she was suffering from a perforated ulcer. Without surgery, she would unquestionably die an unpleasant death, but given her advanced age and other factors, the situation appeared so grave to Suzanne, me, and the rest of her family that we felt that her chances of sur-viving surgery were slim. Frankly, she looked to be so terribly ill that we had all but given her up. Thus, only a couple of days after burying Jennifer, Suzanne faced what seemed to be the likelihood of losing her mother as well. Everyone's emo-tions were overloaded, and coping abilities were pushed to the limit. The physi-cian, however, felt that Helen's chances of coming through surgery were good, and since the only alternative for her was a painful, certain death, the family opted for surgery. Happily, after many tense hours at the hospital, we learned that she had come through the surgery very well. Within a reasonable period of time, she would recover to the point that she would be able to return to her nursing home.

This entire episode, which would have been harrowing under any circum-stances, was doubly so given Jenny's death. The result, especially for Suzanne, was that emotions were thrown into utter confusion and her grieving process for Jenny was temporarily impeded or derailed. For me, in addition to being deeply concerned about Suzanne and feeling unable to exert any kind of control over anything, the long visits in Helen's hospital room, and the activity and equip-ment—the various sights and smells—on the ward, aroused in me disturbing and painful recollections of the once happy months I had spent visiting Jenny at Hunt-ington before her move home. Since Jenny's death, all those formerly beautiful memories haunted me deeply.

While we were in Kentucky, Suzanne and I stayed the entire time with the Roggenkamps in Anchorage. In addition to the hours we spent with Helen at the hospital in Louisville, there is little to remember about the remainder of that week except our visits to Jenny's grave and my feelings of inexpressible loss, with all of the accompanying thoughts and emotions, which sometimes made me numb and almost inert, and at others pierced me in the form of fresh, agonizing realiza-tions that Jenny was gone.

One odd thing happened at the Roggenkamps' home while we were sitting around in the den one evening. After it had gotten completely dark outside, there was a loud knock at the front door, but when Jim went to look, no one was there. After going outside and walking around the entire house, he returned to announce that he had found no one. Since the house was situated in the middle of a very large piece of property with little place to conceal oneself, it was highly unlikely that someone had knocked on the door and then run to hide. Besides, nothing like that had ever happened before in all the years that they had lived there. We all looked at each other, and I know that we were all thinking something similar. Whether this strange occurrence was some kind of psychic manifestation associated with Jenny's death, I cannot say. However, I am open to the possibility that it was.

After Jenny's burial on Monday, Suzanne and I drove back to Gethsemani at least twice later in the week. On one occasion, Charlie accompanied us, and on another, Dale Roggenkamp went with us, and perhaps Nancy and Erica as well. On the day Dale drove with us, the weather was uncertain. The morning started out sunny and clear, and remained so until after we had reached the abbey. We spent some time by Jenny's grave and then walked around. Although the sky overhead was bright blue and clear, ominous clouds began to pile up and approach us from the west. Finally, it started to sprinkle lightly and, except for me, every-one began to head back toward the car. I had walked back to Jenny's grave and remained there as the rain began to come. The others sat in the car as the raindrops started to fall thicker and harder. Somehow, when I stood at the grave, and espe-cially when I sat on the grass next it, I felt very close to my daughter. It was almost like she was alive and we were there together, and for a few moments I could feel an unexpected but deeply welcomed peace. I did not want to leave her. Finally, the rain came down really hard, and although I could not have cared less about getting wet, I felt like the time had come for me to go back to the car. I could sense the others waiting.

After we left Gethsemani, we stopped in Bardstown to get something to eat. Bardstown was a rural, quaint, and charming small town. And although the little restaurant we found was delightful and the waitress was very nice, I noticed that little things seemed to keep going wrong. I became irritated when they were out of what I ordered, or when there were short delays, little mistakes—nothing really to get upset about. But after a while I found myself getting deeply angry. I felt like I wanted to explode and give somebody hell. I mentioned this to Suzanne and Dale, and in doing so I realized immediately that this kind of gunpowder feeling I had was not at all about the service in the restaurant. It was about my despair and, at that moment, the rage at Jenny's death surfacing from deep inside of me. How could anyone I loved so much be taken from me like that? How could God do such a thing to me? How could Jenny leave me like that? As I sat there asking myself those kinds of questions, I realized that the act of seeing where the anger was coming from helped to drain some of it off, to take some of the force out of it, at least for the time.

I Return to L. A.

That was my second full week away from work. Although I tried not to think about the office, I was aware, underneath everything else that was going on, that my work was piling up, that no one else would be doing it, and that my managers were probably beginning to wonder when I was coming back. I did not want to go back; I did not give a damn about going back. But I knew that the longer I stayed away, the more critical the problem would become, since my work seriously impacted the company's cash flow, and the more irksome the cleanup would be for me. Reluctantly, I started to think about having to return to Los Angeles.

I talked things over with Suzanne. Although her mother was now stable, Suzanne felt that it was far too early to leave her, and I agreed. Therefore, I decided to go back to Los Angeles alone on the following Saturday so that I could be at work the following week. Suzanne would return a week or so after me, once she had some peace of mind about her mother's health. Suzanne mentioned her concern about my going back alone to the condo, and at her suggestion I called Julie Schmidt in Los Angeles, a nurse who, in addition to being a very close friend of Suzanne's and a godmother to Jenny, was someone whom I had gotten to know and like very much. Julie readily agreed to come and stay with me for a day or so, and told me to call her on the Saturday afternoon that I arrived back in L.A.

At the end of the week, I was deeply reluctant to leave Anchorage. Dale and Jim had been wonderful to Suzanne and me, and it was hard to say goodbye and leave a household that seemed like home. In addition to going back without Suzanne, my departure meant saying goodbye to Gethsemani, the beautiful, holy place whose sacred ground held the body of my daughter. But at least I had the consolation—and it was a very important one—that she could not possibly be in a better place, and that her grave would be cared for with reverence and love by the best of people.

On Saturday, August 24, I flew alone back to Los Angeles. From the time I said goodbye at Standiford Field in Louisville and boarded the plane until I walked in the door of the condo in L.A. late in the afternoon and called Julie, I felt utterly desolate. The plane ride seemed unusually long. I did not talk to anyone, and yet I found it impossible to sleep. Los Angeles International Airport, as always, was noisy and chaotic, an assault on the senses that I never looked forward to. But that time it was especially overwhelming, and I was relieved when I finally boarded the shuttle that would take me home. During the ride, the driver and I got to talking, and I finally offered to him that I was returning from burying my three-year-old daughter.

Finally, I was dropped off outside of the condo with my luggage, and the shuttle drove away. For a few minutes I stood almost motionless, looking around. Everything seemed terribly still, somehow. It was a quiet, peaceful afternoon, sunny, cool and pleasant. No one was around. The tranquility somehow heightened my feelings, which I find hard to describe. It was the first time I had really been alone since the day Jenny died more than two weeks before, and now I was standing on the very spot where I had laid her body on the floor of the van from the county. Standing there, it was as if she were everywhere, all around me, saturating my every thought and perception. And yet there was the pregnant emptiness that seemed to have settled on everything—that stark, inexpressible, uncompromising void. How utterly empty the world was without her!

I picked up my things and walked up the sidewalk to the front door. Unlocking it slowly and deliberately, I went inside and set my luggage down. Confronted by the stillness, I walked slowly through every room. I went down the stairs and stood in Jenny's room, looking at the empty crib with its clean linens. My eyes moved from object to object—the sofa and Jenny's dresser, covered with stuffed animals and dolls; the toy box; the set of shelves; the radio that had played her tapes at bedtime.

I rescued myself from the encroaching silence by calling Julie almost right away. She came over within a couple of hours and we went out to get something to eat. I do not know what I would have done without her company. We talked a lot. She was very understanding and stayed the night, as I had hoped she would. The next morning, Sunday, I hated to see her leave. Julie sensed how alone and directionless I felt, and she offered to come back that afternoon after attending to some commitments. I readily accepted, and she ended up staying the night again. On Monday morning, we said goodbye; she returned to her regular routines, and I faced the difficult and extraordinarily painful task of going back to my job and moving through a life that had lost all meaning, joy, and light.

Later Things

Emptiness

During my first week back in Los Angeles, I went to the office during the day, tried to pick up the pieces, and endeavored to get my mind focused on work at least enough that I could execute the most critical tasks. Everyone pretty much stayed out of my way, which was exactly what I wanted. As far as I remember, I went home alone to the condo each night. Suzanne flew back a week after my return. By then, to everyone's surprise and relief, her mother was in stable condition and recovering remarkably well from her surgery. Within a short time, Suzanne also resumed her job at Huntington, something extraordinarily difficult for her.

On August 30, I received a letter from our Children's Social Worker asking me to sign and return an attached affidavit regarding Jennifer's funeral expenses, a bill for which had been submitted to the Los Angeles County Department of Children's Services by Cabot and Sons. By signing the affidavit, I would be agreeing that the bill was correct, that the county would pay a certain portion, and that I would be responsible for paying the remainder, which was a little over seven hundred dollars. I was deeply irritated, but wrote a dignified letter of response the same day, stating that I was unable to sign the affidavit, and making reference to the following facts.

I reminded the CSW that, when I telephoned him on August 9, the morning of Jennifer's death, his exact words were, "Make whatever funeral arrangements you wish, and the county will pay for it." I had proceeded on those instructions in good faith, securing the services of Cabot and Sons upon a recommendation of Father Mike Wakefield, and therefore regarded the full amount of the bill as the county's responsibility. I further pointed out that I had already paid a number of expenses out of my own pocket, namely, $1,385 to the Joseph L. Greenwell Funeral Home in New Haven, Kentucky, and that, in addition to that, I would be paying him for Jenny's headstone. Also, Suzanne had made a contribution to the abbey of Our Lady of Gethsemani after we were granted permission to bury Jenny there. I cited that the expenses we had already incurred, above and beyond the money the county was asking us to pay toward the Cabot and Sons bill, were in excess of $1,800, not including more than $800 in airfare for Suzanne and me to fly to Kentucky. I mailed back my response hoping that I would not hear from the county again.

Not long after my return to Los Angeles, I made a trip to All Saints Children's Center to collect Jenny's things, including her spare clothing, sheets and blankets, medical supplies, and so on. Although I felt agonizing pain just at the thought of going there, and even though I knew it would be difficult, I was not prepared for the impact. I looked at the play yard and remembered seeing Jenny there, on the slide and swings. Now, in my mind, I could see her there again, her sweet little form playing here or there, perhaps sitting in the sand. When I went inside the building, the first memory that rushed over me was of carrying Jenny inside in the mornings and signing our names on the register. The power of it was so physical that I almost passed out. It nearly suffocated me. I went to the other end of the hall, near the office, and looked into the playroom where the children gathered in the mornings, and saw all of the familiar little faces—except one. I felt sick. Going to the office, I found a couple of the staff who I liked very much and who had been very special to Jenny. We spoke only briefly, because as each second passed I felt a pressure building inside of me. I tried not to let go before leaving, but I was overcome and tears filled my eyes. I excused myself, saying quickly that I probably should not have come back so soon and that I had to get out.

The staff had given me Jenny's belongings, along with a couple of other things I looked at when I got home later. One was a beautiful, touching record of Jenny's days at All Saints. In July, just a month before Jenny died, the staff had placed a large sheet of white paper, about three feet by four feet, on the ground and, after having some of the children dip their bare feet in finger paint of various colors, had them walk across the paper, leaving their footprints behind. The teachers had then written the children's names by each footprint and traced lines showing each child's path. Several beautiful colors of paint had been used. After drying, the work had been entitled "Pitter Patter of Little Feet" and taped up on one of the walls. After Jenny's death, the center had been kind enough to give it to Suzanne and me. Among the interwoven paths of footprints, were six lovely little impressions where Jenny had walked. It was a lovely gift, and I was deeply touched. To the paper I added the words, "Jenny, Six Footprints, July 1991, All Saints Children's Center," then carefully rolled it up and placed it in a long piece of cardboard tubing that I had for safekeeping.

The other gift from the center was something the children themselves had helped to make and was dated Friday, August 16, a week after Jenny's death. I do not know exactly how the teachers explained to the children that Jenny would not be coming back, but I am sure that they had been truthful with them and somehow communicated the fact that she had died. By way of acknowledging Jenny, many large hearts of varying size had been cut out of construction paper, each one representing one of Jenny's classmates. Upon each heart, a child had drawn some kind of picture or design, and one of the teachers had written a loving message to Jenny from that child. The hearts had all been tied together with strands of ribbon. I have never forgotten one of the messages to Jenny from a little boy named Stephen, whom I did not know: "I love you and I'm sorry I hit you and kick you." Carefully and lovingly, I placed the farewell gift in a large folder I had made for Jenny's artwork.

As the days passed, I felt the gaping hole in my life more and more painfully. Jenny filled my heart and mind every second of every day. When I opened my eyes in the morning, she was with me—and the terrible, merciless, unrelenting reality of her absence; I dwelt on her every waking moment and fell asleep each night with my heart aching for her. I had been so deeply involved with Jenny and the demands of her daily care that I did not really become fully aware of the incredible momentum I had developed until her sudden death brought everything to a soul-jarring and permanent halt.

Suddenly, in the space of that one night that would change my life forever, all of the dear and cherished routines became longer necessary, and ended. How deeply I missed doing even the most mundane things!—telephoning the medical supply company each week and ordering the things Jenny needed; coming home one night each week to find the large boxes on our front doorstep; carrying them downstairs and, always with the "assistance" of my little helper, unpacking, stacking, and storing colostomy bags, gauze, tubing, sterile swabs, surgical tape, gastrostomy bags, feedings, and so on.

No longer was there the happiness of seeing Jenny run to me at All Saints Children's Center at the end of the day, or putting her to bed each night, or a thousand other things that had brought indescribable joy and meaning into my life; no dear little voice that, each Saturday morning when I had hoped that I might grab a little extra sleep, had called out "Daddy" persistently from the other room until I responded.

Amid the pall that settled over our lives and which colored our every act and thought, I remember an incident that took place within a couple of weeks after Suzanne's return to Los Angeles. It was the first time after Jenny's death that Suzanne and I experienced friction with each other. Both of us had been careful not to upset each other unnecessarily; we both had an awareness of the fragility of the other person. We were feeling our way along, not knowing what to expect in terms of our own emotions, nor having any idea what would become of us.

However, one afternoon around dinner time, something happened. We were in the kitchen. Suzanne was standing at the sink, and I was seated atop the bar stool that stood a feet feet away, near the edge of the dining room. I must have made a comment to Suzanne about something that was causing me concern or irritation, and she responded in a fashion that was typical of her clinical, passive-aggressive aloofness, tinged with resentment.

That kind of interchange had taken place thousands of times during our marriage. The whole thing would have been insignificant under other circumstances. But given the timing, it brought to the surface an agonizing realization. As I sat there on the bar stool, my eyes happened to be focused on the end of the supporting wall between the kitchen and the living room on the other side. Suddenly I remembered how Jenny used to bounce around that corner as she came into the dining room or kitchen from the living room. I remembered how her face looked—her beautiful, infectious smile and her sparkling eyes looking up at me. I thought of how reassuring—how comforting and healing—it would be to see her shining face at that moment, to bask in her presence, to pick her up and hold her in my arms.

Jenny would never walk around that corner again! Never again would I see her face or touch her! She would never sleep in her bed again. I would never hear her voice. This realization hit me like a tidal wave, and I felt utterly sick inside. It pressed up against me, from all around, as it had again and again over the past days, so that wherever I might turn or no matter what I was doing, it was there in front of me. And with this pain came also a coldness—a desolate perception that my life had returned to the emptiness that had characterized it before Jenny had transformed it and rescued me from that pit of nothingness. Now, my precious little savior was gone. I was alone again.

Looking for Support

It was difficult for Suzanne and me to comfort or support each other. It was not that we didn't want to, but we had not had much practice during our marriage, and each of us was struggling so much with our own individual grief that not much was left over. We continued going to the therapy sessions with Dr. Wortz that we had begun in early July. This was an important and meaningful outlet. In addition to knowing our backgrounds and our situation from having worked with us before Jenny's death, he was truly understanding and compassionate and very skilled. The focus now was on dealing with our loss, and Dr. Wortz sought to help us do this both individually and as a couple. Suzanne's ambivalence toward Jennifer and me was probably not discussed at all. None of us brought it up, and I do not even remember Suzanne and I talking about it outside the sessions. It seemed largely irrelevant now, given the way things had worked out and our need to find a way to live with our immediate emotions and an overwhelming sense of loss. In time, however, the issue of what had happened during the month before Suzanne went to Gethsemani would return to haunt me.

Suzanne and I also searched for other means of emotional support. I felt a deep need to find people who could understand what I was feeling. One good friend of mine, Gillian McKenna, strongly urged me to have at least one appointment with a particular psychiatrist who, according to Gillian, specialized in bereavement therapy. This might have turned out to be a very good thing, but I never found out because, despite my friend's prompting over many months, I never followed up on Gillian's suggestion. There was nothing very mysterious about my inability to seek out this therapist. The main obstacle, in my mind, and one big enough to squelch the idea, was simply that she was located in Santa Monica, a hard drive from my side of L.A., especially considering the formidable evening rush hour traffic. I could not deal with facing that drive every week, and I never found the necessary motivation.

Nevertheless, I needed some kind of added support. And what made me feel this so acutely was my realization that the support I had counted on was not there. During this critical period, I learned a great deal about human psychology, about how people understand and relate to death, and about how they relate to those whose lives have been touched by the loss of a loved one—especially a child.

I had never counted on much support in my work place. The corporate philosophy—one I have always found unrealistic, abhorrent, and ridiculous—was that personal feelings are left at home. Everything was geared to the highly competitive consulting environment—to surviving both corporately and individually. In my own experience, deep and lasting friendships rarely were born in such environments.

More importantly, when Jenny died, I also lost an entire circle of people who had come to mean a great deal to me, including a large part of the nursing staff on the pediatric unit at Huntington; the medical social workers and child life therapists there, Dr. Laurance, and Sue Collins in Las Vegas. Jenny's death meant the end of our social calls to the hospital. When Jenny was alive, she had to check into the pediatric ward every two or three months for several days, at which times I visited frequently and had the opportunity to talk at length with the nurses and staff there.

It was terribly painful to let all of that go. I longed to see them and socialize with them, and I missed the pediatric ward—its sounds, smells, and activities, and all that it represented. As days turned into weeks, I realized that no one was going to call to see how I was doing. I do not know exactly what I expected, but I felt disillusioned and sad when not even those who were closest to Jenny called me.

On several occasions during the weeks following Jenny's death, I called the hospital and left messages for two of the nurses, Carol and Cindy, whom Jenny had adored and who had been mothers to Jenny while she lived at Huntington. Neither of them ever called me back. Actually, I had not even seen Cindy since before Jennifer's death. She did not come to the funeral mass, and despite the calls, notes, and the verbal messages I have occasionally left at the hospital up until as recently as September 1995, I have never received a word of response.

I also had little contact with Sue Collins after Jenny died. I invited her to stop and visit us when she came to town, but she never accepted. During the one serious phone conversation we had, at my initiation, she had little to say. There were two beautiful photos in Jennifer's album which Sue had taken of her at our home in March 1991. Sue had the negatives, and once or twice I called her to see if either she would have more prints made for me (for which I said I would gladly pay her, of course), or, if that were not convenient, if I could borrow the negatives long enough to get more prints made myself. It finally became obvious enough to me that, for reasons I still do not understand, Sue was not willing to put forth any effort, and I finally gave up. I had to have copies made from the prints in my possession, which yielded inferior results.

This also calls to mind a young man who worked at Huntington as a physical therapist and who had known Jenny very well. Although I was not close to him, our relationship was certainly friendly, and Suzanne was well acquainted with him. After Jenny's death, one of the medical social workers at Huntington told me that he had taken many photos of Jenny during her residence at Huntington, and I wanted to get copies. But again, he was not cooperative, and gave so many excuses over a number of weeks that I finally tired of his evasiveness and gave up. I could not and still do not understand why some people were unwilling to go at all out of their way to provide, at no cost to themselves, photos of a little girl that would be deeply treasured by her bereaved father.

Fortunately, not everyone was that distant toward me. Some of the nurses and staff were very kind when I stopped by Huntington occasionally. As time passed, they seemed to become even friendlier, probably because some of the most acutely painful associations—at least for them—had been mitigated by passing months and years. I might add that my visits back to Huntington since Jenny's death have been very sparing, two or three times a year at most.

In fairness to the nurses and staff at Huntington who loved Jenny and cared for her so long, and by whom I might have felt a little abandoned after Jenny's death, I clearly acknowledge that they did nothing deliberately unkind. I admit that, at times, I even wondered if what I perceived as the fading away of their friendship and support was an indication that they resented me, perhaps unconsciously, for Jenny's death. However, I believe they were just trying to get on with their own lives as best they could, and I do not doubt that many of them felt deep pain and genuine loss. It would be naive and disrespectful not to assume so. After all, they had to live with death—especially the death of children—in their work, perhaps not every day, but much more often than most people. Certainly, their professions required them to steel themselves in whatever way necessary to function effectively. And again, I acknowledge not only the love and care they gave Jenny, but the unselfish support they gave Suzanne and me when we took Jenny from them and brought her home.

For Suzanne, Huntington was a very different issue. She worked there and came into daily contact with the people I have spoken of. But for Suzanne, understandably, this was difficult and painful because she was reminded of Jenny at every turn. The hospital was saturated with memories of her. In fact, after Jenny's death, Suzanne wondered if she would even be able to return to work at the hospital. This, of course, had to be her choice, but when she discussed it with me, I offered my feeling that, even though it would be hard, she should return to work, at least for a time, to try to work through some of the feelings and memories. Right or wrong, I felt that, in the long run, this would be in her best interests. In the end she opted to stay and remained at Huntington until early 1994. But it was hard for her. People with the best intentions stopped her constantly at first to make inquiries and offer condolences. For a long time, she could not even bring herself to go to the fourth-floor pediatric ward. Once or twice she saw little children there who resembled Jenny— riding in one of the little red wagons. This must have torn her apart.

As for the people in my life outside of Huntington, there was little support, at least in terms of numbers. In some cases, the people who showed the most compassion were friends with whom I had been out of touch for a while. Often, the deepest, most meaningful, lasting friendships have not required much maintenance and have sometimes weathered long periods of little or no contact because they have been based on some spiritual affinity or chemistry that resists the corrosiveness of time. Therefore, ironically, some of the people to whom I was closest never knew Jenny, never saw me during the period that she was physically a part of my life, and, in the case of Gillian McKenna, heard about Jenny only after her death, through a mutual friend.

Gillian, with whom I had been out of touch for a very long time, telephoned me unexpectedly at work on Friday, August 16, the day before I left L.A. to bury Jennifer at Gethsemani in Kentucky. She had heard about Jenny and her death through a mutual friend and had called me out of compassion and very deep concern. It was, in fact, this reaching out on her part that started a whole new dimension to our friendship and set it upon a path toward an irreversible crystallization. Four years later, Gillian is one of my dearest friends. She has been a support and confidant through many difficult times.

Another close friend, Dawn Grant, came to know about Jenny only at the end of June, when we talked on the telephone after being out of touch for months. We did not talk again until I called to tell her that Jenny had died. My other very close friend, Jerry Alber, whom I had known for twenty-five years, had never known Jenny because he lived in Chicago, but he had known all about her during her presence in my life. Jerry was and still is like a spiritual brother.

However, when Jenny died, Jerry seemed unavailable emotionally. I was disappointed to find little support from him. In fact, a letter which I received from him on January 3, 1992, seemed so strange, uncomprehending, and almost antagonistic toward the grief I was feeling that inwardly I felt entirely cut off from him and, by the end of February, after having no communication with him, I wondered if our friendship had even ended forever. However, on June 18, 1992, I called him, prompted by some very sad and traumatic episodes which had just taken place in my life (including the death of a pet). At that time, our friendship immediately picked up again after several months of no contact, a pattern that has manifested itself throughout our long relationship and which I now simply accept as one aspect of the mechanics through which our souls interact.

In retrospect, I came to realize that Jerry's emotional distance was not personal, nor probably conscious. I have accepted that everyone is different and has different strengths and weaknesses. It is unfair and unrealistic to expect anyone—a friend, or lover, or a mate—to meet all our collective expectations of what we need in other people. And what one friend cannot offer, perhaps another can.

Throughout my adult life, it has been difficult for my mother to accept or understand some of the changes I have gone through. For instance, she has never digested the fact that I stopped being a professional musician. She sees that as a waste, irrespective of what I have done since. I have been hearing about this for years. And, since I had never showed much interest in having children, she failed—understandably, perhaps—to grasp the incredible significance Jennifer had for me. What seemed at first almost like indifference on my mother's part to this terrible loss in my life turned into downright callousness a few months later. It was only many months after Jenny's passing that my mother really began to grasp how much I had loved Jenny and acknowledged it.

Yet Dale and Jim Roggenkamp, both during the emotionally difficult weeks before Jenny's death and thereafter, acted toward me just as they always had during the past many years of our friendship—openly, warmly, honestly, and compassionately. Even though they live in Kentucky, half the continent from Los Angeles, I feel as close to them today as when I lived in Louisville, and if ever there were two people who made me feel like their home was mine, it was Dale and Jim. Not only when Suzanne and I stayed with them during the week that Jenny was buried at Gethsemani, but during the whole critical, painful period right after Jenny's death and for months afterward, their love and understanding gave me more support than they ever imagined. I thank them with all my heart.

During the first painful and chaotic weeks after our return from Kentucky, Suzanne and I went through a sifting process with friends and acquaintances in terms of who would and would not be nearby emotionally. Suzanne and I both encountered a void in our lives at the point where we instinctively sought comfort and support in our bereavement; and it was a void that needed filling. Ironically, this void came to be filled largely by strangers.

The Compassionate Friends

I cannot remember where or how Suzanne and I first became aware of the existence of grief support groups, or even who was first to hear of such a thing. Nevertheless, by the beginning of September, we had come across the Compassionate Friends, a support group, in their own words, "for parents whose children have died." I first contacted them by telephone on September 5. They explained that they met in the evening twice a month, on the second Thursday, in small groups, at different members' homes, and on the fourth Thursday, in a larger group, at a regular location such as an auditorium, civic center, or hospital. Their organization, which had chapters across the Los Angeles area, suggested the Verdugo Hills Chapter in La Crescenta, which was within very reasonable geographic range of our home. This chapter held their large, monthly meetings at Verdugo Hills Hospital and was divided into smaller, more intimate groups of ten to twenty individuals each who met in various homes. Suzanne and I were put in touch with one of these smaller groups which was headed by a lady named Diane Keane (whose daughter had committed suicide several years earlier). One or two of the homes in this group turned out to be practically next door to us.

On Thursday, September 12, 1991, Suzanne and I went to our first home meeting. It was held in a large, comfortable den, and drinks and light refreshments were served. About fifteen people attended, and the furniture was arranged so that everyone could sit more or less in a circle, facing each other. Shortly after 7:00 P.M., everyone had arrived. At one point, as if by unspoken consensus, everyone quieted down and got settled in anticipation of the start of the meeting. I noticed a feeling of tension in the room, a kind of nervous anticipation or apprehension. Suzanne felt it too. Later, I came to understand that this happened at the outset of every meeting.

After the leader spoke, she invited each person to introduce themselves and to recount briefly whom they had lost and by what circumstances. This, also, was a standard element of each meeting. One by one, each of us spoke. If someone felt too emotional to speak about the circumstances of the death of their child or simply preferred not to share their experience that particular night, that was fine. No one was under any kind of pressure or scrutiny. Some of the people offered only a sentence or two; others spoke at length. Again, no one was pushed or censored. Some who shared were quiet and composed, while more than one who spoke became deeply emotional almost immediately. Tears were common. When our turn came, Suzanne and I introduced ourselves, and I explained that we had just lost Jennifer, our foster daughter. Everyone seemed to accept immediately and without question that we loved and missed her just as we would have our own biological daughter.

During this first meeting and immediately afterward, Suzanne and I had the same reactions. First, there was so much grief in the room that we felt overwhelmed. Given that our own bereavement was so intense and painful, we asked ourselves later why we would want to subject ourselves to all the added grief that the others expressed there. Second, although a number of the other participants had experienced losses relatively recently, some had been coming to the meetings for years and, in a few cases, seemed as emotional as those who had come around only in the last few weeks. This seemed odd. Actually, it seemed unnatural, as if there were some normal period of time for grieving the loss of a loved one and they had exceeded it.

Even before the meeting, Suzanne and I had begun to ask ourselves and others such questions as what a normal grieving period was, how we were likely to act, what we were supposed to be feeling, and at what point in time. Was it normal to feel this way or that way? How long would our pain last? When could we expect to start feeling better? We had no objective yardstick upon which to judge the people at that meeting. And despite the fact that I could not envision myself ever feeling better about losing Jenny, I nevertheless found it strange that people were still going to support groups over the death of a child years after the fact. It seemed a little sick, both to Suzanne and me, and we both felt that in such cases those people might benefit from professional psychiatric help to get their lives more in the present and back on track. Thus Suzanne and I both questioned the purpose and efficacy of such a group, whether it was healthy, and, above all, whether or not it was appropriate for us. After all, we were "normal" people. We did not wish to be a part of some gathering that fed on its own pain and the pain of others for years on end, or whose social life and whole raison d'être centered around a morbid attitude toward death.

Finally, immediately after the meeting and for most of the next day, Suzanne and I both felt drained and possibly worse than before we had gone. We asked ourselves what the point was in going if it only made us feel worse.

After people had introduced themselves that evening and said whatever they chose about themselves and the child they had lost, the meeting progressed informally and was characterized chiefly by a free-flowing dialogue. The tension that had been so evident at the outset had diminished as the self-introductions proceeded, and had vanished by the time they had ended. A wide variety of circumstances of death and ages at the time of death were represented at this small meeting—suicides of adult children, drug overdoses of teenagers, accidents, cancer and other diseases, and even murder victims.

That particular evening, there was either a short film or slide presentation. Everyone was very supportive and understanding and extremely friendly. After various announcements, the meeting ended on a cordial note. We were encouraged to come back and put ourselves on a mailing list to receive free publications of the organization and notices about the dates, locations, and details of future meetings. We were even given names of several members to call at any time if we needed emotional support or help.

Nevertheless, over the next day or so, and for all of the reasons I have described above, Suzanne and I decided that the Compassionate Friends was not for us. I think that Suzanne had made her mind up immediately after the meeting. However, as the days passed, and as I lived with my grief moment to moment without abatement, with little support from friends, I became a bit humbled in my initial assessment of the group. First of all, I knew from experience that, in individual therapy, the most productive sessions sometimes left one utterly drained for a day or two, and often feeling somewhat worse than before the session. Therefore, I felt that not to go back to the meeting at least once more, just because it had made me feel even lower that evening and part of the next day, was not sound judgment. And besides, the meeting may have done me some good.

Also, I recognized a tiny element of pride that had made me reluctant to go back. Despite much loneliness throughout my life, I had nevertheless a strong, individualistic predilection that had often made me a loner. I had never liked groups, organizations, or clubs of any kind, and despite my own acknowledgement of an almost chronic lack of fellowship of various kinds in my life, I resisted any kind of membership. As ridiculous or irrational as it may sound, I suspect that, for the same reason, I backed away from returning to the group because of some misdirected sense of pride. It was as if I should be able to handle my sadness and grief myself. And yet, I had sought out the Compassionate Friends precisely because I had wanted help and support. Thus, when I identified this conflict, I was able to deal with it and set it aside as an inappropriate reason for not giving the meetings another chance.

Thus, when October came, I had made up my mind to go to at least one more meeting of the Compassionate Friends. I asked Suzanne if she would like to go with me, but she had decided that the meetings were not for her, and never attended another one. In addition to other differences in our make-ups, Suzanne was more reserved than I in terms of articulating personal or intimate feelings in an open setting. On the other hand, despite my tendencies during certain periods toward an almost hermitic lifestyle, I tended to be quite open, even in a public setting, when it came to talking about personal feelings. This may have been another reason that I was willing to try the group again.

I returned to a subsequent meeting of the Compassionate Friends, this time in a different home, on the second Thursday of October. I was more prepared; I knew what to expect this time, and I experienced much less personal tension. I now had an inner assurance that the environment of the gathering would be empathetic and supportive. Many of the same people from the previous meeting were there, and one or two new people as well. The same general format was followed. The part of the meeting taken up by open discussion took a different turn. I gained new insights into the nature of grieving and what it meant to different people to lose a child. I was glad that I had decided to come back, and after that, I went regularly to the home meetings for several months. At least one of the later meetings was held in my home, but I do not remember if Suzanne sat in on that one or if she was even home that night.

I derived great benefits from the home meetings, and I even noticed that I started to look forward to them. However, although I made halfhearted commitments almost every month to attend the larger gatherings at Verdugo Hills Hospital on the fourth Thursday, I never made it to any of them. Despite my decision not to attend, the larger meetings sounded very appealing. They were more structured, always featured some kind of formal presentation or guest speaker, and offered one the opportunity to meet more people.

The Compassionate Friends also organized many types of outings and social functions for its members during the course of the year, and in this respect, I am sure that the organization was of great value to many people. As for me, I restricted my involvement to the monthly meetings at various homes. I was not ready for a social life. Outside the meetings, I found no meaning or happiness. And I remained reticent about building any kind of social structure in my life that centered on Jenny's death as its foundation.

Nevertheless, I attended the monthly home meetings. They were one of the most important factors in my gaining critical insights into the grieving process and in coming to understand my own inner life after Jenny's death. This insight was gained gradually over a period of months as different aspects of grief were discussed in successive meetings.

Some of my initial discomfort and resistance to returning to the meetings lay in the fact that, by going to the meetings at all, I was acknowledging something which, on a certain emotional level, I did not want to admit with finality—that Jenny was really dead. She was gone and would not come back. This terrible reality, I came to learn, was something to be faced in stages, and at various levels of realization, one of which was my decision to continue my involvement with the Compassionate Friends. A significant task therefore, and a long and difficult and painful one, was reorganizing my life around the unmitigable fact of Jenny's death.

The loss of a child is the worst loss imaginable. This was pointed out during the first meeting I attended and was emphasized in the later meetings. For those who have lost a child, regardless of the child's age or the circumstances of its death, it is crucial to understand this point. The group supported and understood that whether Jenny was my biological daughter was utterly irrelevant. Jenny and I were as much father and daughter as any child and parent who ever lived, and we shared more closeness and love than was experienced in many biological parent-child relationships. Jenny's death was the greatest loss of my lifetime. I had lost my father in 1969, and although this had been traumatic, it could never have prepared me for the sledgehammer blow of Jenny's death.

Many people are not able to comprehend the full significance of the loss of a child, since they have not experienced it. This is especially true for people who have never had children. Suzanne had a close friend who was a loving, generous person who had two children of her own, but who never understood the depth and the ongoing nature of Suzanne's grief. My own mother has never comprehended what Jenny meant to me. Experience is truly the best teacher, and when one's child dies, a harsh and unforgettable learning experience indeed—other parents who have suffered a similar loss are the most empathetic. The place where one will come most closely into contact with these parents is in a grief support group like the Compassionate Friends. Only there can the pain of a bereaved parent be the most fully voiced and understood.

I gained another important insight from grief support meetings. The notion that there is some kind of normal or set grieving period is fallacious and inappropriate. As the years go by, I perceive the shallowness of such platitudes as "time heals all," and the groundlessness of such ideas that, in time, one "gets over" such cataclysmic events. For some people, it is appropriate to go to grief support meetings for months or even years if it is in accordance with their own personal nature and needs. When I remember the beautiful things that have happened in my life, I do not (hopefully) get over them—I never forget them or the meaning they brought. Rather, I embrace them, build upon them, and reshape my life around them. Why then, would I not acknowledge, embrace, and build upon suffering in the same manner?—except perhaps to deny it or try to run away from it, which is in opposition to personal growth and evolution.

Beyond the Physical World

In addition to seeking emotional support during the first months after Jenny's death, when I was feeling an especially intense sense of loss, I also began to search for meaning. From November 1990, when I first met Jenny, until the end of August 1991, after I had returned from burying her at Gethsemani and resumed the everyday routine of living (if I could call it living), I had been involved in such a whirlwind of activity that even the idea of searching out or contemplating "meaning," in some deep metaphysical sense, of what was going on never occurred to me. My days had been filled with immediate matters and physical realities demanded my constant attention and energies—the bureaucracy of the county, filling out endless documents for foster home licensing, ordering colostomy bags and sterile swabs, refining techniques for the application of gauze dressings, getting Jenny to and from day care, and, above all, trying to keep her healthy.

All that had come to an end with brutal abruptness. But the momentum had continued for a couple more weeks; in a sense, Jenny's care continued for a while longer. But when I returned to Los Angeles, my physical care of Jenny was over, and in its place was a gaping hole in my life. I began to wonder about things.

On one level, no meaning beyond what had actually happened over the last ten months was necessary. Essentially, a wonderful, needy little baby girl had come into my life. I had fallen in love with her and Suzanne and I had brought her home and cared for her, giving her everything that we could. In turn, she had loved us, filled our lives with light, and turned our world upside down. Then, she had died. She was gone forever, and I was left with a mixture of beautiful, cherished memories and indescribable pain.

The love that I felt for Jenny could stand by itself and the beauty of the relationship that we had. Those things could endure, and had unshakable reality and meaning in themselves. We had come together, each of us with great needs of different kinds, and each of us had answered the needs of the other in a profound and beautiful way. Then, suddenly, Jenny went on to an existence beyond mine. I was deeply bereaved, but there was no mystery about what had happened.

And yet I found myself wondering about the forces that had brought us together—about whatever noumenal realities, underlying the drama that had played itself out in our lives, might have shaped and guided the procession of events in my relationship with Jennifer. To say that what had taken place was not enough for me was both true and not true. In one way, I accepted the past ten months at face value, as complete, self-sufficient, beautiful, and even "perfect" in some sense—despite the pain—because of what Jenny and I had shared. But my inner self, which had always, from childhood, sought answers to life's most difficult mysteries, began to ask questions.

I remember one evening very vividly, when I was sitting on the large rug on the floor of my garage-become-den. I am sure that there were things spread out on the rug all around me, and although I do not remember precisely what I was doing, I am certain that it had something to do with Jenny. Perhaps I was arranging something in her photo album or organizing all the sympathy cards that Suzanne and I had received, or going through papers. I do not know. But what I remember unmistakably is that, at one point I was sitting quietly, motionlessly, looking toward the brightly lit desk against the wall, but deep in thought. And at that moment, something in me made a decision and became mobilized. I knew that I could not remain in the limbo that I was in; I had to find some answers.

That scene took place during the last week in August, after I had returned from Kentucky. I know this because the dates on various papers I have kept show that by September 1, and off and on for the next ten days, I was making contact with three individuals who were deeply involved in the metaphysical, or occult, world—a medium, an astrologer, and a channeler.

Although my career, or careers, have taken many turns, including music and the performing arts, writing, design, and various kinds of business pursuits, and although I have, over the course of my life, practiced disciplines of many kinds and moved among widely diverse circles of people, there is one thread which has woven all of these experiences into some kind of coherent, multifaceted whole. This thread is a spiritual quest that began in August 1964, when I was fifteen years old.

I was suddenly and unexpectedly caught up and initiated into a mystical world of perception. My life was turned upside-down overnight and took on the character of a quest. Ongoing even today, thirty-one years later, this search—for answers to what I experienced as a youth, for understanding, and for new and expanded perceptions—has taken many turns. My experiences, which I have written about in *Darkness Is Light Enough* (Galde Press, 1996), have included encounters with a Hindu swami, a Native American medicine man, psychics, and others, and have included first-hand knowledge of many forms of magic and hallucinogenic drugs, Buddhism, Hinduism, various Christian sects, including the charismatics, mystical visions beyond the dogmas of any organized religion, and lifelong relationships with places of power, yogic disciplines, and Eastern teachings.

Although I have done voluminous research and reading in the realms of the spiritual, the metaphysical, and the occult, I believe that nothing can substitute for firsthand knowledge and experience. I am a realist. I am skeptical of anything that smacks of metaphysical nonsense, and I do not believe that the problems of the personality or the soul can be solved by escaping into a world of mental gymnastics or preoccupation with the psychic.

On the other hand, I know as clearly and as deeply as I know anything that we are surrounded by incredible realities which we cannot ordinarily see or understand. Most of the forces that govern our lives are beyond our range of normal perception in a world that is at the same time above and coexistent with our own. I believe in reincarnation, which I will discuss later in more detail.

Finally, I have known for many years that there are certain gifted individuals who have real powers and who can aid one at times when, as in my own case, I have felt a deep and genuine need to call upon the abilities of others to gain knowledge of a special kind. I have had numerous personal direct experiences with such people whom I know to be absolutely genuine and to have abilities that range from average to astounding. And, I am fully aware that there are, in fact, many in the psychic fields who are self-deluded or inept at best, and, at worst, deliberate, unscrupulous frauds.

I will not waste energy trying to defend my view with respect to metaphysics in general or psychics in particular, nor in attempting to demonstrate that I have enough intelligence and experience to distinguish the real from the unreal, or a person with genuine psychic abilities from a fraud. Readers will understand or not understand, according to their own experiences and world views. During the weeks immediately following Jenny's passing, I came to the realization that I was going to explore the possibility of finding people who could help me see beyond the normal boundaries of things—this time, because of my deep and ever-growing desire to understand what had brought Jennifer and me together, how she had come to have the physical difficulties that she did, and what role her dead Siamese twin, Wendy, had played in all this.

Thus, on Sunday, September 1, 1991, I obtained the telephone number of an astrologer in Topack, Arizona, who had come highly recommended by two of Suzanne's closest friends, one of whom was Zippy Frankel. I called her the same day and explained to her all about Jenny: her relationship with me, her subsequent death, and the fact that I was seeking answers to questions surrounding all of this. I learned that Nicki Mellette came to Los Angeles periodically to give readings.

Accordingly, I made an appointment to see her. I also agreed to call her back in a few days to give her precise times of birth for Suzanne, Jenny, and me (I already felt that I knew the precise time that Jenny had died within a few minutes), so that she could work up our various astrological charts. During our phone conversation, Nicki mentioned that she knew of an excellent British medium who came to Long Beach every year to give readings and whom I might be interested in seeing.

In the meantime, on Tuesday, I called an organization known as Concept: Synergy in Palm Beach, Florida, to obtain a reading with a man named Jach Pursel, a widely sought-after, world-class channeler of international reputation and phenomenal ability, through whom a nonphysical entity named Lazaris channeled exclusively.

Although I was determined to explore as many avenues as possible with respect to my questions about Jenny, I felt strongly that, if anyone in the world could provide answers, it would be Jach Pursel. I had first learned about him from Suzanne. I had already had one reading with Jach Pursel by telephone in 1983 when Suzanne and I were living in Louisville. Even then, due to his vast reputation and the demand for his services, I was fortunate to get an appointment at all, and, as I remember, I had to wait some time for the reading.

During that reading, Jach had answered questions about many areas of my life, providing some very dramatic information and insights into a realm of personal mystical experiences and their connection with various past lives of mine that I had written about in a manuscript which at that time had been completed for about fifteen months. What he told me was so insightful with respect to the manuscript that I transcribed the relevant portions of the reading (which was recorded on his end and then sent to me) and incorporated them into an epilogue which was included when the book was finally published under the title of *Darkness Is Light Enough,* to which I have previously referred.

Eight years later, I decided to seek out Jach Pursel again. Appointments with Lazaris were far from easy to obtain. The person with whom I spoke at Concept: Synergy on September 3 noted that I felt my need was critical, since it involved the death of a child. Later that day he called back and told me that I would be granted an emergency reading with Lazaris within the next couple of months. Meanwhile, I would have to be patient until they contacted me again.

On September 10, I again telephoned Nicki Mellette the astrologer to give her the exact times of birth for Suzanne, Jenny, and me. She provided the name of the British medium to whom she had previously referred and some background information about her. Freda Fell, the medium in question, traveled each year from England to the United States to give readings and, during her stays in Long Beach, saw clients at the Universal Mind Science Church on 8th Street. Nicki recommended her strongly and explained that, during one period in the past, Freda had stayed with her for eight years during her U.S. visits, when Nicki had studied various psychic sciences with her.

I called the UMS Church the same day, learned that Freda Fell was in Long Beach, and made an appointment for a reading one week before my appointment with Nicki. I was told to bring a ninety-minute cassette tape so that I could have a record of the reading.

Thus, if it was possible to learn anything about Jenny from people in the psychic or occult fields, I felt that I was on my way. With confirmed appointments for a medium and an astrologer, and high optimism for a reading in the near future with Jach Pursel, the channeler, I felt that I had done the right thing. Actually, although I had seen a number of psychics in my life, most of whom were pretty good, I had never visited a medium or an astrologer. As far as mediums were concerned, I really had no preconceived notions, except that I did not want to be taken in by any frauds.

I had always shunned the idea of going into an endeavor in a half-hearted manner, and it seemed that a great deal of time and study would be required before proficiency could be acquired in the discipline of astrology. Given my strong interest in other esoteric areas, I had not explored the field. Besides, I was turned off by dabblers, and astrology seemed to draw them more than any other occult practice, probably due largely to its vulgarization through newspaper horoscopes and the plethora of slick paperbacks available on the subject.

Thus, when the occult arts become entertainment, bastardized through popularization with the masses, as has been the case with popular astrology and the current "psychic telephone networks," I walk away—at least from all forms as represented through cheap marketing and its promises of romance, sex, power, money, and happiness forever after. However, I have always been receptive to astrology, and to the preparation and study of astrological charts, as long as the work is done by, or in conjunction with, serious, competent people.

A Medium

My appointment with Freda Fell arrived. The afternoon of Wednesday, September 18, was sunny and pleasant. I left my office downtown early. I did not want to be rushed on the freeway, and I wanted to be peaceful and calm when I got to the church. In my car on the seat next to me were the directions I had written down for getting there, a blank cassette tape, and a small, carved, soapstone container from India, which I had bought at one of the little gift shops run by Self-Realization Fellowship. I had acquired the decorated little box as a vessel for holding Jennifer's hair and fingernail clippings, which the funeral director had set aside. After placing the relics inside of it, I had permanently sealed the lid on with powerful glue to avoid any possibility of accidental spillage.

I arrived in Long Beach and found the address without any difficulty. The Universal Mind Science Church, located on a quiet street corner, was a simple, unostentatious, but dignified gray building. I parked and went inside. The lady in the office greeted me, accepted my donation, which had been requested in exchange for the reading, and asked me to be seated. A few minutes passed while I sat with my tape and soapstone box in hand. Just before 3:00 o'clock she escorted me out the same door through which I had entered and down the sidewalk to another door at the top of some steps. She ushered me inside and left.

I looked around the room, which was pleasantly illumined by natural light that came in through the side windows. It was about the size of a small den, plain, and austerely furnished, with only two straight-backed chairs that had been placed about eight to ten feet apart facing each other. There was little else in the room to distract the attention, and one had the impression that this was deliberate—that the ambiance of the room had been created specifically for mediumistic readings. There was something that I liked about the starkness, mitigated only slightly by the two chairs that stood empty and waiting, creating an almost confrontational, though nonthreatening, setting. The intent and function of this simple, unadorned room could be clearly sensed. This appealed to me.

I heard a rustle in the hallway, and Freda Fell entered. She was short, probably in her late sixties, with gray hair and extraordinarily intense blue eyes that immediately arrested my attention. There was something about them, something in their peculiar intensity and the sense that they were focused just beyond what most of us ordinarily see, which said that this person had spent a great deal of time in trance states. We introduced ourselves and spoke momentarily. She asked me if I had brought a tape recorder, and I replied that I had not, but only a tape, since it had been my understanding that a recorder would be available. But a tape machine could not be found that day, and so I was not able to record the session. I would have liked to have a tape to refer to later, but it was not to be, so I just accepted that things were as they were and made a few brief notes later that evening at home.

At one moment, while we were still standing and talking, Freda, looking puzzled and then almost alarmed, suddenly said sharply to me, "What's that smell? There's something in here that smells like liniment!" She seemed almost horrified. I thought for a moment and then remembered that the lid of the soapstone box I had with me had been lightly anointed with some kind of oil. After sealing the box, which had been some time ago, I had rubbed a couple drops of scented oil, probably patchouli or rose, into the lid. But the aroma had grown faint since then, and, possibly because I was so accustomed to it and to the smells of incense, and so on, I had not even noticed it as we stood there in the room, talking together.

Freda's reaction actually reminded me of the vampires in the movies who draw back in horror when they are confronted with a crucifix or a mirror. She was extremely sensitive to smells, both physically and psychically, and the scented oil had really thrown her. I explained to her that I had brought something which had a scent, and she demanded that I get it out of the room immediately. Not even explaining to her the nature of what was in my possession, I carried my soapstone box outside, and placed it carefully and inconspicuously in a corner at the top of the steps. I retrieved it right after the reading.

With the crisis resolved, things became calm as we sat facing each other and talked. Freda explained how she worked. The first thing she said was that I could not ask her about this or that person. I could not mention any names, or lead her in any specific direction. Therefore, she would pass on any and all impressions that she received, but if she got nothing regarding a specific person I might have in mind (Jenny, of course), I would have to accept that. In addition, I was not to interrupt her with questions during the main portion of the reading. She stated that at various times she would pause after telling me something and ask me if I understood what she had said. I was to answer straightforwardly, with a simple yes or a no. Although I am not certain, I believe she told me that I could pose some questions toward the end of the reading.

My first reaction to what Freda had said was disappointment and concern. After all, I had really come only to find out about Jenny. No other information mattered to me. Obviously, my sole reason for bringing the little box with Jenny's hair and fingernail clippings was to provide Freda with an object that might supply a powerful means for some kind of psychic contact. But, given that Freda did not work that way, the box now could serve no purpose (unless, perhaps, despite its apparently upsetting effect, it had initiated some kind of mediumistic connection, anyway). I knew how I would feel if nothing came through of its own accord about Jenny. At the same time, I realized that, since I could not ask questions or make comments that might supply Freda with leads, she was completely on her own to succeed or fail without my input. This strongly argued for her authenticity and integrity.

We became quiet. The room was very still. The silence seemed intense and somehow pregnant. As I watched Freda closely, two things happened. Almost immediately, she went into a trance. There was nothing dramatic about it, and Freda did not announce it or make any gestures, but I could tell, unmistakably, by her eyes. They became glazed over and glassy; she was not acting. I do not even think she saw the room. She was focused somewhere else, beyond what I could see.

Within a very short time, I could clearly sense another presence in the room, behind her—a strong energy of some kind. Someone else was there; a disembodied consciousness, and perhaps more than one. Of this I am certain. There were no cues and I was not the victim of any kind of suggestion; I'd had enough occult experiences to recognize what was happening. Whatever was there was offering information to Freda, and thus, she began to voice the impressions and messages coming to her.

Immediately, Freda picked up on things that could only refer to Jenny. She clearly saw the recent death of a very young child, a little girl. At first, she commented that there might be some circumstances of violence around the death, and in connection with that I think she used the term, "foul play." This concerned me, but in the same breath, she corrected herself by saying that she had seen people like policemen and paramedics (who, of course, had all been at my house the day Jenny died), and that what she felt was the sudden and unexpected nature of the death and the intensity of the shock and grief it had engendered. Without any comments or coaching from me, Freda continued to articulate the other things that she saw, making specific reference to the fact that Jenny had spent much of her life in a hospital, that she had been almost a kind of diva there, and that the nurses had loved her deeply. She also specifically identified some kind of eliminative disorder. After she made certain comments, Freda would ask me if I had understood, and I said yes.

At some point, Freda must have asked me Jennifer's name, which I told her, and after which, in the briefest possible way, I clarified the nature of the relationship. In addition to this, Freda said that Jennifer had been sent to us for a very special purpose, that she had finished her cycle, and that now I must finish mine. She also made a number of general comments intended to be comforting and which one would want to hear and believe in any case, such as that Jenny was fine and happy where she was. One thing Freda did say that caught my attention was that she felt that Suzanne, Jenny, and I had all been together before in a past life.

In addition to everything that came up with respect to Jennifer, Freda Fell also made extensive references to Suzanne, to my father, who had been deceased for more than twenty-two years at that time, and to many of my own personal idiosyncrasies and habits, including a briefcase that I had, all the paperwork in it, and the manner in which I would often devote an amount of attention and energy to that kind of thing which could only be called obsessive. The things she said about my youth, specifically my relationship with my father, caused me pain and sadness, because she spoke the truth. She told me emphatically that my father was in the room with us and that he was beseeching me to believe how much he really loved me. I also received some very poignant advice from him on how to improve my relationship with Suzanne.

Freda described Suzanne as sensitive but masked. This was certainly true, and she went on to amplify this with a number of statements. Additional comments were made about the nature of our relationship, its problems, and what we needed to work on. Undoubtedly, the most significant utterances with respect to Suzanne that came to light were the ones that referred to the ambivalence and inner turmoil she had experienced with respect to Jennifer and me just before Jenny died. Freda stressed very strongly that Suzanne's doubts about being able to sustain responsibility in caring for Jenny stemmed from a deep inner pain that she felt about the likely unalterability of Jenny's medical condition and therefore the likelihood that she would not live a long time. At the same time, Freda implored me not to harbor blame toward Suzanne over this and the resultant conflicts we'd had. Rather, she said, I should work diligently toward improving our relationship, adding that this was what Jenny would have wanted. Freda's references to these personal and interpersonal conflicts were especially interesting, given that I had made no comments whatever about Suzanne's doubts or the ensuing problems.

An hour had passed. The reading came to an end, and after thanking Freda, I left the church, retrieved my little box, and headed home. During the drive back and later that evening, as well as in the coming days, I had time to reflect over everything that had taken place that afternoon. In many ways I was impressed. It could not be denied that, without any fishing on her part, Freda had given me a great deal of detailed and absolutely accurate information that could only have come from supernormal means. In some sense, she was, without question, authentic. Granted, she had also supplied a number of comments that were nonspecific in nature and which could have applied to almost any situation. However, at least in my mind, this could not detract from the rest of the reading.

But were her abilities mediumistic, psychic, or purely telepathic in nature, or some combination? Although the detailed information she relayed was accurate and true (or could be assumed to be true, for instance that my father really did love me very much), it could all have been picked up either psychically or telepathically from my own mind without the instrumentality of a third party such as a disembodied spirit. And, since everything Freda had told me had already been known to me, I felt even more strongly that purely psychic or telepathic abilities might be indicated and not necessarily mediumship.

If mediumship were involved, I should be able to acquire specific information about circumstances and events that were unknown to me and which were part of the world beyond, such as detailed facts about where Jenny's spirit went after her death, who she was with, and what she was doing and thinking. Even this kind of information could be received without mediumship. Some ordinary psychics were able to access such knowledge. I had, in fact, had contact in past years with individuals who were profoundly psychic, who did not claim any specifically mediumistic talents, and who had told me far more about the after-death states of various individuals than Freda had.

Given that I already knew everything Freda had told me, it seemed more likely that she was merely telepathic, rather than psychic or mediumistic. This did not detract from her obvious abilities; it only recategorized them in my mind and left the same bottom line, which was that I still had learned next to nothing about Jennifer's present state of existence.

However, in fairness to Freda, I clearly sensed another presence in the room with us. So the question remains unresolved. Nevertheless, the reading with Freda, who clearly possessed psychic gifts of some type, had been worthwhile, thought-provoking, and characterized by some very sensible and sound advice. And in addition to pondering what she had said and making a few notes, I relayed the content of the reading to Suzanne, especially the portion that had offered light on the confusion and turmoil which she had experienced in her struggle to come to terms with her feelings about Jenny.

After the reading, when I arrived home that evening an envelope was waiting for me that had been mailed from Joseph Greenwell, the undertaker in New Haven, Kentucky. Enclosed were two photographs of Jenny's grave at Gethsemani with her new headstone in place. I had received drawings for the marker during the first week in September, approved them, and mailed them back. Seeing the photo, with Jenny's name and the dates of her birth and death on the gray headstone, produced a jolt, another confirmation that she was really gone. Looking at the dates, June 24, 1988–August 9, 1991, brought home once again how brief Jenny's life had been, and that my time with her had been even shorter. I also thought about the incredible amount of living we had done together in just ten months.

On September 19, I received another letter from our children's social worker expressing his regret that the county would be able to pay Jenny's funeral expenses only up to the maximum specified in his previous letter. It further stated that, until I signed and returned the attached (again) affidavit, I could not be reimbursed for any of the expenses. In other words, unless I cooperated by signing an agreement to their terms, the county would not pay for any of the expenses, leaving me holding the bag for the full amount. In addition to the affidavit, a copy of a page from the Los Angeles County DPSS BHI Handbook (whatever that was) was attached, citing maximum reimbursement to foster parents for funeral expenses, in the event that they "may want a funeral for the child other than as provided by the county." (I shuddered to think what a county funeral and burial would be like!)

Although the tone of the letter was very polite, I was angered by it because I saw it as an attempt by the CSW to go back on his word by hiding behind rules and regulations that he was citing to me after the fact. However, primarily because I did not want to see Cabot and Sons get caught between me and the county, and not wanting to create a delay in payment to them, since they had worked so hard, I wrote a letter of response the same day, stating that I was signing the affidavit and returning it, and that the county could pay Cabot and Sons directly for their portion of the expenses. Then, however, proceeding in a somewhat legalistic but combative manner, I again raised the issues that I had voiced in my first letter (a copy of which I attached); namely, his verbal commitment to pay all expenses, and the amounts of money Suzanne and I had already spent. I accused him of going back on his word.

Then I went on to document that, after Jenny's death, a colleague of his had excused his error by saying that he (our CSW, that is) was "under a lot of pressure" on August 9 because he was getting ready to go on his vacation. Referring to that conversation in the letter, I wrote, "My comment (to the colleague) was that I, also, was under a lot of pressure that day. My home was full of policemen, paramedics, personnel from the coroner's office, doctors, and many other people, and my child was lying dead in her crib."

Then, addressing the CSW directly, I continued, "I suppose the implication is that, even under those conditions, I should have thought to sit down and study

Section 44-267.3, "For Reimbursement to Foster Parents or Direct Payment for Funeral Expenses" (which you have provided to me with your 9/18/91 letter), of the L.A. County DPSS BHI Handbook, which of course I do not have anyway. Do you feel that citing this policy makes it okay that you gave me erroneous advice?"

Pushing things even further, I cited the nightmare that Suzanne and I had to go through to get Jenny's body in time for the funeral, and that we had at times been treated with unbelievable callousness by the DCS office. I made reference to the woman who had described the whole affair as a PBS docudrama and who had lamented the fact that she had had to have lunch at her desk two days in a row in order to get the job done. In closing the letter, I described the DCS personnel as having "a demeanor that seems utterly devoid of compassion or basic human concern for our grief." I acknowledged that it was the primary responsibility of the DCS to look out for the needs of the child, as it should be. But I added that a show of some concern for our feelings would, under the circumstances, have been nice. I closed my letter by declining the CSW's offer for me to call him and discuss matters any further, and I did not correspond with him ever again.

Perhaps it seems petty to the reader that I went so far out of my way to declare war on the Los Angeles County Department of Children's Services, or especially petty that I would argue over a few hundred dollars of expenses when the burial of my daughter was concerned. In looking back at all of this many times later, I have also asked myself why I got so bent out of shape, and why I spent so much time and energy generating a lot of rhetoric and documentation that was most likely doomed to failure from the start. In response, I can only say, especially in retrospect, that the issue was never really money. I hope it is obvious that I would gladly pay whatever costs necessary to give my precious child a beautiful burial. I was just angry—angry at Jenny's death, and angry at the county because of the way they had treated Suzanne and me. Thus, when the CSW inadvertently backed himself into a corner, I used the opportunity to focus, for a short time, the energy of my grief and my chagrin at what I saw as the total lack of interpersonal skills in the Department of Children's Services on him. If he ever reads this book, I hope he will forgive me. After all, his job cannot be an easy one.

An Astrologer

Another week passed, and I was deeply gratified and relieved when the same day that my appointment was scheduled with Nicki the astrologer, I received a telephone call from Concept: Synergy notifying me that I had been granted an appointment for a reading with Lazaris on Saturday, October 12, 1991, from 9:15 to 9:30 A.M., Los Angeles time. The reading would be brief, but I had only one issue—Jenny.

That afternoon, around 5:00, I left home to arrive in Long Beach by 6:30, the time of my appointment with Nicki. I found her to be very pragmatic and down-to-earth, yet knowledgeable and sensitive with respect to the occult disciplines—a good combination. Originally from Kentucky, she now lived in Topack, Arizona, but spent a good deal of time in Los Angeles, giving readings to her clients there. She had previously been affiliated with the Universal Mind Science Church for fourteen years, where I had had my reading with Freda, who had stayed with Nicki over an eight-year period during her visits from England, and with whom Nicki had studied various esoteric arts.

Nicki's primary area of expertise was astrology, and she was well versed in related areas, including spiritual and past-life counseling and communication with the dead. It was obvious that she was well prepared for my reading with her and that she had done a great deal of research. She had many pages of handwritten notes, computer-generated astrological charts for Suzanne, Jennifer, and myself, and other supporting materials. In compliance with her instructions, I had brought a ninety-minute cassette tape. She said that she always insisted that her readings with her clients be recorded for their benefit, and she had an excellent recording device at hand.

A couple of weeks after my reading with Nicki, after I had had time to reflect upon and digest its contents, I put her tape and other materials away and did not refer to them again until September 1995, when I carefully went over everything again in order to relate here what took place during my session with her. I put most of those things away for several years because of the intensity of the emotions and memories they could arouse, and it was only when I began the work of writing the book that I found that I was finally ready to open myself again to all of those experiences and memories.

Thus, in September 1995, I sat down with Nicki's tape and listened to it carefully, making detailed notes. My visit with Nicki was almost two hours long, and we filled most of the ninety-minute tape with the main body of the reading. It covered many areas and jumped from one topic to another, often incorporating fairly sophisticated references to astrological principles and terms and the charts she had prepared.

Nicki began by explaining that she had examined many connections between Suzanne, Jennifer, and me. Almost immediately, she referred to Jennifer twice as "Tina" and corrected herself. With respect to Jenny's birth, Nicki pointed out the theory that the phenomenon of Siamese twins suggested a very strong karmic entanglement, possibly with strong hatred involved, and that Wendy, the twin that was born dead, possibly needed to have the birth experience, for whatever reason, and then end it. Again, Nicki referred to Jenny as Tina. Nicki also stressed that Jenny (again referred to as Tina) left this world of her own choice; that, although perhaps she could have stayed for a while longer, she elected to go.

Nicki said that the fact of Jennifer staying as long as she did in this life had to do with Suzanne and me. She felt that the strongest love tie was between Jenny and myself, and that we had shared deep love relationships in past lives, possibly even as husband and wife. Nicki also suggested the possibility that Suzanne, Jennifer, and Wendy, the dead Siamese twin, had been sisters in a previous incarnation; that there were indications to that effect, and that the relationship had been out of balance and needed to be fixed this time around. Nicki said that Suzanne's help was needed here, and that in many ways, she and Jenny were very much alike inside. Nicki suggested that, although she concealed it very well, Suzanne had a deep inferiority complex, and a long memory in terms of past hurts.

Nicki stressed how much I had needed Jenny's love, how I had needed the experience of being loved in the way that Jenny had cared so deeply for me. Jenny's and my sun conjunctions pointed to perhaps five or six previous lifetimes together. With respect to this, I related to Nicki how powerfully compelled I had felt from the very beginning to take Jenny as my own daughter, the indescribable importance and significance for me of caring for her, the anxiety I had experienced when Suzanne had expressed doubts about remaining involved, and finally, my ultimatum to Suzanne that I would raise Jenny alone, if necessary. I did not say these things with animosity; I only felt that Nicki should be given as full a picture as possible. And actually, she had already seen much of what I told her in the astrological charts.

Nicki emphasized what she called the strong "soul love" between Jenny and me. She also suggested that Suzanne's particular personality type, in contrast to mine, permitted her to abstract, to stand back more from the situation and possibly to lose patience.

When Nicki referred to Jennifer again as "Tina," she paused and said, "That's odd. Why do I keep doing that?" I asked Nicki if she knew anyone named Tina, and she said no.

Nicki talked about my with relationship with Jennifer in terms of the planets. The sun signified spirit and essence; the moon, emotional responses. In many ways, my sun ruled Jenny's moon. A Venus-sun connection showed particularly the strength of my love for Jenny; my sun on her Venus revealed that her love for me was just as strong, and that she had in all probability been my daughter before.

Jennifer's Neptune was close to Suzanne's love planet, signifying Suzanne's somewhat colder nature of feeling. Regarding this, Nicki said that one of Jenny's purposes in Suzanne's life was to give Suzanne the opportunity to transmute her physical love into universal spiritual love and compassion. In reality, all indications were that the whole picture had been set up for all three of us—Suzanne, Jenny, and me. Suzanne and Jenny might have experienced some problems in a former incarnation, and Suzanne might have been her biological mother before and some kind of separation had taken place.

According to all the astrological indications, my initial and powerful feelings that Jenny was meant for me and that she was to be mine to take care of occurred exactly when the cycle of energy was just right to trigger them.

Nicki expressed once again the depth of feeling between Jennifer and me. And with respect to this, she introduced the idea of the "Yod" (a term used in astrology, and, I assume, taken from the tenth letter of the Hebrew alphabet), which she referred to as the "finger of God," and which she said appeared unmistakably in the charts in connection with my relationship to Jenny, confirming the dynamic interaction of our souls. She underscored this phenomenon by saying that my Mars—the symbol of force and initiating energy—conjuncted with Jennifer's Jupiter in the aspect of her higher mind and depth as a soul. At this point, Nicki temporarily shifted gears; but she would return later in the reading to the deep significance of the Yod.

The indications in the charts were that Jenny had been some kind of spiritual counselor in previous incarnations. Also, Nicki saw suggestions that Suzanne had formerly been an American Indian. Regarding my relationship with Jenny, Nicki was inclined to believe that we had been together previously in the medieval period, when chivalry was a prominent aspect of the culture. For Jenny, Nicki definitely saw past incarnations in Eastern countries, Great Britain, Greece, possibly France, and certainly in Atlantis. She also confirmed something of which I was already absolutely convinced—that Jenny was a very old soul. With respect to my own past, previous incarnations in Eastern settings were very obvious.

Nicki tied my Taurus rising to my strong sense of commitment and loyalty. Suzanne's chart showed a temperament that could be characterized by up-and-down rides. Nicki also made it clear that I could benefit from working on forgiving various forms of resentments that I might hold, and that I should let go of such feelings.

Then a discussion followed about some basic astrological principles. Suzanne's chart showed seven different fixed aspects, indicating that she was not one to change easily. Again, Nicki brought up the possibility that, in previous lives, Suzanne had been Jenny's mother or that they had been sisters. This time around, Suzanne needed to be here to be a nurse for Jenny, to assist her in her medical condition; this aspect seemed much more dominant than the emotional level. Therefore, Suzanne's attitude that perhaps she could not sustain the connection with Jenny might be a manifestation of some deep, inner, perhaps unconscious sense that the situation was lasting longer than it should.

Nicki stated unequivocally that Jenny had no intention of staying long in this present incarnation, but that she did need to reconnect with both Suzanne and me to teach us something and to demonstrate to both of us that very special kind of love of which she was capable. She added that, in my case, Jenny probably touched and brought to life a part of me that I did not even know existed. In my mind, this was absolutely true. My relationship with Jenny had activated powerful, nurturing, parental traits which, before knowing Jenny, I probably would have denied even having.

With respect to this, I related to Nicki the unmistakable parallel in my life between Jenny and the extraordinary mystical experiences I'd had as a youth. The perceptions—I could really call them revelations—of my early years had revealed to me a cosmic, universal love that permeated all of existence and which was at the same time both personal and impersonal. But afterward, and for twenty-six years, I could never find anything in human relationships that could compare with that kind of love—until Jenny came into my life. Then, the cosmic became human. Without any doubt, and to my inexpressible joy, the love that had flowed between Jenny's heart and mine was fully and in every way of the quality, strength, and beauty that I had formerly known only in rarified and extremely infrequent states of perception. The chasm between my mystical and human experiences had finally been bridged.

My sharing of these experiences with Nicki brought her around again to the idea of the Yod, the finger of God. Citing that Mars, the eighth house in my chart and gateway to my higher mind, ruled my moon, Nicki affirmed that I needed to have a certain kind of experience, one which I really could not ascertain, but which (and she added that this would sound strange to me) would inevitably carry with it some hurt. The experience would call for certain adjustments on my part, and would, in one sense, be absolutely out of my hands. Thus, the Yod.

Again, Nicki stressed that, seen from one perspective, the experience of Jenny was totally out of my hands, that I could do nothing about it, and that I could have nothing to do with Jenny being brought into my life. I might convey this concept more clearly by saying that I was powerless to prevent the events which would take place (not that, of course, I would have wanted to, insofar as having Jenny come into my life); that they were fated to be. But I hasten to add that, in my mind, they were absolutely destined, not because Jenny and I were pawns of the designs of some higher power, but precisely because our own personal karmas, our own past lives together, and our powerful love for each other had caused it all to be. Those very same forces had ultimately been set into motion by our own souls, our own actions, and the extraordinary power of the love that connected us.

Nicki went on to emphasize the deep importance of responding to the Yod. I called to mind again and related to her the events of November 3, 1990, when I had stood at the kitchen stove and felt the hand of fate, and also my response of terrible concern, months later, over Suzanne's doubts, because of the certainty in my own soul that to upset or interfere with our care of Jenny would, as far as I was concerned, bring about a tragedy of cosmic proportions and generate horrible karmic repercussions. (If this sounds melodramatic to anyone, I cannot help it and do not apologize for it. That is exactly how I felt, to the depths of my being.)

Nicki expressed how the Yod had a powerful regenerative effect on my emotional life. I told her how I was afraid that I might revert to the way I had been before Jenny had come into my life. Nicki told me that this would never happen; not to worry; that I could never go back. She said that once a certain spiritual height is achieved, although you may fall to a degree here and there, you never revert to your former state. Nicki said that such spiritual experiences were blessings to let us know what it feels like "up there." She was absolutely right. My own life attested that, once one gets even a glimpse of the glorious existence that is possible, one is never the same and can never settle for less; and somehow, one finds the impetus to pursue, for lifetimes if necessary, the path that leads back to such a state of being.

I then mentioned to Nicki that, during my session with Freda Fell the previous week, she had described my relationship with Jenny as "soul-searing." I felt then, as I do today, that one could not have coined a better term to characterize the attraction between our spirits.

Again, Nicki pointed out my loving, nurturing side. She asked me what kind of a relationship I had had with my parents when I was a child, and I responded by telling her briefly how it had lacked almost any physical intimacy. Nicki suggested that the opportunity that I had been given to care for Jennifer had been very therapeutic in this respect, and I agreed wholeheartedly. Certainly, in tending to Jenny's medical problems and needs as a child, I had also ministered to the emotionally deprived child in myself. It rang very true when Nicki commented that, in my own heart and soul, I had been both a daddy and mommy to Jenny. This was not to suggest in any way that Suzanne had not performed her role well as a mother—only that my own newly aroused parental instincts had been so strong as to encompass the whole mother-father range of feeling.

The discussion then focused on Suzanne. Explaining that Suzanne had a strong chart, but in some ways a difficult chart, Nicki went on to say that the entire year had been very tiring for Suzanne, that she was emotionally worn out, and that, in addition to the rocky present, the next few months would be difficult and stressful. Nicki felt that someone close to Suzanne could die around the end of the year. Suzanne's mother, Helen, had been quite ill in August, but she was doing better. She did live for quite some time after that in reasonably good health, despite her unfortunate mental deterioration, which had been occurring for some years. Nicki correctly identified the issue of Suzanne's circulation, because she had a lot of difficulty keeping warm in cold weather. (Suzanne and I had always had an ongoing struggle during the colder months, given that, even with the heat off, I was completely comfortable, and that, with the house at a cozy temperature for her, I felt like I was suffocating.)

I had offered little information about Suzanne to Nicki, but her ongoing comments and insights were remarkably accurate. Nicki further pointed out that it would be of benefit to Suzanne to learn how to transfer the use of her power (power had, in many ways, always been an issue in our marriage); and, that she had a tendency (as many of us do) to judge falsely and too quickly, the result sometimes being a perception of someone that was way off. Nicki referred to Suzanne's tendency not to show depression, in contradistinction to my own behavior patterns, and said again that, at that time, Jenny's death and her mother's recent illness had taken a very heavy emotional toll. Finally, Nicki felt that Suzanne had, in past incarnations, worked in some kind of a counseling role and was fairly certain that Suzanne and Jenny had known each other before. I also felt that this was quite likely. (Interestingly, no one in the psychic field has ever mentioned to me something of which I myself am very certain, namely, that Suzanne had most likely spent previous lives in France as both a member of the aristocracy and as a religious renunciant of some kind, possibly in the same lifetime.)

Nicki mentioned soul groups—the concept that various souls tend to incarnate with each other lifetime after lifetime. (I have come to believe this deeply.) Although this part of the conversation was not clear, Nicki said that much could be learned about a particular incarnation by looking at an individual's chart and studying the eclipse which had occurred six months prior to birth, which, in Jenny's case, was Piscean. Nicki concluded that Suzanne was in a position to learn a great deal from Jenny, especially given that Suzanne's chart showed such strong nursing inclinations. Nicki commented about what a surprise Jenny had been to me, and that it was because Suzanne was a nurse—a key factor—that I had come to know about Jenny's existence. (I have wondered if Jenny would have found her way to me by another means if the situation had been different. I can only defer to the wisdom of the soul and accept that Jenny did find me.) Nicki emphasized that my soul relationship with Jenny went at least as far back as Atlantis. Again, there were strong indications of Eastern incarnations, religious orders, and various schools of self-development.

She also made reference to Edgar Cayce, the famous "sleeping prophet," and his idea that stillbirths (Wendy, the Siamese twin) often indicated that a soul just needed the experience of death and the transition from one world to the other; and that such a circumstance was certainly the result of a decision made by the soul in question to have such an experience.

Nicki affirmed that, as long as I lived, the love of Jennifer's spirit would flow to me. Regarding this and other comments of a positive, reassuring nature Nicki had made, I stressed that although I regarded her as honest and not the kind of person who would say things just because I might want to hear them, I did not want to feel better about anything at the cost of being misled. I wanted to know the truth. Then I mentioned my practice of yoga in Jenny's room, and that I had vowed to continue the meditations through the end of the year, at which time I would reassess whether or not I wanted to continue. Finally, I asked Nicki, "Does she remember me? Does she remember and feel my love? Does she know how deeply I miss her? Is there still a relationship (from her side)?"

Nicki promised that she would never tell me lies, and said that she expressed what she saw, neither more nor less. First, she stressed that, in the Divine Mind, there was no separation; it did not exist. Second, she said that love was the strongest tie in the universe, and that, any time I thought of Jennifer, there would be love. The love between us would endure always. She added that I did not have to make promises or do disciplines for Jennifer; that that was something I should do for myself.

Nicki said that, although I would never love Jenny any less, the intensity would change in time, and I would feel a letting go. Some of this made me feel uncomfortable. More than four years after her death, the intensity of my feelings for Jenny has not diminished. Yet I do not think I am clinging to Jenny or holding her back. Nicki stated that this letting go would have to be so, adding that, as long as I thought of Jenny and loved her, she was no further away than my thought.

Explaining to me that her first introduction into metaphysics had been in the realm of spirit communication, Nicki knew for certain that we live on and that we cannot die. God was love and life, and we were all a part of God. After death we would awaken to realize that we were part of the Divine Mind.

Nicki momentarily returned to the lack of intimacy and demonstrated love in my childhood, that in the past I had often felt I did not deserve love, and that, even after Jenny's passing, I was still undergoing a great regeneration process.

Referring to the entire situation with Jenny, her care, and to the idea of the Yod, Nicki said unequivocally, "You did this thing correctly!"

Then Nicki turned to alignment of the planets the day Jenny died. She said that for all intents and purposes, Jennifer was my child and that she was mine to keep while she was here. I had felt this deeply in my soul almost from the very beginning. Nicki asserted that she could show me, astrologically, why Jenny's heart simply stopped on August 9, and that nothing I could have done would have made any difference. Jenny had elected to go at that time. I mentioned the episode in the car on the Thursday afternoon before Jenny's death, when I was bringing her home from day care and had such a difficult time awakening her. Nicki said that Jenny was trying to go then, that she was ready to go when Mercury went retrograde on August 8.

Next, Nicki addressed the issue of the positions of the planets at "Jennifer's first breath." According to her, at birth, Jenny's energy was "scattered all over the chart." Nicki took some time to explain that this was not typical of everyone's chart, and, as an example, showed me how, at my birth, the planets had been grouped together in certain coherent patterns.

Nicki then directed the conversation to me. Her strong feeling was that my present lifetime was one of fruition and stabilization, one in which I should, and would make things count, as opposed to a recent past lifetime in which I had not followed through to finish things I had begun. (I usually finish what I start.) Then Nicki returned again to my childhood, saying that I had blocked out past hurts and the lack of love I had experienced. She suggested that vast periods of my childhood were probably blocked from my memory, which was true. In the past, I had reflected that periods spanning years of my childhood were nothing but voids in my memory! I was often surprised at what other people could remember of their times as children. (I have often wondered—although I have never asked—exactly what my mother meant when she told me one time, after I had become an adult, that, when I cried so much as a baby, probably due to an inappropriate nutritional formula, "had there been a lake in our back yard, I would have jumped in with you in my arms and drowned us both.")

Nicki talked about how I had loved to take care of Jenny as a way of physically demonstrating my love for her. And she talked about the importance of my starting to forgive my mother and father for any perceived hurts to me (which I have done more and more, especially since Jenny came into my life). Nicki pointed out that I was now tied to an Aquarius (Suzanne), and that people born under this sign were not particularly good at demonstrating their love. I explained the dynamics of our marriage to Nicki in a little more detail, and commented that it was not so much that Suzanne was unwilling, but rather that I felt she did not take any initiative. I, in turn, had grown hesitant about making the overtures because I was afraid of rejection.

When Nicki continued on the theme of how Jenny had shown me her love, I asked her, "What in God's name will I do now?" I could not envision how I could survive in the days to come without Jenny's love and nearness, and without taking care of her. Nicki and I talked about the grieving process, and she asked me if I were involved in any kind of therapy or grief support. I told her that Suzanne and I were seeing Dr. Wortz, who was excellent, and that at that time we had already been to one of the meetings of the Compassionate Friends. I added that Suzanne and I felt uncertain about the grief support meetings, and that, even though the loss of Jenny had been terrible, it appeared that our tragedy was less traumatic than that of parents who had lost children through murder or suicide. I also voiced some of the insights I had gained during my reading with Freda Fell.

Nicki encouraged me to stick with the grief support for a while before I made up my mind (which I did, and about which I am very glad), and gently urged me not to rush the grieving process. Then she told me Jenny was in the room with us, trying to send me her love. Nicki mentioned the tiny pink light that she had detected in the room, appearing now and then, subtly, floating in the air, and then disappearing again after a second or so—the same little light I had seen, unmistakably, in Jenny's room a few days after her death, and that I had continued to see from time to time in various parts of the house (which still appears to me today).

I talked about how brilliant Jenny was, how remarkably perceptive and intelligent. Nicki commented about her refined spirit, and added that Jenny had needed her brief, three-year trip into this plane; that knowing exactly what the problem had been was unimportant. It was important only to know the she had most definitely "completed the job."

Nicki then returned to the subject of the astrological conditions surrounding Jenny's birth. Jenny had five mutable planets in a T-square, something that "restricts ability to work." I reminded Nicki of the extent and gravity of Jenny's medical problems, and the difficulties at birth. The T-square had created a chain reaction resulting in five simultaneous problems which, in spite of Jenny's strong soul, manifested in the form of great physical difficulties. She commented that a teacher with whom she had formerly studied astrology had once said, "The horoscope is the contract that the soul signs in order to come into a body and have an experience."

Regarding the five mutable planets in question (Venus, Mercury, Mars, Pluto, and Neptune), Nicki stated that a spiritual principle was attached to each one of them. Venus symbolized love, compassion, forgiveness, and a harmonious relationship; Mercury was associated with humility and attitude; Mars represented motive, or motivation; Pluto was tied with self-knowledge and development, right insight in one's inner self, and power; and, Neptune signified sacrifice. Four out of these five mutable planets in Jenny's birth chart—Venus, Mercury, Pluto, and Neptune—were in retrograde, a condition which, according to Nicki, signified that some things had been mishandled spiritually, and that a "refresher course" was needed.

Regarding Pluto (self-knowledge and development, right insight in one's inner self, and power), Nicki wondered aloud if perhaps Jennifer had, in another life, somehow used power in a wrong way with a sibling. With respect to Neptune (symbolizing sacrifice, but in retrograde, and opposing the sun—very bad), Nicki speculated about the possibility that Jennifer had not been good to her children in a past incarnation. Nicki sensed that Jennifer had been here in another life pretty recently, and that one possible theory would be the misuse of alcohol or drugs. Might she perhaps even have been responsible for a death? Of course, I thought right away of Jenny's mother, Rosa, whose life had been seriously damaged through the use of drugs. Whatever the truth, Nicki felt that Jenny needed, in this short lifetime, to "retouch all of those bases during the little while that she was here."

Nicki was adamant in her assertion that I would have felt my intense love for Jennifer whether she had been one, two, or thirty years of age. Referring to the trines (a trine, astrologically speaking, referring to a favorable positioning of two planets, or the astrological aspect of two planets when 120 degrees apart) between planets in Jenny's and my charts, Nicki called them a "blessing," a "gift from God," an energy flow, which was "mine to keep." Commenting that Uranus was the strongest possible attraction a person could have, she pointed out that Jennifer's moon at twenty-nine degrees Libra was in exact trine to my Uranus at twenty-nine degrees Gemini. Thus, again, I would have loved Jenny even if she were fifty years old. It was deeply important that our two souls meet in this lifetime, and through the workings of the Yod, she had been powerfully instrumental in breaking up the attraction to certain conditions that I was holding in my life, so that I could change my emotional state for the better.

I commented that Jennifer was a "loving, light-radiating being." Nicki responded by saying that this was so because Jennifer had "brought her spirit with her;" that it was there all the time; and that all who looked at her saw Christ, saw love, saw understanding. She commented that charismatic spirits transmitted love, and that, often, those around them "fell in love with pure love." Jenny had radiated the Christ love and facilitated my awareness of that kind of love. She transformed me, helped me to overcome my emotional lethargy, and therefore to return to my yogic disciplines. I admitted that over the years I had sloughed off in terms of any kind of methodical practice of meditation. To overcome that, I had vowed to do kriya yoga at least until the end of the year, and then reexamine things.

Nicki and I talked a little more about Universal Mind Science Church, in which she had been deeply involved over a period of fourteen years, and then we turned to other topics. I wondered about ever having another child through foster parenting or adoption. Suzanne had had a hysterectomy several years earlier, so a biological child of our own was out of the question. Nicki reminded me of something that I already knew, but which was very important; namely, that I could never duplicate the experience with Jenny. She had been a great blessing and utterly unique. She was a one-of-a-kind, mountaintop experience.

Nicki commented on my good spiritual energy, and that it was important for me to meditate. Jenny had opened a spiritual door and there was no going back.

I then asked Nicki about contact with Jenny in future lifetimes, or on some other level of existence when this life was over. Nicki responded by saying that love binds, and therefore that there would be contact. Souls would meet again, especially if there were any unfinished business between them. I wondered about future contact with Jenny even if there were no specific karmic ties. Nicki said there would still be spiritual contact. This seemed right to me, given that I would continue to love Jenny always and send my energy and thoughts to her.

Nicki said that when I "first went to spirit" (right after death), the ones that I loved most would meet me. Nicki believed that, after that, various souls gravitated to the planes most suited to their individual natures.

Nicki asked me unexpectedly if I did any writing. I commented that I had published a scholarly book in 1978 through Indiana University Press, and that in 1982 I had completed a large metaphysical manuscript, based entirely on personal experiences, which was still unpublished at that time. (It was subsequently published by Galde Press, Inc., in 1996.)

"The reason I asked," Nicki said, "is that I just heard Jenny's voice in my head, saying, 'If you write, Daddy, I'll help you.'" Nicki commented that perhaps Jenny would inspire me to write, but my only response at the time was that I could not force it. The idea of doing any more writing was an unpleasant thought at that time. Nicki said that the desire to write would "catch me unaware, when I least expected it." As it turned out, Nicki's words were prophetic!

In a very gentle way, Nicki said again that, in time, I would be able to let go of Jenny enough, at least, not to hold her back. She added that, at that time, Jenny could come and go, and that there was nothing wrong whatever with my reaching out to her, as long as I did not bind her down. Nicki suggested, correctly, that I did not let go of relationships easily, and that it was possible to let go and get back even better. I expressed what was one of my deepest fears at that time: that I did not want to be empty the rest of my life. Nicki assured me that I would not be, and that now I had become aware of my nurturing abilities.

On a whim, I had bought a book on palmistry a few weeks before Jenny's death. I had two very dominant lines, one on each hand, that were entirely absent on any other hands that I had ever seen during my life, except those of a music professor whom I had known well during my college years. I asked Nicki if she knew anything about the subject, but we got sidetracked and never returned to it.

Nicki said that my chart clearly showed mystical abilities, and that these might manifest themselves in the areas of meditation and dreams. This certainly was true. In some ways, these tendencies were to become more pronounced in the future, especially with dreams.

The reading ended, and I thanked Nicki warmly. She gave me the charts she had prepared. The time I had spent with her would provide much food for thought. Over the next couple of days, I shared some of the information with Suzanne. Now, four years later, I appreciate more than ever the scope and quality of the information I got from Nicki.

I began to focus on October 12, the day of my telephone reading with Jach Pursel. In the meantime, other events occurred that would have deep and lasting significance in my life.

Treasures

After Jenny's death, certain things that spoke strongly of her, which I had taken for granted while she was alive, became treasures in my eyes. I am speaking chiefly about artwork she had done at Huntington and later at All Saints Children's Center. A lot of it had been taped up on doors at home or in my office at work. As time went on, I had several of these pieces professionally mounted and framed and hung them in my home. These paintings were quite beautiful—full of life, motion, and color: the very delicate and subtle "Foam Painting" from Huntington (age two years, one month, before I had known her), hanging in my bedroom, and the only piece I have from her Huntington days; the exuberant "Brush Painting" from All Saints (age two years, eleven months); and, the "Car Painting" (age three years), and her untitled painting (three years, one month), also from All Saints, framed together and hanging under the "Brush Painting," which looks remarkably like a stand of brilliantly colored flowers (Jenny's "fowers"). The "Car Painting" strongly reminds me of the blur effect created when a car is photographed while moving at high speed.

I had not thrown out any of Jenny's paintings from All Saints, and the ones that were not framed and hung in the months after her death were stored, carefully and chronologically, in a large folio. There is a series of pencil and crayon drawings that was done at home over the summer—mostly just scribbles, but nevertheless precious to me, and one of which is a crude crayon tracing I made of Jenny's hand with a ring drawn on one finger. I have always remembered how she looked up and smiled at me after I drew it. Also, inside a large cookie tin that Jenny used to play with are a few pages from a little notepad upon which she had scribbled in pencil. One day a few weeks after Jenny died, I was rummaging through some paperwork of my own and happened to come upon them accidentally, having completely forgotten about them. I was stunned to see them again so unexpectedly. They were nothing more than a few scribbles, but to me they were deeply meaningful—a powerful reminder that Jenny had really lived in the world and become my daughter. I put them in her cookie tin to keep forever.

I realized that so much artwork Jenny had done at Huntington had been thrown away, but it was a loss that could not be undone. I also thought back to all the things I had made for Jenny that I had not kept, like the reams of computer-generated love notes and printouts of her name in various fonts that I had done at work and taken to the hospital to give to her while she was still living there. Thank God I kept the things I did!

My photographs of Jenny were precious. I had been bad about saving negatives, but fortunately, Dora Anne Mills, a pediatrician from Huntington who had taken some wonderful pictures at our house on the occasion of Jenny's third birthday party, not only gave us prints a few days later, but the negatives as well. Thus, thanks to her great thoughtfulness, I was able to have many quality reprints of various sizes made, several of which are hanging on my walls. I had hung some of Jenny's photos and a painting at work after her death, but later I felt that I wanted everything connected with Jenny to stay in the privacy of my own home, so I took the photos home and hung them there, along with the painting. The few other photographs of Jenny that were hung at home had to be reproduced from the larger collection of prints in her photo album, a process that yielded adequate but not spectacular results.

When I opened my mail on October 4, 1991, I experienced an emotional jolt. The State of California Department of Social Services had sent our license to operate and maintain a foster family home. It was dated October 3 and covered the period of July 9, 1991, through July 8, 1992. I felt great sadness, realizing the irony of receiving something for which I had worked so hard only after it had become irrelevant. Jenny had been dead for almost two months.

My Return and Lifelong Commitment to Meditation

On October 6, something extraordinary happened. To explain what took place, I must backtrack three and a half weeks to about a month after Jenny's death, on September 11, 1991 (the day before Suzanne and I went to our first meeting at the Compassionate Friends), the day on which I resumed the practice of kriya yoga. I had first learned these powerful meditation techniques soon after entering college through Swami Nirmalananda Giri, a member of the Giri order of monks in India. He was to play an important role in my life for some time after that, and although I eventually lost touch with him, I practiced the techniques from then on, although sporadically and with long interruptions sometimes lasting years. In spite of my spotty practice, I had great faith in the power of these techniques, and returned to them often, especially in times of great distress. I eventually became connected with the Self-Realization Fellowship, whose U.S. headquarters were in Los Angeles, and through whom I formally applied for the yoga teachings I had formerly learned.

Although I practiced some kriya yoga in 1990 (halting a few weeks after starting individual therapy with Edward Wortz), and again between late January and the end of June 1991, I have almost no recollection of this. During the latter period, any practice that I would have done must have been sparse indeed, given the fact that Jenny came home in February, and that I was incredibly busy during those months. My records show that, in July, I had even looked briefly into palmistry and the tarot, although I cannot imagine why. The only reason I actually recollect this is because I remember looking at Jennifer's palms once or twice.

After Jenny's death, I had to find something to hold on to. Jenny's room had remained unaltered. I had created a place to meditate in her room by placing some folded blankets and my meditation cushion up against the sofa bed that faced her crib. Enhancing my ritual with candles and incense, I began meditating in her room.

I decided that, since Jenny and I were separated by her death, and given my total unwillingness to accept this barrier between us, along with the feeling that she could not come to me, I would somehow have to empower myself to come closer to her. I would have to dedicate myself to the task of evolving spiritually and psychically, of raising myself to her level, so to speak, so that in some way she and I would remain connected. I could not accept the idea that her death was the end of our relationship. These are the feelings with which I began yoga meditation again.

At first, I meditated as I felt the need, with fair regularity. But early on I vowed that I would continue doing daily practice until the end of the year, when I would look at things again and decide whether or not to continue the meditations. It was during that first couple of weeks of meditation that I had my readings with Freda Fell and Nicki Mellette. On October 6, about three and a half weeks after I had resumed meditating, an extraordinary thing happened that would change my life. In the evening, I was seated on the floor in Jenny's room on my blanket, cross-legged and facing her crib, meditating. It was fairly dark, but the room was softly illumined by burning candles and the fragrance of incense filled the air. Suddenly, I had the overwhelming feeling of Jenny's presence. I could feel her spirit there with me. In my mind, I felt her urging me to make a commitment, a vow, to practice kriya yoga meditation every day for the rest of my life!

I was overcome with excitement by her nearness, as if she were inside of my mind, and I lost all awareness of the outer world. I felt unable to react to this sudden prompting, and after struggling to get my bearings, I could only respond by speaking to her within my heart and saying, "That is an awesome commitment. I am not ready to make it. But I will certainly keep my promise to do the practice every day until the end of December, and then see how I feel." Instead of going away, her urging became more intense. I could not avoid what seemed to be almost a plea from her—her spirit implored me in an almost imperative way to accede. For a few moments I sat in silence, engulfed in Jenny's presence and realizing unmistakably the force of her desire. And then I knew, clearly and deeply, that it was my path, my destiny, to say yes to her. And so that evening, in that moment, deep in meditation and in Jenny's presence, I vowed to her that I would practice kriya yoga meditation every day for the rest of my life.

Shortly afterward, I sought some meditation beads. The beads I had used for twenty-three years, a gift from my teacher from India, had been buried with Jenny. Some of the techniques I practiced involved a large number of repetitions that I could only count by using beads. I spent a lot of time in the jewelry district of downtown Los Angeles, a few blocks from the office where I worked, and although a lot of possibilities caught my attention, I was unsatisfied by anything that I had seen.

I felt that I could find anything I needed in the huge jewelry district if I looked long enough, but I was growing weary after several unsuccessful excursions. Finally, one hot afternoon when I had taken time from work to look again, as I stood in the burning sun on a street corner, wondering where to go next, I suddenly felt Jennifer's presence. It was very strong, much like it had been when she came to me during meditation, and I felt guided to cross the street and enter a vast building, formerly a theater, whose cavernous interior had been converted into many dozens of stalls and booths where all kinds of jewelry were displayed. Without hesitation, I navigated my way past many counters, along passageways, down stairs, turning in this direction and that, until I found myself in a far corner of the building, almost hidden away, where I discovered a counter belonging to an Asian woman. There before me was every kind of beautiful bead imaginable—strings and strings of them. My search was over. I was certain Jennifer had led me there. I was deeply attracted to the lapis lazuli beads, since this gemstone had always been my favorite, with its deep blue, spiritual color. I purchased the beads I needed and returned later to pick them up after they had been strung. That evening at home, I added knotted pieces of thread at the desired intervals. I have used these beads in my yoga meditations ever since, and I prize them highly because of their beauty and spiritual significance, but especially because I was led to them by Jenny.

I decided to involve Jenny, in a very special way, every day, in a portion of my yoga disciplines. During daily meditation, when it came time to perform a number of cycles of advanced pranayama exercises (breathing techniques designed specifically for the development of conscious control and manipulation of energy currents in the body, and leading to certain desired psychic states and the acceleration of one's spiritual evolution), I did a portion of them while holding Jenny in my consciousness in such a way that, hopefully, she would also derive spiritual benefit.

It became a permanent part of my routine, and I have always performed it in the faith that in some way I was helping Jenny spiritually, or at least sending her a daily stream of loving energy.

$\mathcal{A}$ Birth and a Channeler

On October 8, 1991, Rosa Pivaral, Jennifer's mother, gave birth to Jessica Christina Pivaral, Jennifer's half sister. I did not learn of this until Saturday afternoon, October 12, after having my telephone reading with Lazaris that morning (making it a very significant day, indeed). Nancy Pivaral, one of Rosa's younger sisters, telephoned me from Malibu to give me the news and commented that Rosa was in jail in Fresno, and that the family in Malibu (that is, herself, her sister, Maria, and Graciela, their mother) would take care of the baby. It was only later that I learned the exact date of Jessica's birth. When Nancy called me, two odd coincidences came to mind. Only a couple of weeks earlier, Nicki Mellette had referred to Jennifer repeatedly as "Tina." Had Nicki psychically sensed the approach of the birth of Jenny's sister, Jessica Christina (Tina?). The coincidence was unsettling. Lazaris also mentioned that Jenny's spirit would be instrumental in guiding four other children into my life at some point. I wondered if Jessica would be one of these.

Jennifer and Jessica had different fathers, and I know almost nothing about Jessica's father except that, at the time of her birth, he, too, like Rosa, was in prison somewhere. I do not even know his name, nor, I believe, does anyone else in Jessica's family, except Rosa. No one ever heard from him again after Jessica was born. With regard to little Jessica, I was deeply intrigued by her appearance in the world, but completely at sea as to how, if at all, she would fit into my life or play a role in it.

Meanwhile, that morning was filled for me with a deep and powerful sense of anticipation. I arose early, and at precisely 9:15 A.M. I dialed the number I had been given by Concept: Synergy to contact Lazaris.* Concept: Synergy made a tape of the reading and sent it to me a few days later. Because the entire reading was only fifteen minutes, and because it was so densely packed with information (which is typical of Lazaris's readings, regardless of the length), I have reproduced it here, word-for-word.

On September 13 and 14, 1995, I painstakingly transcribed the Lazaris tape, having not listened to it since a few months after Jennifer's death. This was not an easy task, given that Lazaris's speech was (typically) extremely rapid, characterized by some kind of accent like an Irish brogue, often run together without punctuation, and with barely a breath, and filled with odd little phrases and unusual mannerisms of speech. It required seven hours to copy it, and I had to listen to many parts of it again and again to get all of it.

---

*Lazaris is a nonphysical entity who has been channeling through Jach Pursel since October 1974. Lazaris holds seminars frequently in major American cities, and has released more than two hundred audio and video tapes and books on a vast variety of metaphysical and spiritual issues. Concept: Synergy, which publishes The Lazaris Material, can send you more information. They can be reached at 1-800-678-2356, or by writing PO Box 3285, Palm Beach, FL 33480.

In addition to wanting to offer all of the information contained in the tape, I felt that to paraphrase or summarize Lazaris's words could not fail to detract from the charm, rhythm, and special quality that characterizes his readings. Hopefully, also, by reproducing the reading verbatim, the "ring of truth" that is clearly perceptible when one listens to his tapes will show through. Thus, my only addition to this material has been to insert punctuation and paragraphs as best I could and where I felt it was appropriate. I present below the reading in its entirety.

LAZARIS: Well, we know there's a number of issues you want to discuss and talk about, so just to begin, Gerald, if you would, just give us your name, your age, and where you're calling from today.

GERALD: Gerald Lishka. I'm forty-one, and I'm calling from Los Angeles, California.

LAZARIS: All right. And of course, the reason we ask your name, to tap into the vibration, though we're aware of the vibration; your age, to separate into the past, the present, and future; and also Los Angeles, its own vibration. We want to separate that which is Gerald, so that we can respond to your particular issues and concerns more directly. And with that, since you're talking, unfortunately, so briefly, let's go right to the issues you'd like to discuss.

GERALD: I really only have one matter, and that's Jennifer Pivaral. She was my foster daughter, and I found her dead in her bed on August 9th. I loved her more than anything on this earth. I miss her terribly, and I'm very desirous of knowing about any past life relationships we had; why she came to me; why she had the severe medical condition that she did; if she remembers me and loves me; and, if I will ever know her or meet her again, in another life, or after this life. Really, anything you can tell me about Jenny.

LAZARIS: All right. And what was her age?

GERALD: She died at just a little over three years.

LAZARIS: Three years. And what did she technically die of?

GERALD: Causes unknown. She had severe medical problems. She didn't eat. She was born a Siamese twin. The twin was born dead. She lived in a hospital for two and a half years with a Broviac catheter. We fed her at night through pumps. She had a digestive disorder. She did not eat, and she had a little colostomy bag and a tube that drained the bile out of her stomach. But she went to day care. She lived a pretty normal life. We don't actually know the cause of death.

LAZARIS: All right. And you were her foster parents?

GERALD: Yes.

LAZARIS: Were you looking to adopt her?

GERALD: Yes.

LAZARIS: And was that part of the plan, in terms of would they have allowed you to do so?

GERALD: Yes.

LAZARIS: All right. All right, and let's look at that in terms of Jennifer and her situation. All right. All right, first of all, yes. First of all, she's doing absolutely splendidly. And as we sense her, she's still a child, in that sensing, and she is—because that's the last body she knew, even though she had it for such a very little time, in that regard. We would suggest here that—oh yes, all right. We would suggest here that, yes, there's a consciousness being born about three years ago, in that sensing, just under that. We would suggest here that, in that regard, she definitely was working off a massive, major bit of karma, with her, what was her Siamese twin, in that sensing. A tremendous amount of karma there, just released in a huge bundle. But, in that sensing, almost overwhelming. Too big, in that sensing. She could not recuperate. She could not, in a sensing, get her gyroscopic balance back again. And therefore, rather wobbled, as it might well be, as you know and can relate to in terms of that sense of wobbling, even in her health concerns, in that regard, like a top wobbling on itself, back and forth, and just could not right herself, just could not get her feet under her, so to speak. And therefore, in that sensing, chose to exit. But even so, has maintained, at least at this point, the child's body, even though she could perhaps return to the previous reincarnational experiences, now that she's still in that.

She's moving, she's laughing, she's playing a lot. She has a favorite color, yellow, so important to her. She just loves yellow, anything yellow, etc. She plays a lot. She's walking, she's running, in that particular sensing. She laughs a lot. Her hands are up in the air. All the time, hands up in the air. Just this delightful sort of energy, having a delightful time. Absolutely so. So she is fine.

And indeed, the death was the right thing for her. She just knew she could not right herself. She just couldn't get her feet under her, and she just couldn't allow herself to go through life, in that sensing, in that much need, in that much dependency, in that sensing. And she intended to work off the karma, perhaps taking on too much. But at least, now, its done. It's over with. She's not going to have to deal with that again. But we would suggest here that she's doing absolutely fine, is totally happy, is playing a lot, as we say, in that sensing, laughing a lot.

Let's look at it in the deeper level.

GERALD: Does she remember me?

LAZARIS: Does she remember you? Absolutely, she does. She's very aware of you, in that particular sensing. And although she's not going to show up again in this lifetime, per se, in that particular sensing, she's going to be there. She's going to influence you. You see, she is a very interesting spirit, in that particular sensing. A very wise spirit. A very old spirit, in that sensing. And therefore, on a very accelerated journey at this particular point.

GERALD: Yes.

LAZARIS: And we would suggest here that she's going to work, in a sense, as a counselor, as a guide for you. And we would suggest here that she's not ready to yet, in that particular sensing. In other words, she's still having, quote, too much fun exploring the mobility, in that particular sensing, and the freedom, in that particular sensing. But in a time period—and this is being October—August, September, October—it's only been two months—we would suggest here that in a time period that is less than a year from her death, and therefore we would almost suggest that we want to tell you it is June, July—June, July of 1992—not that she'll get serious, etc.—but she will at that time start taking on certain responsibilities, in that sensing, in her relationship with you. Yes, she misses you, in that sensing, but in a positive sense of that, because she knows she's going to be working with you, in that sensing. And she will work in a guidance way. What she's going to do is a number of things.

First of all, she's going to give you a lot of magical ability, in that sensing, the magical part of her, the magical child that she was, the magic that she even could work even in her limited stay itself, very much there. And we would suggest here that she's going to be of an influence that will be sort of a hint of magic that comes into your life, and when you need something to occur, etc., she'll be the one sort of, quote, behind it. She'll be there.

Also, she'll bring a certain wonder—a certain wonder, a certain naiveté, a certain innocent, childlike quality, understandably so. But she's going to bring that back to you, in that sensing. She's going to bring back to you a lightness, in that particular sensing, as you used to, once upon a time, in your past, be able to take things fairly lightly. Not just since Jennifer's death, no, but even before that, you, Gerald, have gotten pretty heavy, in that sensing, pretty difficult to take yourself and life lightly. She's going to return that—the gift of laughter, the gift of joy to you.

And we would suggest here she's going to, quote, look out for you, in that sensing. She's going to be, sort of—things that could have gone wrong, but don't, in that sensing. So she's going to take on that roll.

And you will sense her. And in that sensing, she'll show up in dreams, she'll show up in meditations, she'll start popping in, in that sensing.

She will also bring people to you, in that sensing, in terms of there seems to be other children that are coming into the vibration. Most definitely so. At least four more. Now, not all at once, please. But, in that sensing, four children that seem very evident around the both of your vibrations, very clearly, that are somehow—and she's going to be involved in the picking and choosing of which ones actually come into your life, and for what purposes, etc., as you are somewhat of a revolving door, a catalyst, yourselves, in that sensing, for helping people. Sometimes getting them on their feet again, sometimes helping them move beyond, and let go, in that sensing, which is what you helped Jennifer do. But she's going to be there, guiding a lot of that, in that work.

You have known each other many times before. We would suggest here that she has been your daughter, she has been your daughter three times. And we would suggest here two of those were very positive, in that particular sensing. One of them wasn't. One was where, indeed, due to circumstances of miscommunication and misjudgment, you were separated from each other, in that particular sensing, and unfortunately never connected again. But, nonetheless, the other two were very positive father-daughter connections, absolutely.

There was a time also—that's three lifetimes—there was also two lifetimes where, indeed, you were students together, in that particular sensing, both male students, in that sensing, because at that time women weren't allowed to go to school. But in that, went at university—at university, studying art and literature, in that particular sensing, and you became fast and glorious friends, in that sensing, and study partners, etc., and there was just this gloriously wonderful, loving relationship. Nothing, nothing sexual about it, but loving relationship between these two, two students, in that sensing. It's just quite incredible.

There was also a time that, in that particular sensing, she was a teacher of yours, in that sensing. In fact, more than once. At least two times. A teacher of yours, in that sensing, in Atlantis, at one time, and also Egypt, in that particular regard. And she had malady then. She was, in that sensing, had a crippling malady where she had virtually no use of her legs, paralyzed from the waist down, in that particular regard. But yet, in that sensing, a brilliant teacher. Many would shun her, and walk away from her, because she was this cripple, in that sensing. But you did not. And there was a great, great rapport that developed between you.

You also saved her life one time, in that particular sensing. And that was a time in France, where, indeed, she was in trouble, because she had a mouth, in that sensing, that just wouldn't keep quiet. And the local priest decided to get even with her, and therefore accused her of witchcraft, though, indeed, she wasn't really involved in such activity, though it wouldn't have been bad if she'd been. But, nonetheless, she was accused. And you, in that sensing, rather single-handedly, helped her to escape, in that particular regard. A jail-break, as it would be, in the high tradition of drama. But, nonetheless, out of town, on the back of your horse, the two of you rode, for you could not let yourself be seen again, ever again, either. Heading into the Swiss Alps, in that sensing, where, indeed, you went your own way. And she forever grateful, in that particular sensing.

And we would suggest you have this long—one, three, six—six, eight, nine—something like that—six, nine, ten, eleven lifetimes, whatever. Many, many of them there.

As you came, in that sensing, she decided to work out a tremendous karma, with the other half, in that sensing, that Siamese portion that was born dead. And we would suggest here that that other part of her—you felt you owed me. You owe me life, in that sensing. You owe me life. It wasn't true. But you owe me a life, damn it! You owe me a life! And so Jennifer said, okay, okay, I'll give you life. I'll give it to you, in that sensing, and we'll be done with this, and stop chasing me through the centuries, as it were! And therefore, born in the Siamese condition, in that particular sensing, there, I gave you life. But it wasn't really a karmic debt, in that particular sense, so, therefore, the life did not sustain itself. That part died at birth—before birth, actually. And we would suggest, but left Jennifer, in that sensing, in this state.

And she said, okay I'll give it a shot. I'll give it a try, etc. But it just was the gyroscopic balance was just too off base, and she just couldn't get it under. And she refused to be an invalid. She refused to be dependent, in that way. She was so, even so—in her three years, she was so reliant in herself. Such an independence there! Such a self-reliance! Such a determination to be so! But she realized, okay, you know, I could stay in this life, and I could probably last another ten, maybe at best, fifteen years, and then I could be a real freak. You know, have all the scientists come look at me. Look at the Siamese twin that lived this long. But, in that sensing, I could cut my losses now. I could do a lot more work for Gerald, in that sensing, who I really want to work with. I could do a lot more for him on other levels than I can here. And therefore, I think I'll cut my losses now. I think I'll just—And so, she did, in that particular regard. And we would suggest here that that's where the energy opens up.

GERALD: Wonderful. Can I ask one other question?

LAZARIS: Certainly so.

GERALD: One comment. I've made a vow to meditate every day for the rest of my life, as a result of this. I just wanted to tell you that. And also, will we meet after this life, or again?

LAZARIS: Most definitely so. We would suggest here, as you make this decision, indeed, a vow, to meditate every day, to give yourself the option, in that sensing, for the varieties of meditation.

GERALD: All right.

LAZARIS: Sometimes, to sit down and meditate in great depth. Other times, to—in the automobile, while you're waiting, here, in that sensing, I can take a brief meditative time. Meditation, that time of quieting, centering, and altering your state of consciousness. It can take many different forms. So, if you find yourself not meditating in the exact form on some particular day, not to beat yourself up, or decide you blew it.

Beyond that, in that sensing, yes. When you decide to leave, which is not for a very long time, she'll be there. Absolutely. And she'll be, in that sensing—what will happen, in the ways, that even though she will have at that time, quote, changed the body form quite substantially, for your point of recognition, in that sensing, when you come through that tunnel, in that sensing, she'll be one of the first ones there, as a little girl, in that particular sensing, waving furiously at you. Then, in that sensing, almost before your eyes, she'll sort of metamorphose into the adult person body form, in that sensing, that you can relate to more fully. More in that sense of counselor-guide. But, in that sensing, absolutely.

Then, on—there's other levels you'll definitely know her, in that particular regard. And we would suggest here that she'll be playing an integral part in your own process of growth at that particular time, as well.

So, no, you won't lose her, in that particular sense, even though she gave up the body. It was just too destined, too destined in this life, in that sensing.

In terms of that you found each other, in that sensing, she wasn't necessarily thinking she would find you, in that sensing. But when she—what threw off, what killed her—when in that sense she realized she took on more than she could handle, in that sensing, then, it was just such a wonderful thing for her to find you—that you're there! Oh, good, you're here, in that sensing! And, in that way, it's just such a lovely, destined connection, in that sensing. And although it seems sad, indeed, it was appropriate that she let go, in that particular sensing. And her way of loving you, in that sensing, was to let go. And your way of loving her was to allow her to let go. Even though I might have wanted you to stay for my own reasons, in that sensing, I'm going to love you enough to let you do what you want. And you have. It's not like, oh, yeah, do that, Gerald. You already have done that. But, in that sensing, the connection is solid. It's there. And it's certainly an eternal one, and will not depart.

And you'll feel her presence so clearly. Not now. You feel it somewhat. But when she's ready to really get going, you'll feel it very strongly. She'll just pop up in dreams, she'll come up and you'll sense her, almost as though you see her out of the corner of the eye, sometimes, wide open, in that sensing. And of course she'll have an impact upon your meditative experiences, absolutely. So, its a very solid and very beautiful thing.

GERALD: All right.

LAZARIS: All right. It's a sad thing, certainly so. But we would suggest here it's also important to realize that death is not failure, in that sensing. It's the ultimate physical healing. But, short of that, it's still not failure, and that, in that sensing, she chose it, in that way. And ironically, as you look at it, in that sensing, she did choose to die in such a way that you would be the one to find her.

GERALD: All right.

LAZARIS: You see. And that's where it fits together.

GERALD: All right. Thank you.

LAZARIS: All right. And we love you very much, and with that, then, we'll close. Sweet love.

GERALD: All right.

LAZARIS: And peace.

GERALD: Bye-bye.

LAZARIS: Good-bye, now.

Thus, the reading ended and I received a tape of it a few days afterward. I was extraordinarily affected by what Lazaris had said, both in and of itself, and in the way it related to some of the things that had come to light in my previous readings with Freda Fell and Nicki Mellette. I believed (as I still do) what Lazaris said to me. Since I cannot prove the truth of what he told me, I simply choose to believe and accept it. Call it my own personalized brand of faith.

What was particularly meaningful and made absolute sense to me on deep intuitional and emotional levels was the string of previous lifetimes Lazaris had described in which Jenny and I had been together. Given my total acceptance of reincarnation, there was no other explanation that could so logically and convincingly explain my immediate and unconditional decision to take Jenny, sight unseen, as my foster daughter, or my accompanying conviction that she was somehow "mine" to have and to care for, and my unshakable perception and attitude that she was literally, in every way, my very own daughter.

After all, according to Lazaris, Jennifer had in fact been my biological daughter in three previous incarnations, and I accepted this completely. In addition, was there not something remarkably ironic and "coincidental"—to say the least—in the idea that we had served and helped each other so many times, and in so many ways, before? If what Lazaris had said was true, then, in addition to my taking care of Jenny both physically and emotionally in this lifetime, I had in the past been her father (three times), a loyal follower even when others had shunned her because of a physical malady (another one!), and, in one lifetime, a friend who had literally saved her life. On the other hand, in addition to the exquisite love and immeasurable spiritual gifts which Jennifer had blessed me with in this life, she had been a teacher and counselor for me in (at least) two previous incarnations.

Of course, Freda, and especially Nicki, had also pointed to past incarnations in which Jenny and I had been together—both Nicki and Lazaris had mentioned France. If Nicki's reference to my having known Jenny during medieval times could be linked with France, it would tie in very well with Lazaris's recounting of my lifetime in France with Jenny, during which I had rescued her from persecution by a religious official.

During the first few weeks after Jenny's death, these questions had been growing in my mind. On a deeper level, what did it all mean? Had there been some grand design behind it, or was this incredible experience with Jenny just some dazzling meteor flash, destined to disappear into a darkness which could yield no understanding or knowledge as suddenly as it had appeared? And what of the future? Would I never again find this soul which I had loved and cherished above all other things?

With the Lazaris reading, coupled with Freda's and Nicki's insights, had come light and meaning. Now it made sense. There had indeed been a past to my relationship with Jenny—a very long and meaningful one—and, according to what I had been told, and the faith and hope I held inside of me, there would be a future relationship as well, in this life, beyond this life, and possibly in future lives. Our meeting in this incarnation had not been random or without design; it had been exquisitely engineered in accord with the laws of the universe and the karma that linked us, by the indwelling intelligence in each of us and the burning love shared between our souls.

On October 24, I received a bill from Cabot and Sons for Jenny's funeral expenses, including the transportation of her body by Delta Airlines to Kentucky, minus what the county had paid. I gladly sent them a check the same day for the balance. They had done a very good job.

On October 25, 1991, I made a formal, written application to Concept: Synergy for another reading with Lazaris sometime in the future, chiefly to discuss Jennifer further, to explore the possibility of adopting or raising other children, and to talk about my own personal evolutionary path and other metaphysical issues. The fact that they were unable to grant this request was in no way a reflection on them, but merely indicative of the great demands on Jach Pursel's time and the number of hours in a given day. The requests they received far outnumbered the number of readings they were able to schedule, especially considering Jach Pursel's additional schedule of speaking engagements. Besides, I was probably being a little greedy and unrealistic—although perhaps forgivably so—in expecting to get another reading any time in the near future. And finally, I had, after all, already learned a great deal from Lazaris—certainly the core and essence of that which I had sought to ascertain and understand. For this, I was deeply grateful.

I Meet Jessica

Responding to an invitation from Nancy Pivaral a few days earlier, I drove to Malibu to see little Jessica Christina Pivaral (then only two and a half weeks old) for the first time on Saturday, October 26, a bright but cloudy day. It was also the first time that I had ever been to Malibu to visit any of Jennifer's family. For some reason, Suzanne did not go with me, and I cannot remember if she had something else to do or if perhaps she was not up to it emotionally. It had after all been only two and a half months since Jenny's death. I, too, was grieving deeply and was on an emotional roller coaster, but I was deeply curious about the new baby, and I did not want to appear rude by not going.

Following Nancy's directions, I took the 10 freeway west all the way to Pacific Coast Highway (PCH), then drove north through Santa Monica and Pacific Palisades (past the Self-Realization Fellowship Lake Shrine near the corner of Sunset and PCH), and far up into Malibu, beyond the point where Kanan-Dume Road came down through the mountains to meet PCH (a forty-eight mile trip from my home). Finally, I made a left turn into a quiet residential area that became increasingly affluent as I neared the ocean. The beautiful ranch-style house where the Pivarals were living sat near the edge of a cliff and overlooked the Pacific. It was on a cul-de-sac at the end of a road and hidden from view from the street by a high, gated wall and extensive gardens. Graciela, Jessica's grandmother, who worked as a maid and caretaker for the elderly lady who owned the house, lived with Nancy and Maria, two of her daughters (Rosa's sisters), in the small apartment above the attached garage. I entered the grounds, parked my car, and walked around the side of the garage and up the stairs.

I had not seen Graciela, Nancy, and Maria since Jenny's funeral mass at Holy Family Church on August 14, and it was good to see them again. Nancy led me to the crib where little Jessica was lying, picked up the tiny form, and handed it to me. I had never held such a young, small baby, and I felt gratified that they trusted me so much. The child, of course, was sweet and adorable. Fortunately, she had been born normal and healthy, with no physical problems or defects of any kind. I stayed and talked for quite a while. When I left, we agreed that we would be in touch again soon.

As I drove back toward Los Angeles, I mulled over my impressions. I was a little surprised that, from the first moment I had seen Jessica, and from then on, I had not felt much of a connection with her. On the way home, I thought that perhaps she was just too little, or that it was just too soon after losing Jenny for me to make an emotional connection with anyone or anything. I told Suzanne about the visit and offered my impressions about Jessica's (and Jennifer's) family.

It was now apparent to me that Graciela and her daughters, Nancy and Maria, were very decent, respectable, caring people. I had seen little of them. Actually, in addition to my contact with them on the day of Jenny's funeral mass, I had only seen them a couple of times many months before that, when Jenny was still living at Huntington and they had come, with other family members, to visit her (as they did every couple of months) at times when I also happened to be there. Jenny did not know who they were, and she was always somewhat overwhelmed and extremely shy when they came around. After taking Jenny home, Suzanne and I had decided that we did not want to have any contact with the family because of all the negative stories we had heard about Jennifer's father.

After visiting them in Malibu, I realized that I needed to correct my perception of them and that judging them because of their association with Jennifer's father had been an error. I was sorry that Suzanne and I had done so, although I suppose it was understandable, and I regretted that we had excluded them from our lives during the months Jenny had lived with us. None of that could be changed, however; Suzanne and I had done what we believed was right. Now we could open the avenue of communication again. They had made the overture by calling us after Jessica was born and then by inviting us to come and see her. Actually, I realized that there was a very real emotional compensation and comfort in being able, at least now, to be closer to the people from whom my dear Jenny had come.

A Crisis

Sometime around the end of October, a particularly dark time for me, I reached a crisis one evening. Suzanne and I did not feel very close to each other and I was feeling especially isolated in my grief. I felt particularly alone and desperate. I drove to South Pasadena and walked along the quiet, dark residential sidewalks. It was an overcast night, and damp. I had my leather jacket on.

As I walked around aimlessly, my sense of hopelessness and aloneness grew, and I found myself really wondering if I ought to consider killing myself. The problem with suicide, however, which had surfaced every time the thought had crossed my mind over the last few weeks, was that my personal religious beliefs made it a completely nonviable option, at least under those circumstances. I felt that such an act would create terrible karmic consequences, and that probably it would drive my spirit even further away from wherever Jenny was and obliterate any chance of being spiritually attuned to her. Nevertheless, I felt the world closing in around me.

Impulsively, I went back to my car and drove to Holy Family Church, a few blocks away. I felt I desperately needed to talk with someone and I thought of Father Mike, who had known Jenny and conducted her funeral mass, and who seemed a good, kind person. I walked up to the rectory behind the church and went inside. The front office was empty except for the receptionist, who noticed that I was very upset. I had been crying earlier. With an urgent tone in my voice, I asked her if Father Mike was there, but he was out for the evening, so there was nothing I could do. Deeply disappointed, I left my name, but no telephone number or message, and went home. I never went back or followed up, nor did I hear from Father Mike. It is entirely possible that he never even knew I had been there. Even if he had known, I had not asked him to call me. He would not have known how upset I had been that night.

Self-Realization Fellowship

On November 3, 1991, I telephoned the Self-Realization Fellowship in Los Angeles, after having been out of touch with the organization for many years.

In October 1967, when I was eighteen years old and a freshman studying piano at the University of Illinois in Urbana, I met Swami Nirmalananda Giri, a monk from India (Giri was the name of his monastic order). I had gone home to Bloomington, Illinois, for the weekend, and my friend and spiritual brother, Jerry Alber, who was then living there, had introduced me to Swami, who was also living there at that time, and whom Jerry had just recently met. (A swami, who may or may not be a monk, is a spiritual teacher, a guru. Conversely, a monk may or may not be a swami. Swami Nirmalananda Giri happened to be both.)

Swami had soon initiated me into various yogic practices, including kriya yoga. Over the next year, I spent a lot of time with him, when I could, practicing various meditation exercises and absorbing Eastern ideas. Swami had other students as well, a few of whom, like Jerry Alber, lived with him in an ashram in Bloomington. Then, in August 1968, Swami returned to India, and Jerry and a number of other people went with him. Swami strongly pressured me to go also, but I was unwilling, for many reasons. Therefore, after arriving in India and writing me a letter stating his final request for me to follow him, and after receiving no response from me, he made good his words, which were that, if I did not go to India, he was terminating our relationship for all time. He never communicated with me again, which left me emotionally traumatized for years.

The techniques he had taught me were very powerful, but my practice was tentative due to the impression left on me by our parting. Eventually, Swami and his followers returned to the United States and formed another ashram. Jerry remained with him for some time, but eventually left, and our friendship resumed. After his return to the U.S., I wrote Swami two letters, one in January 1978, when I was living in Detroit with my first wife, and the other in January 1979, when I was living in Louisville and just getting my balance back as the result of our divorce, which had taken place in the fall of 1978. Swami did not answer either letter, the second of which had been a request from me to address some technical questions regarding the correct practice of meditation techniques, since I had not had any supervision for many years.

Therefore, in January 1979, I contacted the Self-Realization Fellowship, the official organization for the dissemination of the teachings of Paramahansa

Yogananda (including kriya yoga). Yogananda had founded SRF several decades earlier. In order to have my questions about the advanced techniques answered, it was necessary for me to start at the beginning with them and receive their lessons by mail (at a very nominal cost). I received my first set of lessons on April 18, 1979, and continued them until April 27, 1981 (several months after I had met Suzanne, whom I would marry in August). I stopped the lessons because, by that point in the SRF teachings, I had, through study, found the answers to my questions.

Then many years ensued, filled with all kinds of experiences, during which I had no more contact with SRF. I did practice the yoga techniques, but in a very spotty manner, with long interruptions, and with no real sense of direction. On November 3, 1991, after ten years of marriage to Suzanne and moving to Los Angeles in 1985, and after the beautiful but shattering experience of having Jenny and then losing her, and finally, after resuming once again, on my own, the practice of kriya yoga on September 11, 1991, and making my subsequent vow to practice it daily for the rest of my life, I renewed my contact with SRF.

I felt a deep need to address two very big issues in my life. The first was, if possible, to put to rest forever the feelings of conflict I still carried, after so many years, about the traumatic ending of my relationship with my former guru and my subsequent reluctance to practice kriya yoga, which was almost like a superstition with me. Ever since our parting, I had held some kind of vague fear that, since I had been spiritually dumped, I might either be practicing the techniques without benefit or, even worse, bring some kind of harm upon myself. Second, I wanted to talk with someone within my own yoga tradition about Jenny, about the commitment I had made to her regarding meditation, about the incredible relationship we had had and what it had been like to lose her, and finally, about where I was going spiritually.

Brother Anandamoy

I made an appointment for November 9 to go to the SRF temple in Pasadena and meet one of the monks in the organization, Brother Anandamoy. I had heard about him through my friend, Dawn Grant, who was also a member of SRF. Not only was he one of the senior people in the organization, but he had actually known and worked with Paramahansa Yogananda himself many years earlier. After Yogananda's death, Anandamoy had continued to work within the organization to participate in its growth and the communication of its exemplary teachings. Kriya yoga was, in fact (and despite my unsteady practice of it in the past), the finest, most powerful and efficacious technique of meditation and inner growth that I had ever come across in all my years of spiritual searching. Anandamoy had an unimpeachable reputation of spiritual integrity based on a lifetime of dedication and experience. I was nervous about meeting him.

I drove to the SRF temple in Pasadena, which was only a few miles from my house. It was a very pleasant day, bright and sunny. The temple (one of several in

Los Angeles) was a simple but appealing structure that had been converted from what had been a Christian church. Inside, in addition to a sanctuary that seated several hundred people, there were rooms for meetings, Sunday school and other types of instruction, a large kitchen, and, outside and in the back, a patio area adjacent to a bookstore and gift shop that were part of the building.

I soon found Brother Anandamoy, who, over his street clothes, was wearing an ocher robe which was the traditional garb for an Indian monk. He was extremely dignified, with snow-white hair and clear, deeply penetrating eyes that gave one the impression that his mind was always intently focused on whatever was at hand. We said hello and he escorted me through the church to a room in the back, where we sat facing each other across a table. He graciously invited me to share with him whatever was on my mind.

I started by saying that I hoped he would not be shocked by some of the things I intended to tell him. He smiled, and answered that he had heard everything over the years, and that there was not much left that could shock him. For an hour, I recounted the major milestones of my life, from my early mystical experiences, through my subsequent search for truth by way of metaphysics, yoga, hallucinogenic drugs, magic, and so on. I included my experiences with Swami Nirmalananda Giri, explaining how I had actually learned the kriya yoga techniques of meditation—which were supposed to be disseminated only through SRF lessons and under their supervision—years before coming into contact with them. Sharing my fears and lack of ability to practice the techniques consistently over the ensuing years as a result of my spiritual abandonment by my guru, I brought him up to date by describing how I had taken many of the SRF lessons between 1979 and 1981, my subsequent move to California, and finally my life-altering experience with Jennifer, her death, and my decision thereafter to resume kriya yoga practice and the vow I had made to her.

Anandamoy never spoke, never moved, and never took his eyes off of me. He sat across from me with folded hands, concentrating totally upon what I was saying. His attention never wavered. I have never had a comparable experience in which someone has given themselves so totally and selflessly. The experience impressed me so deeply that it had a major influence on how I listen to others.

When I finished talking, Anandamoy and I spoke very meaningfully. He provided many valuable insights into my issues. When I left, I felt clear about my practice of kriya yoga. Although I would always be grateful to Swami Nirmalananda Giri for bringing such valuable techniques into my life, I would never again feel traumatized by the ending of our relationship or have reservations about my right to follow my yogic path independently. Anandamoy had pointed out that, since I had acquired the teachings through the SRF, Paramahansa Yogananda was really my spiritual teacher and guardian, and I was entitled to practice the techniques.

My inner focus became aligned. I could keep my vow to Jennifer without reservation, and I felt I was on a spiritual path that had stability, integrity, and purpose. I knew there would be difficult, painful times ahead, probably for a long time. That was to be expected. But I had a sense of where I was going on my inner journey. And, Anandamoy had been deeply understanding and kind in response to my story about Jenny, her death, and my bereavement, and supportive with respect to my motives for resuming my kriya practice and my vow to her. Karma, reincarnation, and the powerful ties between certain souls from life to life were elements in his world view, just as in mine. It was easy to share with him my metaphysical feelings about my relationship with Jenny and the nature of my love for her.

I realized that there were additional, advanced kriya techniques I had not yet learned which were the culmination of the teachings.

I felt a profound appreciation of Anandamoy as a person and as a deeply committed spiritual seeker and leader. My memory of his kindness has not faded.

$\mathcal{A}$ Dead End

In November 1991, the Los Angeles television news broadcasts carried the story of a little boy a couple of years old who had a rare disease requiring a bone marrow transplant, and who, in time, would die if a donor were not found. Through blood sampling, the chances of finding a donor to match the various tissue characteristics of the child were only one in many thousands. A center was set up twenty or twenty-five miles east of where I lived, where people could go to give blood samples.

When I saw the news coverage, I decided immediately that I would donate blood. After losing Jenny, I thought how wonderful it would be if it turned out that I was the one to match the characteristics of the little boy and ended up donating the needed bone marrow. On a gray, rainy Saturday morning I set out to find the center for giving blood, which had been set up in a building that was part of a small college. When I arrived at the campus, I found it extremely difficult to locate the right building. The signage and street layout was confusing, and by the time I had finally gotten parked reasonably near to where I should be and had asked many people where the place was, I was out of sorts.

When at last I arrived by foot at the right place, I found lines of people waiting to donate blood samples. I wandered among the many hundreds of people for some time before I could even determine where the end of a line was. There seemed to be little guidance or information available, and no one appeared to be in charge. As I stood there waiting, I realized that the whole affair was, in terms of coherence or efficient management, a disaster. In a short time, I knew that I would be there all day. Frankly, it was not really the waiting that bothered me, but the fact that the operation had been so badly bungled. My irritation slowly escalated, and I found myself in a foul mood.

At one point, the father of the little boy walked by with his child in his arms, greeting people and stopping now and then to talk with someone. When I saw them, I felt nothing whatever inside. After they had passed by and I had stood around in line a while longer contemplating the growing throng of people, most of whom obviously were resigned—and happily so—to camping out there for the day, and all of whom for some reason I found extremely irritating, I came to another realization. I did not belong there. A few more minutes passed. Then, I stepped out of line, walked to my car, and left.

As I drove home, I experienced a growing and incomprehensible disgust. As time passed, a deep sadness surfaced within me, which had been masked by my irritation. Finally, I became clearly aware of how much I missed Jenny, and that nothing could change that, including going out as I had that day on what was really a misguided personal crusade. Not that there was anything wrong in wanting to help that little child. What was wrong was my motive. I came to the realization that, having been the center of Jenny's life, I wanted to have that kind of feeling again. I wanted to be the "savior" of that little boy, but in a way that was rather selfish and driven by my ego.

I had not had those kinds of selfish sentiments with Jenny. My relationship with her and the fact of her coming into my life were destined, and on an entirely different level of experience. In the case of the little boy, however, I finally realized some things that, although understandable, were unflattering. I had been guided by the wrong motives, and I had foolishly thought that, perhaps by coming to his rescue, I would be embarking upon some kind of lifestyle that would involve going around saving children. I had also resented those people because I felt insignificant and anonymous among them. That massive crowd had brought home to me that my chances of being the hero of the day were slim indeed; and that probably had as much to do with my leaving as anything, although I did not realize that at the time.

When I got home, I told Suzanne what had happened without going into detail, and that I had decided not to stay. I heard no more as to whether a donor was found or what happened with the child. I sincerely hope things worked out for that poor little boy, and that, given my foolishness and selfishness, I was not the donor he was looking for. Deep in my heart, I felt I was not. If I really had thought I was the one, I would have stayed all day and all night. I would have wanted someone else to do the same thing for Jenny. My ego and my sense of reality got an adjustment that day, and I realize now that it was really too soon after Jenny's death for me to think clearly or have a clear sense of direction.

Thanksgiving, and a Baptism

Suzanne and I invited the Pivaral family for dinner on Thanksgiving. Graciela, Nancy, and Maria brought Jessica (then just over seven weeks old) and several guests. Rosa, still in jail, had asked if Suzanne and I would be Jessica's godparents. We were happy and touched and readily agreed. It was both a sad and rewarding day for Suzanne and me. Jennifer's death was fresh in our minds, and I was aware of her absence every moment of the day, as I am certain Suzanne was also. At the same time, it was a good, positive thing that we had come closer to Jennifer's family, and it was now evident that there could be a lasting, meaningful relationship between us. As we ate the wonderful meal that Suzanne had prepared and later as we sat around talking and taking pictures, I often looked around and reflected that, although the sadness of Jenny's death was with me literally moment to moment, touching every thought and action, some design in all of this had given me the consolation of knowing her family, and now, even the opportunity to play a meaningful role in her little sister's life. It was true that Jenny had not really known any of these people, except to have seen them a few times at Huntington. Nevertheless, it really meant something that they were her family, and that perhaps I might further show my love for her by embracing them.

On Sunday, December 15, in the early afternoon, Jessica Christina Pivaral was baptized by Father Mike at Holy Family Church in South Pasadena. (I still have her certificate of baptism and candle from that event.) Suzanne and I, Graciela, Nancy, Maria, and several others who had come with them were in attendance. Afterward, we all went back to Vallejo Villas for dinner. Now more than ever, a strong and meaningful bond had been created between the Pivarals and us.

Heartfelt

On Monday, December 16, 1991, I went for the first time to a meeting sponsored by Heartfelt, a grief support organization for bereaved parents similar to the Compassionate Friends. I cannot remember why I sought them out. I was still going to the Compassionate Friends home meetings and getting a lot from them; I was happy with that organization. Perhaps I was interested to see what they were about and if they offered anything different than the Compassionate Friends.

Heartfelt met in private homes during the evening on the third Monday of every month, and as far as I know there were no other larger meetings on alternate dates. The format was similar to that of the Compassionate Friends. Heartfelt also published supporting literature and offered each member the names of certain other members, to whom they referred as "support parents," and who could be called in times of emotional crises. The particular Heartfelt group with which I was involved always met at the same home in Alhambra, a few miles from where I lived.

I did not feel apprehensive at the first meeting, since I was a veteran of the Compassionate Friends meetings. At Heartfelt, also, there were refreshments, an opening statement, self-introductions and accounts of personal experiences, and a general discussion open to all.

What I experienced at Heartfelt reinforced and complemented what I was learning at the Compassionate Friends. At times, I became deeply and passionately involved in discussions. Perhaps partly because I had started out at the

Compassionate Friends, I felt more loyal to that group and came to recognize that I had somewhat of a preference for their meetings. My preference for the Compassionate Friends was purely subjective, and my references to them are not to be interpreted in any way as a rating or comparison. Both were excellent, and each served a necessary and meaningful purpose.

From the middle of December 1991, I went to monthly meetings held by each group until the end of February 1992. Since the Compassionate Friends met every second Thursday, and Heartfelt every third Monday, the meetings were acceptably spaced. Each knew that I was attending the other's meetings, and no one from either organization raised any objections.

Dr. Ribe

On December 18, 1991, I went to the Los Angeles County Coroner's Office to meet with the pathologist who had performed Jennifer's autopsy. Neither Suzanne nor I, nor anyone else really knew why Jenny had died. Suzanne and I understood that, given her medical problems, there might be any number of causes. And although knowing why she died could not bring her back or lessen our sense of loss, we felt the need to find out as much as we could. By not knowing, I was haunted by a sense that something was not settled, not at peace.

I had been trying for weeks to get the appointment. My phone calls were never returned. I had begun to wonder if the pathologist was avoiding me for some reason, but eventually he contacted me, and I was able to understand that his schedule was impossibly hectic. When we finally met, he struck me as a very compassionate person, and it was obvious that he was willing to take whatever time was needed to discuss Jenny's case thoroughly.

In addition to the apprehension—even dread—that I felt in going to this meeting, because I knew that the things to be discussed would be very painful, I was troubled by another issue. Some days, perhaps weeks, before this meeting, I had a phone conversation with Dr. Laurance during which he told me that he had spoken with the pathologist. I could sense that Dr. Laurance was trying to say something to me that he found difficult. Before proceeding with what he had to say, he asked me to try not to be upset. According to Dr. Laurance, the pathologist had listed Jenny's official cause of death as an intracranial hemorrhage. Although, as Dr. Laurance explained, there could be any number of medical explanations for intracranial hemorrhages, which may be fatal but often are not, one cause could be child abuse.

If, for example, a child were taken by the shoulders and severely or repeatedly shaken so that its head was jerked about, an intracranial hemorrhage could result and might cause death. And even though the pathologist was only doing his job by asking Dr. Laurance about the character of Jenny's caretakers—namely, Suzanne and me—I was appalled at the idea that anyone, under any circumstances, might suspect that Suzanne or I had caused Jenny harm. It was not at all that I was afraid of addressing anyone's concerns or questions, but rather that, given how deeply I had loved Jenny and cared for her, I could not bear the idea of anyone thinking that I could abuse her in any way. Dr. Laurance said that he had assured the pathologist that Suzanne and I were beyond reproach as parents. Again, he advised me not to overreact, and said that he felt that Suzanne's and my care of Jenny would not be an issue. In retrospect, I am sure that his hesitation in discussing the matter was primarily that he knew how hurt I would be. I appreciated Dr. Laurance's reassuring words; however, what he told me continued to trouble me until my appointment with the pathologist.

The setting and tone of my meeting with the pathologist has, from the day of our talk until now, always had an odd, almost surreal quality in my mind. For one thing, the Los Angeles County coroner's office is located practically next to the county hospital where Jennifer was born. I drove past both these buildings every day on my way to work. Seeing the hospital had always reminded me of Jenny, but before the meeting with the pathologist, I had never really paid any attention to the coroner's office. It was only upon getting the appointment that I realized it would be in a building I saw every day—and which was a two-minute walk from where Jenny had been born. Even now, years later, I think of Jenny every time I pass the hospital and the coroner's office, and always with a sense of irony. It is as if Jenny's life began and ended, having come full circle, in practically the same place. But when I think about this, I always remind myself that, between the beginning and ending of that life, Jenny lived an incredible and meaningful existence that changed me forever.

The other thing that made the meeting seem so dreamlike was the overwhelming incongruity of discussing something as cold and clinical as an autopsy in the sterile, impersonal, institutional setting to which I had come, and the idea that all of this centered upon the most treasured person and the deepest loss of my life. Dr. Ribe's demeanor made a world of difference. As I write this, I have just had a telephone conversation with him. Acting on a strong impulse, I was able to reach him at the coroner's office, and I told him that I felt deeply how important it was that people like himself be told that their kindness, sensitivity, and compassion can and do make an unforgettable difference in the lives of people with whom they come into contact. We had a wonderful talk, and I assured him that I would deliver a copy of this book to him when it was published.

After meeting Dr. Ribe, I followed him into a large room with a number of tables and chairs, bookshelves, records, and so on. After we sat down, I explained to him my relationship with Jennifer and said that I had come in search of answers (if there really were any) as to why Jenny had died. I took extensive notes during the long, detailed conversation that followed.

Dr. Ribe explained that he had listed the official cause of Jenny's death as "intracranial hemorrhage, old or new," saying that, in Jenny's case, an old hemorrhage could even be a complication from her difficult birth. He described her autopsy as complex and revealing many abnormalities, and explained that an intracranial hemorrhage was probably or possibly partly involved in the cause of death. Had he not found any intracranial hemorrhages, he would have attributed Jenny's death to the condition of her heart and lungs, which he considered big issues and that could have caused her to die suddenly and at any time.

Jenny's heart was abnormally large, possibly from anemia, or from low protein and high glucose levels from infancy. Both sides were enlarged. The right side showed chronic strain and some pulmonary-vascular hypertension, possibly caused by past bouts with sepsis. Eschemic changes under the right ventricle showed acute strain. Her lungs showed some signs of high blood pressure, probably from past pneumonia, and also signs of oxygen toxicity, caused most likely from some asphyxiation at birth. In addition, her kidneys showed some atrophy from prenatal or neonatal causes; her liver, although its bile duct seemed normal, was somewhat enlarged, something to be expected with TPN; and, she had a fibrotic pancreas with an obliterated pancreatic duct, and with an unusual scar-like lump which was possibly a proliferation of smooth muscle or a surgical leftover associated with her twin. In addition, Jennifer's body showed much internal scarring from surgeries.

Dr. Ribe was interested in my comments regarding a couple of falls that Jenny had had. One had been a tumble down some carpeted stairs in our home, from which she had shown no signs of injury. Another, a few weeks before she died, had been one reported to us by her day care center, when she had fallen off a slide onto the sand. Although in his opinion either of these incidents could have resulted in one of the more recent intracranial hemorrhages he had found, he could draw no firm conclusions.

According to Dr. Ribe, given the complexity of the issues and Jenny's fragile medical condition, her death could have been caused by almost anything, or any combination of things—neurological, metabolic, glucose, and so on. I asked about the possibility of a bad batch of TPN. He said that, even had this been the case, it would be possible for nothing to show up in an autopsy. We concluded that at least the bags of TPN I had used earlier in the week prior to Jenny's death were all right.

He also took many notes during our talk, as I recounted Jenny's medical background, including her two strange seizures that occurred on the Saturday and Sunday prior to her death on Friday, and the details of her unexplainable behavior on the Thursday night just before she died. He agreed with my theory that Jenny's leaving Huntington and coming home to live with us could have shortened her life due to the increased activity, strain, and compressed feeding hours. But he also readily concurred that the quality of her life had been enormously improved. (Since Jenny's death, I have often had the thought that her body was strained from the processing of all the TPN at night, while she was sleeping—when her body should have been resting. Of course, the alternatives of hooking her up to feedings during the daytime for many hours or at more than one time of the day would have profoundly limited her lifestyle and presented extraordinary logistical problems, especially in a home setting.)

When we had finished, Dr. Ribe stressed that he was always available to talk if further questions should arise. I could order a complete, typed autopsy report if I wanted it, but I felt that was unnecessary, given the scope and detail of the conversation we had coupled with my notes. And besides, I felt that having any more details than I already had might make me even sadder, and unnecessarily so. Dr. Ribe told me that many things might have caused Jennifer's death, that a more precise determination was not possible, and that, given that it was necessary to list something as Jenny's official cause of death, the intracranial hemorrhages were as logical a choice as any. No one will ever know for sure why Jenny died when she did.

Dr. Ribe tried unsuccessfully to help me with one other issue relating to Jenny. I had wanted to retrieve her clothing and the colostomy bag, gastrostomy tube, the sections of feeding lines, and the plastic pan with its bottle and related tubing that had been taken with her when her body was removed from my house. By December 31, I gave up, with regret and deep disappointment, on the possibility of ever recovering any of these things. All of them were very important to me, but especially the Mickey Mouse T-shirt—one of two that she had—that she was wearing when she died. I tried every imaginable official, agency, division, and office in the county to no avail. I got nothing but a runaround, lots of conflicting excuses, and even the claim that Jenny's body came in without clothing—which was actually confirmed in an official report! I was told that even the photo taken of her body by the county showed her without the T-shirt. I regret that I have never had the chance to tell whomever threw away or stole that T-shirt what it meant to me. I have heard many stories from people, including bereaved parents in support groups, about similar experiences with the County of Los Angeles.

My meeting with Dr. Ribe left me feeling deeply sad and very drained. I discussed everything that evening with Suzanne. I especially remember the pain I felt that day (I still feel it today) upon realizing the multitude of things that had been wrong inside Jenny's body. It was as if my poor daughter had been a walking time bomb, just waiting to explode from one problem or another, and who, in spite of all our hopes for her, never had a chance of growing up. She was so radiant looking! And yet, all along, behind those shining eyes and that sweet smile, within her beautiful little body, lay the seeds of her early death. Then and now, there is something in this which, to me, is inexpressibly sad. And yet if I had to do it all over again, I would without a second's hesitation. Because Jenny was the most precious and beautiful treasure that ever blessed my life—she was utterly special, absolutely irreplaceable, and more deserving of love than any being I have even known.

Year's End

During the latter part of December, I went to a meeting sponsored by Los Angeles County regarding the adoption of children through the county. Frankly, I am not certain why I went, since neither Suzanne nor I were anywhere near emotionally ready to consider such a thing. On the other hand, I believe that the emptiness I felt inside required some kind of active response. Although my going to the meeting was purely investigative in nature, it was nevertheless something that I could do to keep alive a hope that, if Suzanne and I should ever be ready to become parents again, there might be avenues.

I had already made a few inquiries about what was involved in private adoptions, but I was quickly shocked into reality when I learned the costs associated with such a procedure. I could not believe that, given all of the child abuse and neglect going on, a decent, responsible couple with love and a home to offer should be required essentially to buy a baby for twenty or thirty thousand dollars. Such fees were entirely beyond our means.

What I learned at the county meeting was that Suzanne and I had little chance of ever adopting a child through such a public agency. One factor against us was our ages. I was already forty-two, and Suzanne was several years older than I. Another thing not in our favor was that we were white. In Los Angeles County, the majority of children eligible for adoption were Afro-American, Hispanic, or Asian, in that order, and the county made every effort to place children in homes with racial make-ups identical to their own. On one hand, I saw a point to this, and on another, I did not. At any rate, our race did everything but increase our chances of eligibility, and, by the end of the meeting, it was quite clear that the likelihood of Suzanne and I ever adopting a child, especially a young one, through the county was slim at best. Nevertheless, over the next few days, I filled out all of the appropriate paperwork and mailed it in. It was, in fact, between two and three years before we heard back from the county, asking if we were still even interested. By that time, we were not.

Parallel to my investigation into the matter of adoption, I was going round and round with the county Department of Children's Services regarding the possibility of future foster parenting. This was in addition to and separate from the little war that I had waged with the DCS over the payment of Jenny's funeral expenses. This time, the issue was that, as I began to look into things, I was simply not getting any answers from the DCS when I asked questions about our status as foster parents or inquired if we would be considered in the future for taking other children. As was true with adoption, Suzanne and I were nowhere near ready for any new responsibilities, but nevertheless I wanted to see what possibilities there might be in the future.

This long, drawn-out episode began three or four months after Jenny's death and was not cleared up until sometime late the following spring or early summer. My questions to various county staff were at first met with responses as if no one knew anything, and I was bounced from person to person and among a number of offices. Then, after a time, attitudes toward my questions became mysteriously and disturbingly evasive. Finally, someone told me that our file was on some kind of hold pending completion of investigation.

Since no one would explain what this meant or the reasons behind it, I became deeply concerned. What was going on? Could they possibly suspect me of murdering Jenny? I played this game with the county for months. Finally, after becoming extremely frustrated, I telephoned one of the top officials in the DCS. After I had given him the whole scenario, he promised to look into the situation without delay and get back to me promptly. When I did not hear back from him after a reasonable period of time, I began calling. It became quickly apparent that he, too, was now avoiding me. Eventually, I felt that I had to protect myself by writing him a long letter, documenting the whole history of the problem and the fact that he, also, had not properly responded to my inquiries. I do not think that I ever heard directly back from him. Eventually, however, many months after the whole affair had started, I received some kind of notification in the mail from the county that the investigation had been closed and that our foster home status had been reinstated to the eligible category.

Later, I learned that certain investigative procedures were always done when a foster child died in a foster care facility, something that seemed reasonable and appropriate. Furthermore, it was customary that, during such an investigation, the facility was placed temporarily on a hold status as far as being considered for future children. And finally, it did not appear, after all, that there had been any suspicion with regard to Suzanne and me or that any unusual investigative efforts had been made in closing the case. The problem was simply that the DCS had been completely unresponsive in addressing any of my concerns and questions, thereby causing me months of anxiety which, in the end, had been utterly unnecessary.

It had been Suzanne's and my intention, if Jenny had lived, to look into adopting her. The big issue, and probably one that could have been successfully addressed in time, would have been alternate funding for some of her care. If we had adopted her, the money that we had been receiving from the county would no longer have been available, and it would have been necessary, most likely, to look into Federal programs. Of course, Jenny's death made all of those issues irrelevant, except that later, I found myself wondering if adopting her would have become another bureaucratic nightmare with the County of Los Angeles. (On the other hand, I should be grateful, and I am, that the government has passed laws and made provisions so that children like Jenny can be taken care of and placed in homes where people love them.)

On December 24, I resumed ordering lessons from the Self-Realization Fellowship.

On Christmas Day, Suzanne gave me two beautiful books, each with Oriental designs on their covers and blank pages inside that could be used as diaries. Her idea was that I use one volume to make drawings and various designs related to my thoughts and feelings about Jenny as the mood hit me. She wanted me to use the other volume as a diary. I have used the books as Suzanne intended. On the inside of the diary, Suzanne wrote the following inscription: "The Child I Care For, A Journal by Gerald R. Lishka, Christmas, 1991." This volume contains entries I chose to make from time to time, including many of my thoughts, feelings, memories, and dreams about Jenny, thoughts I wrote down in the form of letters to her, cards I bought for her on her birthdays after her death, letters to and from her mother, Rosa, and other things.

When I look at these volumes now, I am very grateful to Suzanne for thinking of such a thing, because I did not. If it were not for her idea, I would have failed to capture many of the things that have gone on inside of me since Jenny's death. It is a cherished record of many of my deepest emotions and experiences. These journal entries are included in this book, dispersed in chronological order among my accounts of the events that prompted the writings. Since I have not reread much of the journal until writing this book, I have been surprised by a number of the things it contains. I had almost forgotten about some of the entries and the events and feelings they describe. In other cases, the content seems almost too personal to let anyone else read. But because I want to portray Jenny's story and my feelings about her as honestly as I can, I have not edited these entries.

I went to the County Registrar Recorder's office on December 28 to order a copy of Jenny's final death certificate. I had received a copy dated August 14, 1991, from Cabot and Sons at the time of Jenny's funeral mass, but the determination of the cause of death had been marked deferred pending investigation. Apparently, although the autopsy had been performed prior to August 14, the day of Jenny's funeral mass, there had not been time to assess its results and fill out and process the final record. And although I had a good idea of what the amended certificate would say, from my visit with Dr. Ribe, I felt a need to see the final version and have a copy for my records. I received Jenny's amended certificate of death on December 30. The cause of death listed was "(a) intracranial hemorrhage," and "(b) old or recent head trauma." "Other significant conditions contributing to death but not related to cause" were listed as "pancreatic fibrosis" and "diabetes mellitus." The document also made reference to a Siamese twin and to Jenny's abdominal reconstruction at birth.

I had expected the business about the intracranial hemorrhage. However, the diabetes mellitus put me off balance, because the pathologist had made no specific reference to it. I looked up "diabetes mellitus" in the dictionary. It was defined as "a chronic disease of pancreatic etiology, marked by insulin deficiency, subsequent inability to utilize carbohydrates, excess sugar in the blood and urine, excessive thirst, hunger, and urination, weakness, emaciation, imperfect combustion of fats resulting in acidosis, and, without insulin injection, eventual coma and death."

I was neither a doctor nor a pathologist, but I had strongly suspected that there was a metabolic cause for Jenny's death, especially given her convulsions on two successive mornings after her pumps had been shut off a few days before her death. I asked myself if it would not have been more logical to list the diabetes as the cause of death, but then I remembered that the pathologist had only the immediate evidence at the time of Jenny's autopsy, and it had not been until December 18, when I had met with Dr. Ribe (long after the amended certificate of death had been completed), that he had been given the benefit of additional insights into Jennifer's strange condition the few days prior to her death.

Some painful and agonizing thoughts flashed through my mind about the people who had overseen Jenny's medical care, sometimes for long periods. They should have been more in tune with her physiology and better able to monitor this condition. I had been told about her chronically low blood sugar levels upon awakening in the mornings during her years of living at the hospital. And, was not low blood sugar a prelude to diabetes? I was getting in over my head, but I shared my disturbing concerns with Suzanne. In the end, we both experienced the same gnawing thoughts, but there was nothing to be done. Our Jenny was dead. Nothing could bring her back. Perhaps that was destined, as the psychics would have me believe, and nothing could have been any different. And, after all, Suzanne and I really believed that all the people who had been involved in Jenny's care had done their very best, and we knew that many of them had loved her deeply.

Journal Entry: Tuesday, December 31, 1991 (first entry)

To Jenny. You are my guru. It was you who gave me the resolve to pledge to do Kriya Yoga, on October 6, 1991, for the rest of my life—every single day. You are one in a billion.

I Return to Jenny's Grave

On January 4, 1992, I flew to Bloomington to visit my mother. Sometime before Jenny's death the previous August, I had made plans to visit my mom soon after Suzanne had returned from her August retreat at Gethsemani. But after Jenny died I cancelled these plans, largely because I was not able emotionally to cope with the idea of the trip and the visit. Such a thing would have been very hard on me, especially given that, if I had gone to Bloomington as planned, it would have been right on the heels of my trip to Gethsemani to bury Jenny. It was just too much. As I had anticipated, my mother was disappointed, to say the least. Frankly, I detected in her response to Jenny's death more of a frustration that my plans for visiting her were thwarted than any real understanding of what Jenny and her death meant to me. I was not entirely surprised at this and decided to set the whole issue aside for the time being.

Then, as the year approached its end, I saw that it would be quite impractical to go to Bloomington prior to January 1, since a trip right at Christmas would have to be short, because of my office responsibilities. Therefore, I postponed my trip until early January. Besides, the truth was that, despite the obvious appropriateness of visiting my mother, who lived alone, over such an important holiday, I had no desire whatsoever to go. Obviously, Christmas that year was a difficult and painful time. I was deeply mourning Jenny's death, and no trip anywhere, to see anyone for any reason, had the slightest appeal.

Thus, with deep reluctance, I finally made the trip to Bloomington in January, knowing full well what it would be like. The longer I postponed it, the more unpleasant the prospect of having to go had grown. Finally, I went to get it over with.

I had gone to Bloomington with the intention of taking a couple of days to drive to Kentucky, where I would stay with the Roggenkamps in Anchorage and visit Jenny's grave at Gethsemani. Going to Gethsemani meant a great deal, and the Roggenkamps were expecting me. However, rather than preparing my mother for this by informing her of my plans prior to my flight home, I avoided the issue by postponing mention of it until I got to Bloomington. Once there, I made matters worse by letting a couple of days pass before saying anything at all. All this avoidance was a mistake, but I dreaded bringing it up, for good reason.

Finally, early one evening after I had been in Bloomington for several days, my mother and I were in a grocery store, buying supplies for the week. Since she was planning out every meal for the next several days, I finally had to tell her that I wanted to go to Kentucky for two days. I clearly remember the ugliness this created. My mother became angry and spiteful.

In an accusing tone of voice, she looked at me and said, "Why do you have to go down there? That's not necessary!"

Instantly, I bitterly recalled years of growing up at home during which all my wants and desires, regardless of whatever emotional meaning they might have for me, were largely decided, sometimes by my father, sometimes by my mother, on the basis of whether or not they were "necessary."

I tried to explain why visiting Jenny's grave was necessary for me. My mother's response, still in the same tone of voice, was to say, "You don't need to go down there! She wasn't even your daughter!"

This was like throwing a lighted match near a keg of dynamite. Of course, I knew what she meant in her own mind—the literalness of what she was saying. I held onto myself—barely—and answered her very matter-of-factly, and just as literally.

"Oh, yes," I assured her with deep conviction, "She was my daughter. And I was her father."

For a second, this totally unexpected response knocked my mother off balance—but not for long.

"What do you mean, she was your daughter?" she said nastily, like I was some kind of fool.

I kept the lid on and repeated myself, calmly but emphatically, "She was my daughter."

Abandoning her tactics of confronting me with brutal facts, she resorted to complaining, peppering her response with a few more caustic remarks and a little blackmail about my infrequent visits home and their brevity.

Standing there, I suddenly saw that trying to justify my trip was not only ineffective, but utterly unnecessary. I was an adult. I could make my own choices;

I did not have to put up with that kind of shit. Still, I did not want to lose my temper and allow the whole interchange—whose tenor was so familiar to me—to degenerate into mindless, hurtful anger.

My response was even, almost kind, but absolutely firm. "You don't have to understand or like what I'm doing. I'm going, and that's all there is to it."

Still angry, and making sure that I knew that she was hurt, her only response left was, "Well, I don't want you to take my car! You can just rent one!"

"That's fine," I said. "I don't want to take your car, anyway. I don't want to be responsible for it."

Although more venom would surface later at opportune moments, that round was over. I was angry, but more than that, I was deeply hurt. I understood that my visits home (due partly to economic and work constraints) were not as often as they should be, and I was sorry that I found it necessary during such visits to break them up into manageable periods by arranging for side trips, visiting a few friends on selected evenings, and so on. But that is how it was. Even though I loved my mother, and although she had been a real friend and support to me through some tough times in my life, being in close proximity for more than short periods—especially in the winter months, when I was stuck indoors—created problems for both of us.

But what really hurt me deeply that night was my mother's inability to relate to my love for Jenny, whom I had regarded as my own child! Could she really believe that Jenny was not a meaningful loss to me since she had not been my biological daughter? And, despite her own unhappy childhood, had she had no experience as my mother that could provide her with any insight into what it might be like to lose a child? What did I mean to her, then? As prepared as I had been for some unpleasantness, I was deeply shaken by this episode and it took me a couple of years to gain a perspective on it. The incident embodied my fears of going home and spending a week—an eternity, in this case—in a setting that would not support, honor, or even acknowledge the deep grief I felt, and which I needed to stay intimately in touch with every moment.

I rented a car and made the five-hour drive to Kentucky on January 7. I stayed with the Roggenkamps for two nights, and on the eighth, Dale and I drove down to Gethsemani. It was a typical December day for Kentucky. The weather was cold, cloudy, and a little damp. Since it was winter, the fields along the way were barren and empty. The woods were dark brown or gray. Everything seemed somber. Dale and I talked most of the way from Anchorage to Trappist. As always, she was a good friend and an understanding companion.

Despite the bleak day, my spirits rose as I began to recognize some of the countryside near the abbey. Something deep inside me seemed to stir strongly to life. It was as if I was going to meet Jenny. Before we drove the last short distance, Dale and I stopped at a little florist shop so that I could buy a bouquet of flowers.

We drove the last bit, and shortly I saw the abbey coming up on my left. My only thought was that Jenny lay within the hillside near the edge of the road. We got within a hundred feet of the entrance and my heart literally leapt inside of my chest. My Beloved was here! We parked the car, and Dale and I walked to Jenny's grave. I stood there silently, holding my flowers, and read the gray marker.

Jennifer Marie
Pivaral-Lishka
June 24, 1988
August 9, 1991
Our Precious Baby

Jenny's full legal name had been Jennifer Janeth Pivaral, but Suzanne had often referred to her affectionately as Jennifer Marie (Marie was Suzanne's middle name). Therefore, when I ordered Jenny's marker, I had included the "Marie" at Suzanne's wish. And, since I felt that it was only right that Jenny's own last name be used, and since I had also wanted to give her my name, I had specified the marker to read "Pivaral-Lishka."

Looking at the inscription, my heart was filled with indescribable tenderness and love. Tears filled my eyes as I became flooded with intense emotion and a crystalline, lucid awareness of Jenny, of who she was and what she meant to me, of the meteoric impact she had had upon my life and my heart. The hurt and grief that had accumulated into muck inside of me and clogged me over the last five months was broken free and washed out of me as I stood there. Baptized in the power and inexpressible purity of the love that filled me—both my love for Jenny and hers for me—the pain was washed away. I felt light, clean, and purified. And for the short time I stood there, I felt that Jenny and I were not separate anymore.

Writing this four years later, the phrase "cleansed in the blood of the Lamb" comes to my mind, but it sounds strange. I am thinking, "We are not cleansed by blood. We are cleansed by love." Love, and only love, is what cleanses, purifies, uplifts, and makes the spirit strong. When I can feel the quality of love Jenny brought, I rise above the loss and the pain. And when I forget it, life again becomes a shadow.

Visiting Jenny's grave was something I needed very much. Seeing her name on that marker made me sad, but it was also confirmation that Jenny had really existed!—she had really been here, had lived with us, had been my daughter. Because after Jenny died, Suzanne and I found ourselves at times almost wondering if it had all been a dream. Her days with us had gone by so quickly, like sands in an hourglass; a few precious, fleeting months of wonder, adventure, trial, and incredible love. And then, suddenly and forever, she was gone. Her name on her marker was proof to me that she was real! I had not dreamed her!

I laid Jenny's flowers on top of her grave. I knew that they would not last long in the cold, but that did not matter to me. Dale and I walked around the grounds for a while and went inside the abbey. Later, I returned to the little cemetery to say goodbye to Jenny. Why could time not miraculously be turned back and I step through a door into some magical world to find Jenny home with us again, going to day care, sleeping in her crib in her pretty room, filling our lives with light?

Such fantasies are sometimes momentarily comforting, but awakening from them can be harsh. I took my time to say goodbye, gently and reverently. The little spot of earth where I stood was sacred ground to me. I wondered when I would return. And very reluctantly, I finally moved away. Dale and I walked back to the car and drove out of the grounds, back toward Anchorage and the rest of the world. My heart and the love which possessed it remained at Gethsemani.

I was very sad to leave the Roggenkamps the following morning. They did everything they could to encourage me to remain one more day, and I wanted to stay more than anything. But I felt obligated to return to Bloomington and guilt would have marred a longer visit. I said goodbye and drove down their long driveway, across the little bridge and frozen stream just before the road, thinking of the white swans that floated there during the summer. I returned to Bloomington, and on January 11, 1992, I flew back to Los Angeles.

Late that evening, after I was back home in Los Angeles, I made the following entry in my journal.

Journal Entry: Saturday, January 11, 1992

Seven intense moments in my life with you:

(1) The first time I ever saw you, in your wagon, in the hall at Huntington Memorial Hospital, on Pediatrics.

(2) The first time I rocked you to sleep in your room at HMH, and you made a pillow from a towel and put it on my shoulder.

(3) The time I lay by your crib at home at night, and I looked tearfully into your eyes and told you how much I loved you. You reached out and sweetly stroked my wet cheek.

(4) The time during your last visit to HMH in August 1991, and you put three marks on a piece of paper as we sat together on the floor of your room, and you said, "I love Daddy." I was so happy for that wonderful gift that I cried. Added Tuesday, May 18, 1993: We had been drawing with crayons. I wrote your name with a crayon on a piece of paper, spelling out each letter as I went: "J-E-N-N-Y." Then, all by yourself, you made three crayon marks on some paper, and said in the same fashion: "I-love-Daddy." I wish so much that I had what we each put on those papers that day! But I will never forget!

(5) Your last day at All Saints Children's Center, Thursday, August 8, 1991. I came to get you in the afternoon. You dropped your toys, ran to me, and proudly showed me to your teachers, like you always did.
   Added Tuesday, May 18, 1993: And I remember how proud you were of me when I would pick you up from All Saints Children's Center

in the afternoons. You would point to me and say "My Daddy" to your teachers (or "My Mommy" when Suzanne came to get you). And Jenny, I was so very, very proud of you, and still am, and always will be!

(6) Our last night together at home—Thursday, August 8, 1991, and very early morning on Friday, August 9, 1991.

(7) The times I have felt the closeness of your soul in my meditations, and my commitment to you and to myself (October 6, 1991) to meditate (Kriya Yoga) all the days of my life.

Through the Winter

On Monday, January 13, 1992, my first Self-Realization Fellowship lessons arrived, picking up the sequence exactly where they had left off when I had discontinued them on April 27, 1981, eleven years earlier. When I received them, I reflected on how much water had passed under the bridge during that intervening time. The lessons would continue to arrive every two weeks until the 12th of July, 1993, at which time I would have the option of applying for instruction in the second, third, and fourth levels of kriya meditation, the final techniques the school had to offer. In addition to receiving the lessons, I would, from time to time, attend the Sunday services at the SRF temple in Pasadena and some of the group meditations that were offered on Sunday and Thursday evenings. My attendance was not regular (I had never felt entirely comfortable around organized groups of people, regardless of their purpose), but I went whenever I felt the need. Once in a while, I would go to the SRF Lake Shrine in Pacific Palisades, only a block from the ocean, where there was a small, lovely lake, a temple, a memorial to Ghandi (which contained a portion of his ashes), a museum, a bookstore, and a gift shop.

Journal Entry: Sunday, February 9, 1992 (the six-month anniversary of your passing, August 9, 1991)

This is my daily prayer, during waking, and during my Kriya practice: that this shall be my last obligatory incarnation, that I shall find Liberation in this lifetime. And that now, and always in the future, incarnate and discarnate, I shall love, guide, and watch over you until you reach the Goal. I am committed to you always. That we shall, upon our mutual Enlightenment, though individuals, exist as one—one mind, one heart, one Consciousness and Perception, for Eternity. You are my true Soul Mate. And until and beyond that Goal, I shall love you, and pray for you, always. And that you shall know my Love, and the Love and Protection of the Kriya Masters. That your Love and Guidance shall reach me and comfort me. That you should be near me always. Jennifer, I love you infinitely!

The Hindu doctrine of reincarnation and the correlating yogic precepts and philosophy assert that a point is eventually reached in a human being's evolution when a certain level of self-realization is attained that frees him from the necessity of future incarnations.

The real goal of yoga is to achieve that freedom and liberation consciously and deliberately, through proven techniques, and hopefully in a greatly accelerated manner, thereby obviating the necessity of having to come back in different bodies uncounted times to endure the dualities of life and death, pleasure and pain, fulfillment and loss, again and again. For many years long before knowing Jennifer, I had asked myself if I might achieve such liberation in this lifetime, and since her death, and because of it, through my new commitment to the practice of yoga, I had focused on this goal anew while seeking simultaneously to draw ever nearer in consciousness to my daughter.

The questions that remain, which have been touched on or at least implied in my reading with Lazaris, and which cannot be answered definitively at this time, are these. Is this my last time? Can I make it so? Was it Jenny's last lifetime? Did she come back, briefly, to burn off one last megadose of karma? If either of us returns, will it be with the other one, or will one us perhaps be able to look after the other from a higher plane, as I believe Jenny is doing for me now? Or, after I die, will we be able to be united in consciousness and move on from that point, with neither soul having ever to come back, except perhaps by choice, to help other souls?

These and other related questions are some of the most profound that could ever be asked about one's own life and future evolution. And although I did not know the answers to them when I made my journal entry (just as I do not know the answers now), it is clear that I had them in mind. And the deepest desires of my heart, which were tied to those questions, are clearly expressed in that entry, just as they are offered up day after day in my prayers and meditations.

My personal records indicate that, after February 1992, I did not go again to the meetings held either by the Compassionate Friends or Heartfelt. I seem vaguely to recollect having returned to the Compassionate Friends once or twice at most at some point after that, probably at some especially critical time in my emotional life. There certainly have been a few times since then until recently (September 1995), that I have telephoned my friend, Diane Keane, from the Compassionate Friends, sometimes just to say hello and at others, because I felt particularly low. Every time I have called her, I am sure that I have stated, in good faith, that I would appear at the next meeting, but I never did. It probably would have helped me if I had stayed true to my word and gone, but when the nights in question came around, I always found myself too drained to recompose myself after a stressful day at the office and venture out again from the house.

By the end of February 1992, I had been practicing kriya yoga with strict regularity for five months. Although my meditations were often very rocky and powerfully infused with emotion and grief aroused by Jennifer's passing, my efforts were paying off. I had just begun to find a new center within myself that could, with long and faithful application, become permanent. And with the beginnings of this new center had come a clearer sense of purpose and direction—a quest for the realization that could overcome all boundaries, all limitations of time, space, and mind, and carry me to a state of being in which all illusions of separateness from my beloved daughter would disappear forever in the light of pure love and knowledge.

My meditations were divided into two one-hour periods, one in the morning and one in the evening. As this schedule became more established and important, I was not wont to violate it or to rush to complete it in order to go out in the evening. At that time, the benefits of meditation came to outweigh what I gleaned from going to the grief support meetings.

Another factor that played an extremely important role in weaning me from the meetings, and which was tied metaphysically to my meditations, was the strong sense of meaning, purpose, and direction which I had come to feel as a result of my metaphysical readings the previous September and October. The medium and the astrologer had provided me with much valuable and thought-provoking material, but my reading with Lazaris, the entity who channeled through Jach Pursel, gave me a deeply meaningful and powerful new perspective on my relationship with Jenny, not only in this life, but in many past lives, and the purpose of everything that had taken place in her short lifetime during which she had touched my existence in such an incredible way. Put another, simpler way, Lazaris gave me insight into the meaning of Jenny's life and death; and, after all, one of the deepest riddles one can ponder is the meaning of life and death, especially when it touches one in the deeply personal way it had touched me.

To those of us who are left behind, death usually confronts us as a closed door through which we cannot pass until our time has come, and beyond which, except in special cases of revelation, enlightenment, or assistance from an entity like Lazaris, we are unable to see. Death, in that sense, in its aspect as an unyielding barrier between us and our departed loved ones, and any knowledge of their condition and subsequent existence, seems the harshest and the most dictatorial—that it should rob us so brazenly, so cruelly, so permanently of everything that we most cherish.

The loss of Jenny and everything she meant would mold me in many ways, and over the next several years there would be, in addition to my day-by-day awareness of Jenny in my heart and mind, many powerful emotions and experiences, both beautiful and painful, that would be engendered through my undiminished love for Jenny and my longing for her.

Journal Entry: Saturday, March 7, 1992

My love for you never wanes, but grows even stronger, more solid, more unshakable. You are the special gem, the unique and precious jewel in my life. A shining star in my firmament, the purest light in the deep reaches of my universe. Because of my Kriya meditations, I am more resolved, irrevocably, that you and I shall exist together forever in Cosmic Bliss, and I am dedicated to that goal.

On March 15, I was fortunate enough to make the acquaintance of another monk at Self-Realization Fellowship, Brother Brahmananda. I shared some of the details of my life with him (far more briefly than I had done with Anandamoy), including my time with Jenny and my renewed yoga practice, which had become well established. As a result of our conversation, and with his concurrence, I dramatically increased the repetitions of certain advanced pranayama exercises that were an integral part of my meditations (the ones, in fact, I practiced in part with Jenny specifically in mind). With a few occasional variations, I have generally sustained this new level of practice to this day, and it has had an unmistakable and powerful effect on my consciousness and the way I have lived my life. (And, whenever I have an occasion to reflect upon the influence that yogic practice has had over my life during the last four years, I am always reminded that it all came to pass through the influence and guidance of Jenny.) Brother Brahmananda and I became friends, and I continued to see him now and then as time passed.

Films of Jenny, and a Tibetan Lama

On March 30th, I went to All Saint's Children's Center in Pasadena with much emotional difficulty in order to borrow the videotape of Suzanne and Jenny that had been made on Thursday, February 21, 1991, the day before Jenny came home to live with us, in which Suzanne had explained all of Jenny's tubing and dressings. Until the day I borrowed it, I had never actually seen the video, and it was quite a shock, to say the least. I was overcome when I saw Jenny's sweet face and her beautiful, fathomless eyes, when I heard her little voice as she interacted with Suzanne. I kept the video for a few days, just long enough to copy it, and then returned it to All Saints, which was an experience in itself. I had probably been back there only once or twice at most since Jenny's death, because, although I really missed a couple of the staff members, it was unbearably painful to go there. Each time I went back, it was like getting run over by a steam roller. The first time I returned, not too long after Jenny's death, in order to collect her things, I thought I would pass out when I walked in. The beautiful memories of her there, playing, and of dropping her off and picking her up, rushed at me and overcame me with devastating power. The effect of the video, too, was so powerful that, after copying and returning it, I put it away and did not touch it again for three years. The impressions I experienced when I first saw the tape are recorded below.

Journal Entry: Monday, March 30, 1992

Today I got the video of you and Mommy at All Saints Children's Center, which was made in early 1991, and which showed how to change your dressings. I felt awed and consumed by your beauty and purity, and by the attraction which I felt toward your soul. You were still a "baby," then; and I was floored to recall the incredible advancement and changes in you, over the next few months, into a "little girl." Only the mystery, beauty, love, and awe which I found at Lake Geneva in my teens can compare at all with my feelings for you and the power you have over me. And I wept to realize (while watching the video) that I could not step through a warp in space and be with you again, right then, and forever more. Because that is all I wanted; nothing could have held me back from you. How unique and irreplaceable you are! And I hurt because it was like I was watching you through a one-way mirror, and I could not get your attention. You could not know I was there, adoring you, missing you. And you could not come and embrace me with your little arms! God, Jenny, how I miss you, and your incomparable love and magnetism. So I am even more resolved to find you again through Kriya meditation, and to be with you for all time. Every day you shall receive my love and devotion and prayers!

On April 19, I drove over to the west L.A. area to see a remarkable film entitled *The Reincarnation of Khensur Rinpoche.* I had stumbled over this documentary a few days earlier, when Suzanne and I were walking one evening past the Rialto Theater in South Pasadena, one of those rare old movie houses that shows vintage films, foreign films, and, in general, cinematographic works that offer a choice to people who, like myself, will no longer accept having their intelligence and sensibilities insulted by the pig food doled out by all but a few American producers.

A flyer just happened to be on the sidewalk in front of the theater, and I picked it up. On it were descriptions of a number of unusual films currently or soon to be shown in the L.A. area, and *The Reincarnation of Khensur Rinpoche,* which immediately gripped my attention, was being given viewings in a small movie house across town.

The film is an extraordinarily beautiful documentary filmed almost by accident. Briefly, it is the story of a Buddhist monk living at that time (early 1990s) in a monastery in Dharamsala, in northern India, then and now a chief religious and cultural center for Tibetans who have fled the brutal occupation of their country by China. The monk is awaiting the rebirth of his former master, Khensur Rinpoche (a common belief in that tradition), who had recently died at an advanced age. A film crew, which happened to be in the area at that time, on another project, heard the story and subsequently made a documentary of it.

A letter had mysteriously been sent to the monastery that told about the birth of a male child in Tibet who manifested definite signs of being an incarnation of a former lama (Tibetan Buddhist monk). Also, various circumstantial evidence and metaphysical signs, including the child's behavior, oracles, divination, and so on, indicated the strong possibility that the little boy was the reincarnated Khensur Rinpoche. Months passed, and finally, when travel across the border into Tibet became politically possible, the monk from Dharamsala, who originally came out of Tibet years ago as a disciple of Khensur Rinpoche, returned on the pretext of other business to investigate the child described in the letter.

It turned out that the child showed unmistakable signs of former religious lives and identified beyond any doubt many possessions of the former lama. In addition, there seemed to be a strong attraction and sense of recognition between the child and the monk from Dharamsala. The child's parents willingly, although tearfully, agreed that the child should be taken back to Dharamsala and raised in a religious setting. The little boy went willingly, even joyfully, and without regret. After the return to Dharamsala, the monk, now certain and deeply happy that he had found his former master in the body of this child, took on the role of his father and lovingly raised him in the monastic setting.

This film, which I believed I was led to discover, had a powerful effect. I identified with the monk's willingness to raise his mentor after he had returned in the body of a Tibetan boy.

The film made me happy. It reinforced my belief that my bond with Jenny originated in past lives, and that our relationship would continue (I hoped forever) in future incarnations together and eventually in mutual liberation and cosmic consciousness. The film tied in with kriya yoga and my reasons for doing it. But in addition, I became obsessed with the film.

I began to have some strange, irrational doubts. Even though I knew it was a documentary, and that the people filmed were the real characters, I began to question my memory of it. Verifying the authenticity of the film became critical in my mind.

I was not able to see the film a second time, which would have enabled me to procure documentation such as I had seen in the flyer. Necessity mobilized me. The theater that had shown the film was not able to tell me much, and no longer had any printed materials relating to it. I asked the manager to give me the phone number of whatever business owned the theater. Through them, I was able to contact the distributor in New York City who handled the film. The end result was that, to my profound relief, I laid to rest all doubts about the genuineness of the film. But in addition, although I could not actually purchase a video of the film due to certain legalities, I was offered a lifetime lease of it by the distributor for a reasonable amount of money. Thus I have in my video library today a copy of *The Reincarnation of Khensur Rinpoche*.

With the film came some detailed literature that gave me further background about it and the circumstances under which it was made. Also enclosed was a beautiful, eight-by-ten black-and-white photo of the little boy (named Tashi Tsering at birth and renamed Phara Tenzin Khentse by the Dalai Lama upon his acceptance into monastic life) in his Tibetan Buddhist garb, which I had mounted and framed.

Below is a journal entry which I made two days after seeing the film.

Journal Entry: Tuesday, April 21, 1992

Two nights ago, on Sunday, April 19, I saw the film, "The Reincarnation of Khensur Rinpoche." It was no accident. I was led to it, and I "knew" that it would have a powerful message for me. The soul of that little boy was enlightened. He *was* the reincarnation of a Master. And in his beguiling face and eyes, I saw you. I saw you in his beauty, his innocence, his assuredness and authority. Jenny, *you* are a Master, and you gave *me* enlightenment! I felt so much love for that child, that I thought I could never feel for a little boy— and it was the kind of adoration I have for *you,* Jennifer. And I realize *so clearly* that *that* is the love between *kindred souls!* You and little Khensur Rinpoche are the same class of being, the same kind of kindred spirit— enlightened beings! I was so *led* to see that film, destined to see it! And it has brought me joy and peace, and moved me closer to you. And like the Buddhist priest who cared for, longed for, waited for the little boy, I wait for you, no matter the time involved! Our relationship, Jenny, is eternal, and though now you are free of your body, our souls vibrate together and are connected. And in a short span of time you and I will be face to face again. *You* are *my* Khensur Rinpoche, and *I am your devoted servant and protector.*

Although it had been disturbing to watch the videotape of Suzanne and Jenny made at All Saints Children's Center, I realized the importance of having it in my possession. Likewise, I was aware that the pediatric ward at Huntington had several videos of Jennifer filmed during her long residence there. The nurses loaned them to me so I could make copies. However, when I watched them, I was even more stunned than I had been upon seeing the All Saints film.

The episodes filmed were on several tapes. I was able to copy them onto one continuous tape in chronological order, with each vignette identified and dated. The final product was a videotape almost two and a half hours in length, with a total of ten different episodes from April 13, 1989 through February 22, 1991. Since I had not seen Jenny until November 1990, eight out of the ten sequences had been shot before I knew her.

The first episode, filmed ten months after Jenny's birth, was entitled "Jenny's First Feeding." Jenny's right hand and wrist were all taped up, apparently to keep some kind of intravenous line in place. Sue Collins, her child life therapist, was there. The nurses and other medical staff had placed her in a high chair, put a little bib on her, and were attempting to get her interested in eating. Apparently, this was the first time this had been tried since she had come to Huntington, and she had never taken any food by mouth before. First, a little piece of ice is gently rubbed on her arm to let her know that she is being given something cold, and then it is placed in her mouth. Then, attempts are made with various kinds of soft foods. In addition to seeming distracted and a bit overwhelmed by all the people watching her, Jenny cried a couple of times and made some sour faces. She was coaxed into sampling a few things, but only in minute quantities. Finally, one of the nurses got the idea to smear some of the food onto the tip of a pacifier, which Jenny willingly put in her mouth. Thus, Jenny got another few small dabs of nourishment this way, but only as a secondary effect from her being attracted to the pacifier. Later, she was shown lying in bed while getting a diaper change and smiling at the video camera.

What hit me so powerfully was that I was not certain that I would have recognized Jenny if I had not known it was her, given that, like any child, she looked very different at ten months of age than at almost two and a half years (Jenny's age when I first met her). It came to me in a new and potent way that the child whom I had loved so deeply for the last ten months of her life had been a total a stranger to me, and vice versa—she had lived for almost two and a half years without knowing about me and without my love. Because of that, as I sat there in front of the television, I even found myself wondering if she had ever really needed me at all. Perhaps I had not been so important in her life.

I found myself wishing with all my heart that, because our time together during the last part of her life had been so brief, I could have been there for her during those many months at Huntington. Yet I was able to spend the time with her that I had, and I knew that it really had made a big difference in her life.

I was also deeply affected by other segments, but since Jenny was completely recognizable to me, that disturbing unfamiliarity was removed. The second episode, "Jenny Blowing Bubbles, Playing, In Crib," dated March 2, 1990 (a year after the first filming), was just eight months before I first saw her. Again, Sue Collins was present (her voice can be heard), but she was not actually in the shots, which is the same for many of the segments. Much of the footage takes place in the pediatric playroom. Jenny is saying words like "baba" (bubbles) and "mama" (to Sue). She touches the proper parts of her face when Sue calls out, "nose," "eye," "mouth," and so on. She blows kisses, smiles, and makes the most hilariously histrionic, adult-like facial expressions imaginable, a behavioral trait that I often noticed. As in several later sequences, her IV pump starts to beep, which a nurse resets. This piece of footage also has a deeply touching sequence of Jenny in her room, in her playpen. She starts messing around with her colostomy bag, for which Sue scolds her. An enormously pathetic and sad expression immediately comes over Jenny's face, and she starts to cry. Watching that, I was reminded of how extraordinarily sensitive Jenny had been during the time I had known her, both with respect to the nurses at the hospital and later, at home, when it came to receiving even the gentlest of reprimands. I usually tried to be very careful and mild in how I corrected her (which was all that was necessary, anyway), and I was always the world's biggest sucker for her tears and sad eyes.

There is an April 4, 1990, sequence of Jenny playing (with Jello, among other things), coloring, painting, and pushing her IV stand around the halls. She calls all the women "mama." Then, on June 13, 1990, "Jenny's First Real Haircut" (a professional job, performed by someone who came to Huntington). June 25, 1990, features "Jenny's Second Birthday Party" (June 24) in the playroom. Typically (and much like me), Jenny is serious in the crowd of people, but she eventually smiles. There is a large cake, none of which Jennifer eats, and many presents. I was deeply touched by this scene, because many of the beautiful dresses and other pieces of clothing that Jennifer eventually brought home from the hospital were given to her that day, and I recognized them in the video. (She did not outgrow most of them.)

Other shots from July through October 1990 include Jenny giving a doll a "shot" with a plastic syringe, saying "ow," and putting a Band-Aid on the doll's arm. She talks a lot more and responds by saying "two" when asked her age in Spanish. There are many scenes of her painting and playing, and at one point she gets her face up close to the camera and says, "On? Off?" While sitting in a chair, she says "I want down," which touched my heart, because, during the months that I visited her at Huntington and arrived to find her occasionally in her crib, that was always the first thing she would say when I walked into her room. In fact, "I want down" was probably the first phrase that she ever articulated to me. The last shots of Jenny playing were taken on October 24, with Sue Collins present. Sue must have left Huntington right after that to take her new job in Las Vegas, because, when I first started visiting Jenny in early November, Sue was gone. Sue and Jenny were very close, and I have often wondered how Sue's leaving really affected Jenny. I knew that Jenny missed Sue, because she would talk about her after she came home to live with Suzanne and me. Jenny cried, sometimes almost hysterically, whenever Sue called on the telephone, and she would joyously anticipate Sue's occasional visits to our home. And, I will never forget when, one day at Vallejo Villas, Jenny came out with, "I want Sue come my house sit on floor!"

Jenny also appears in a December 27, 1990, sequence (about eight weeks after I had come into her life), one of the pediatric nurses' last day at the hospital. I had been in Bloomington, Illinois, from the twenty-second through the twenty-sixth, visiting my mother for the Christmas holidays, and had just returned to L.A. late on the evening of the twenty-sixth. I came to visit Jenny late in the afternoon on the twenty-seventh, an hour or two after the video sequence had been filmed.

The last portion of the videotape is footage of the joyous going-home party that the pediatric ward gave for Jenny in the playroom (and which spilled out into the hallway) on Friday, February 22, 1991. The love and unselfish support of the nurses and other staff is clearly evident. They were really behind Suzanne, Jenny, and me. I know that they had wished for a very long time that Jenny would find parents. Suzanne and I are in the film, and one scene is of Jenny sitting on Suzanne's lap with her head resting on Suzanne's shoulder. Jenny is wearing her beautiful, dark blue dress with white polka dots. (I have photographs of her, later that afternoon, still in the dress, but standing barefoot in her room at home, looking up at my camera and beaming radiantly. God, what a happy, hectic, wonderful day that was!) At one point during the celebration, Jenny registered surprise when she noticed that she was on television! Someone had found the videotape of her second birthday party (eight months earlier), and was playing it on the VCR in the playroom.

I was able to get a very poignant, sometimes disturbing, sense of Jenny's history and her life at Huntington. When watching this footage, I noticed how many people were in Jenny's life, how many caretakers and role models, how many "mommies" (both male and female). In one sense, this was wonderful, because it meant that so many nurses and other staff members at Huntington gave Jenny their time, attention, and love; and this was a very significant factor in why Jenny developed as remarkably as she did. Yet despite all the attention and Jenny definitely having her favorite people (like Sue Collins, Carol Taylor, and Cindy Thelander), there was something in her face and eyes and whole demeanor that seemed to say, "I need *a* mommy and *a* daddy. I need two parents who will pay attention to me and love me not just for eight or nine hours a day, five days a week, but every minute of my life. I need a home. I need a mother and father who will give me their complete devotion and unconditional love."

All the sorrow I have felt since Jenny's death is redeemed for me in the knowledge that Suzanne and I were given the opportunity to offer Jenny that love and security. That was a priceless gift, one that can never be taken away. My heart is profoundly soothed and compensated by this knowledge. When Jennifer came home to live with Suzanne and me, she blossomed like a beautiful flower. Over a few months, she was transformed into a radiant little girl. I am eternally thankful that we were able to give her that.

A few days after finishing the tape, I put it away. Much time would have to pass before I would feel ready, emotionally, to see it once more. I would, in fact, watch it again only after three and a half years, when I would turn to it in the process of writing this book.

A Fast, an Initiation, Dreams, and a Bonding

On April 28, the day I borrowed the tapes, I began a fast that I continued until May 6, when I drank only liquids, consisting of water, fresh fruit juices, vegetable broth, and herb tea. I made such fasts once every two or three years to rejuvenate my mind and body. This particular fast, which I was able to accomplish only by making a promise to Jenny that I would complete it, was done at that time because I had decided to attend a kriya yoga group initiation at the Self-Realization Fellowship on May 9, and I felt that cleansing myself beforehand would increase the benefits derived from the ceremony. I clearly remember this fasting period because it coincided with the devastating civil unrest that took place in Los Angeles that summer as the result of the infamous Rodney King incident, one manifestation of which was extensive burning and looting across the city. During the time that the fires were burning, even though none of them were anywhere near where we lived, I had to keep all the windows in the house tightly shut to keep out tiny bits of ash and the strong smell of smoke. The event at SRF had originally been planned for a couple of weeks earlier and was rescheduled because of the volatile situation in L.A.

The kriya initiation ceremony was held in the evening at the Mother Center, a sizeable estate owned by the organization and located in an area of Los Angeles known as Mount Washington. From the grounds, situated atop some great hills, and upon which were located an administration center and the residences for the monks, one could look far south across much of the city. Although the ceremony was not mandatory, since the advanced techniques taught that night were also passed on through the printed lessons, I decided to attend as a result of my desire to commemorate my return to meditation.

I drove to the Mother Center and walked in carrying my offerings of fresh fruit and flowers. A hundred people were there that evening. We went together into the room where the ceremony was to be held. During the whole time I was there, I held Jenny close in my heart, and when we were given the opportunity to ask in prayer for something we deeply desired, I voiced inwardly my supreme wish that Jenny's soul and mine should be bonded in love, as one, for all time. After going to bed, I had a dream that was a direct result of the yoga ceremony. It is described in the following journal entry.

Journal Entry: Monday, May 11, 1992 (I think you've shown up in other dreams, as an older girl.)

I must record the two strange dreams that I've had lately. One was several days ago. In the dream, I had some special shoes. When I wore them, I could fly. I remember walking up some stairs in a house in the dream to "launch" myself from a second-story window, but waking previous to the attempt. There was an unidentified girl in the dream, very much in the background of it all, but whom I seemed to love a lot. She was perhaps a teenager. She had short, black hair like yours.

On Saturday, May 9, 1992, two nights ago, I went to Kriya initiation at SRF Mother Center in Los Angeles. During the ceremony, I was told to make one wish. That wish, of course, was that your soul and mine should be *One,* with God, *now* and *forever.* And when I offered my fruits, as a symbol of bad karma to be burned, I held you in mind as well. (I was the apple, you were the mango, and the two of us together were the banana.) I was very psychically and spiritually attuned to you.

That night I had the second dream. I was back in Louisville, selling cars at Brown Brothers Cadillac. I was so shocked to realize I had come "full circle," so to speak. In the dream, I even recalled the similar previous dreams, but thought, "Now it's really happened, and I've left California." But despite everything, it all didn't seem too bad. There was a sales manager there, but I was the *only* salesman in the building or on the lot! A customer(s) arrived on the lot, and I rushed out to claim them. It was a beautiful *young* woman with *long,* straight black hair. (Hispanic? Maybe.) She was *very* physical and loving toward me, but not flirtatious or sexual. I was overwhelmed at her affection, her openness, her boldness, her lack of pretense or inhibition. At one point, she drew very close, on the right side of me, putting her left arm around my waist, hugging me close, overflowing with joy and affection. She placed the side of her face against mine, and I felt her skin and her hair. Her hair smelled *wonderful!* It was the *only* experience of my forty-two-plus years *of smelling anything* in a dream! And this was *overwhelming!*

I *know* that this was your soul contacting mine through this dream! (as, I believe, in the other dream, and possibly in earlier ones also). I was the *only* salesman, the *only* one for you—chosen for you, and you for me! And I used to smell *your* wonderful hair that way! And, you approached me from the *right* side. I *always* held you on my *right* hip, your face close to mine! And your *love* was *always* so *open,* so unrestrained, so uninhibited! Perhaps for contrast your wonderful soul came to me in the most barren of settings; perhaps you came to me in Louisville because your body is buried near there. This dream occurred *exactly* nine months after your passing (August 9, 1991-May 9, 1992)! Almost like a gestation and rebirth! I *know* that your soul is reaching out and touching mine in these dreams! All the clues add up, like a puzzle! I *know* it was *you,* Jenny! The fact that you are older in these dreams makes me even more certain that it really *is* you, because if I merely were dreaming *about* you, you would, I feel, appear in your three-year-old form. I feel *rejuvenated* through the touching of our souls on this deep level! I am *always* here for you! Come to me *always!*

On Sunday, May 17, Suzanne and I drove to Malibu to visit the Pivarals, and especially Jessica Christina, who was seven months old. As far as I can remember, we had not seen them since Jessica's baptism the previous December. I had not felt a strong connection with Jessica Christina when I first saw her. And, that feeling had remained pretty much the same at Thanksgiving and during her December baptism. As the ensuing months passed, I thought about Jessica and her family, but there was no sense of growing emotional attachment on my part. Naturally, I cared about Jessica. However, until then, the freshness of my grief for Jenny was such that it would have been difficult for me to feel much of a connection with anyone or anything else.

Thus, to my great surprise, when Suzanne and I went to Malibu on May 17, I fell in love with Jessica as soon as I laid eyes on her. It was that simple and that quick. I cannot explain it, so I can say only that, whatever the reason, it was time for it to happen. That afternoon, my heart opened to her, and I loved her from that time on. The following weekend, May 23 and 24, Jessica spent the weekend with Suzanne and me in our home. We drove out to Malibu and picked her up on Saturday and returned her Sunday afternoon. Obviously, Graciela had a great deal of trust in us, because Suzanne and I were the only people to whom she was willing to entrust the baby. That was almost three and a half years ago. Since that time,

Jessica has come to visit at Vallejo Villas regularly, every third or fourth weekend, and Suzanne and I have made trips to Malibu to see her. Jessica Christina Pivaral came to be an integral and deeply meaningful part of our lives.

Sebastian Dies

On Monday, June 15, 1992, I had Sebastian, my beautiful Manx cat, put to sleep. I had acquired him when he was nine months old, on April 17, 1988. He was a beautiful cat—with long, snow-white fur, lovely blue eyes, and the most loving, loyal heart imaginable. He followed me about the house like a dog, but he was extremely intelligent and his personality was remarkably human. He quickly figured out things that Sarada, my other cat, never had, such as how to open cupboards and sliding doors. He had been an indoor-outdoor cat, but when I got him, I had him neutered and his front claws removed. Thus he became strictly an indoor animal.

I had heard about Sebastian from a friend at work who acted as a kind of liaison between people who wanted to get rid of pets and those who would accept them, and she put me in touch with the young woman who owned him. Taking Sebastian was like taking Jenny. I made the decision without seeing him; somehow, I felt he was meant for me. I think that the woman giving him away probably misled me about him; that is, she did not make me aware of certain problematic habits of his, although that seems irrelevant now, since I probably would have taken him anyway. He was so adorable and looked just like a big, white bunny hopping around, with his large hind legs and short tail.

However, I was shocked to discover one day that he had been urinating for some time on the back of the cushion of my easy chair. I cleaned the chair up, but only with effort. Then I noticed he was urinating on the carpet. We were renting an apartment, and since we were moving, I did not get too upset and hoped that a new environment would cure the problem.

After Suzanne, the two cats, and I moved into our condominium at Vallejo Villas, Sebastian's problem continued despite the change of scene and two litter boxes. I constantly checked about the house, smelling for urine and using every product I could find to clean and deodorize the rugs, and spraying the areas to discourage him from further transgressions. Nothing worked. Suzanne was also concerned and wondered how long I was going to put up with the problem. I could not give the cat to anyone else, for his own sake.

In time, the issue became more complicated because Sebastian began having sporadic bouts with feline urological syndrome (FUS), a common condition in male cats in which protein plugs form in the bladder because the urine gets too alkaline. The ureter becomes blocked, urination is impossible, and the animal develops a great deal of pain. The situation must be addressed immediately by a veterinarian or the pet will die. During the four years I had him, I took Sebastian to the emergency room at the vet many times, sometimes in the middle of the night, to have him sedated, catheterized, and observed. Then I would take him home until the next bout, perhaps three months later, perhaps considerably longer. In the meantime, I had Sebastian (and Sarada, the other cat) on special, high-ash diets to keep their urine more acidic, and I continued to patrol the house incessantly,

Sebastian's problems worsened. I was at my wit's end and Suzanne had lost all patience. Finally, in spring 1992, several months after Jenny's death, I telephoned a San Diego veterinarian specializing in animal behavior and paid a hefty fee to obtain advice on what I could do for Sebastian. As a result, I began experimenting with a number of litter boxes filled with different types of litter in different locations. However, every time I dared to think I had found an answer, Sebastian would destroy my hopes by urinating on something else, sometimes right in front of me, as nonchalantly as one could imagine. He obviously did not understand that there was a problem. In fact, sometimes in that past I had become furious, scolding him harshly or even swatting him with a towel, but I abandoned such methods because I saw clearly that nothing was gained and the poor animal just could not make the connection between the behavior and the punishment. The behaviorist also confirmed that such methods would prove fruitless.

Finally, the behaviorist recommended that I restrict Sebastian to one room for a number of days, giving him access to only one litter box at a time and experimenting with various kinds of sand. I had to keep him in one of the bathrooms, since they were the only uncarpeted areas in the house. Frankly, he did not seem to mind being shut in. There was plenty of light and fresh air, and he appeared quite content when I came home after work and let him out. However, it was possible that the experiments would have to be continued for a long time before anything conclusive—positive or negative—could be determined, and in the meantime, the poor cat had to be confined almost exclusively to one bathroom. I began to feel more desperate and agonized about the situation.

Then, the morning of Monday, June 15, 1992, while Sebastian was still undergoing his confinement in my bathroom, I detected from his behavior that his ureter was blocked again. As usual, there was some perceived crisis at my office which necessitated my going straight to work, so I asked Suzanne to take Sebastian to our vet. As I started to walk up the stairs to leave for work, I turned around. Sebastian was reclining on the floor in Jenny's room, near my meditation cushion. As I looked at him, a part of me I had never consciously acknowledged knew that it was the last time I would see him alive. I knew it, and yet I did not feel it; something prevented me from acknowledging the thought, and I left for work.

Later that morning, Suzanne called from the vet's office. He had been taking care of our cats for years, so he was well aware of Sebastian's problems, both the urinating and the FUS. Suzanne said his advice was that we have Sebastian put to sleep. I said no at first, but then I began to feel uncertain. I trusted our vet's opinion. He was one of the best we had known, and he loved animals very much. I told Suzanne to put him on the phone. He explained to me very kindly that, in addition to the strong possibility that we would never find the answer to Sebastian's behavior disorder, he would most likely continue to have FUS—since nothing we had done seemed to help—and that it would make his life miserable. Of course, we could have him unblocked and wait for the next time, but the vet believed the problem would become more frequent.

I sat at my desk in a terrible quandary. For the first time in my life, I allowed other factors besides the animal's own welfare to influence me. My own vexations and frustrations from the years of problems, the fear of having our home destroyed by cat urine, and the mounting expenses were taking their toll. If those had been the only issues, I know that I would have told the vet to save Sebastian and give him another chance. But now, I was being told that I was just setting him up for more suffering. Should I act, or should I give Sebastian another chance?

I told the vet to be absolutely truthful; I did not want an easy way out. Did he really believe in his heart that putting Sebastian to sleep was the best thing? He said yes. Then, as odd or perhaps as illogical as it may sound, after he had assured me that he could simply put Sebastian to sleep painlessly by injection, I asked him a question that could decide the issue for me. I said to him, "Can I have his body? I want to bury him myself." The vet said that this would not be a problem.

Years earlier, in Kentucky, one of my deeply loved cats got cancer and had to be put to sleep. Even though I was in living in L.A. by then, Suzanne, who was still in Kentucky, could have arranged to bury her. However, the vet there had said that the law required that he dispose of the body. That had disturbed me, but I had had no choice. Kitty was terribly sick.

Suzanne had told the vet about Jenny's recent death, and that, especially on top of that, this was an agonizing decision for me. He waited patiently for my answer. Finally, feeling rotten, I said, "All right, then. Put him to sleep. I will come after work and get his body." Tears came to my eyes. I hung up the phone and sobbed. The minutes passed, and I felt troubled and unsure about my decision. Impulsively, I telephoned the Self-Realization Fellowship and was able to get hold of Brother Anandamoy. We talked for several minutes, and after explaining the situation with Sebastian, he made a number of observations and ended by assuring me that I should not feel troubled about my decision. We said goodbye.

After hanging up, I was still troubled. Finally, I decided Sebastian should have another chance. I felt great relief. I had made a decision I could best live with. Sebastian trusted me; I could not fail him. In a great hurry, I dialed the vet, but I was too late. Sebastian had just been put to sleep. With terrible sadness and regret, I put down the phone. I felt a deep, wrenching guilt. I felt like shit. I had let him down—something I thought I could never do. It was a bright, clear day, but for me, it was dark and grim. I cried a great deal.

After work, I went to the veterinary clinic. I was ushered into a room in the back, where I sat and waited. The lady from the front desk came in carrying the large wicker basket that we used to transport our cats. I opened the lid. Inside was

Sebastian's body, wrapped in newspapers. I did not look at it, but picked up the basket, went to my car, and drove home.

I changed clothes, took a shovel and the wicker basket, and climbed the high hill behind our home. From its broad, level top, I could see the mountains to the north, Long Beach and the distant ocean to the south. The hilltop was very quiet. No one climbed there, and it was wild, with scattered trees, patches of shrubbery and tall grass, and a few flowers.

After looking around for several minutes, I selected a suitable spot, fairly secluded and near some trees, and began to dig. The ground was very hard lime-stone and rocky dirt and my shovel had a flat blade. It was very tough going. I worked for a long time, sweating and growing short of breath. There was a faint taste of blood in my mouth. The more I dug, and the more unyielding the ground became, the more emotion I felt. As I dug, striking the ground with all the force I could muster, I sobbed, almost gasping for air. Finally, the hole was deep enough, and I collapsed onto the hard ground. I removed the lid from the basket and looked inside. Carefully, I lifted out the newspapers and unwrapped them.

When I saw Sebastian, I was completely overcome and cried pathetically. I had never seen him look more beautiful. His face showed an extraordinary peace. His white fur glowed in the late afternoon sunlight. There was a tiny drop of blood at the edge of one nostril. Otherwise, one would have thought that he was simply asleep. After I was able to get myself under control, I kissed him, laid his body very gently in the bottom of the hole I had dug, and after taking a last, long look at him, I carefully covered him with dirt, using my hands, until the hole was filled in. Then, still sobbing, I tamped down the soil and raked in the remaining dirt and stones with the shovel. When the grave was flat and completely unnoticeable, I camouflaged it further with loose rock and brush. No one would ever know it was there or disturb it, and it was deep enough that coyotes would not detect it.

I did a little kriya meditation for Sebastian, and finally left only with deep reluctance. In my heart I did not feel I had done the right thing. Years have passed, but it has always troubled me. The consequences of my decision were irrevoca-ble, and I have had to live with them, no matter how disturbing.

The sentiments which I felt afterward were captured in an entry in Jenny's journal which I made the following day:

Journal Entry: Tuesday, June 16, 1992

Yesterday (Monday, June 15, 1992), in the late afternoon, I buried Sebastian on top of the hill behind our home. He looked so beautiful and at peace! Some-thing in his quiet, show-white form, so regal and dignified! He was so loyal to me! Now I realize how very, very much I loved him! I hate death! It is cruel, brutal, irrevocable. And yet I wonder, and sense that there is great wisdom behind the force that brings death. Tonight I returned to the hilltop to check Sebastian's grave, and sat and sobbed and wept and talked to him. It was so hard to dig his little grave in those hard rocks, but I dug as deeply as I could, then laid him in gently, after kissing him, and covered him carefully, all the while sobbing and feeling like I would faint. I could taste blood after the exertion of digging his grave. As I sat tonight, talking to him, I felt that the hilltop was lonely—and yet, so very peaceful and beautiful, with the sky and grass and birds—and that somehow it would appeal to him. I filled in his grave carefully yesterday, then leveled it off and covered it with many branches and leaves to hide it from people and animals. I will check on him often.

As I sat there, imploring his understanding, forgiveness, and love, many thoughts came to me. (I must tell you that the grief I have felt was, it seems, as intense as my grief when you died, Jenny.) My thoughts were directed to realize how his life paralleled yours—how I committed to you both and took you into my heart sight unseen! You were both meant for me, destined for me. I see it clearly now. But God, what agony when the bodies that house those dear souls die and we are left behind in this lonely, deeply troubled world! You were both sick. And when you both died, it seems that, although on one level I sensed what was happening, yet on another level Death numbed me, dulled me, made me stupid, perhaps so that I would not interfere with the passing of the soul. I have, in both your cases, asked myself if I did enough, chastised myself for each incident of frustration and impatience. I only hope that the love I have for you both far outweighs my moments of weakness.

Sebastian was always so quiet and unobtrusive, but his absence is so painfully felt. I was so anguished on the hilltop tonight! How I wanted him back! How I agonized to reverse time and events! Because I had called the Vet back to say I had changed my mind about having him put to sleep—but it was too late! Time had run out! I just pray with all my soul that what happened, how it all worked out, was right. But I remain troubled. I will pray for Sebastian in my Kriya meditations as I have continually prayed for you. I did Kriya last night on the hilltop for Sebastian after I buried him. How wretched I feel inside! I accuse myself and wonder if I should have tried to get Sebastian fixed up, if I should have continued the fight. I gave in, and I blame myself for it. I pray that, in my ignorance and humanity and imperfection, the right thing was done for him. I remember how I questioned myself as a father for months after the night I lost you! I love you both so very much! How terribly I miss you both! Jenny, I really love Jessica Christina. Can you make her a real part of my life? I pray to you, Jenny, for love and healing, and protection in all things. Please intercede for Sebastian, also, and convey to him my love in an absolute and unmistakable way! Love him! Love me!

Sebastian, like Jenny, was a special soul. I remember him each day in my meditations, along with the other beloved souls, both human and nonhuman, who have passed through my life. I would be very grateful for the opportunity to serve Sebastian again one day in such a way that would leave me with a clearer conscience than I have had to live with this time.

Father's Day, and a Birthday

Journal Entry: Sunday, June 21, 1992, Father's Day, A Note from Suzanne

From Heaven…
To My Daddy.

God our Father, in your wisdom and love you made all things. Bless my Daddy. Let the example of his love shine forth. Grant that all his family, friends, and coworkers may honor him always with a spirit of profound respect.

> I love you always, Daddy.

> Jenny

Journal Entry: Tuesday, June 23, 1992

Tomorrow, Wednesday, June 24, 1992, is your fourth birthday, Jenny. If you were here, you would be so much taller, and I know you would be talking so much! This is a hard, lonely world. What with Sebastian's death (Monday, June 15, 1992), the terrible work environment in my office (you always used to ask me to hang your drawings and paintings in my office—and I did), and our car wreck on Father's Day (Sunday, June 21, 1992), life has really been the pits. I hope that at least you are so very happy—on vacation—where you are. And I hope you are loving me all the time and praying for me! I will be thinking of you all day tomorrow. I am thinking about all the beautiful presents I would have bought you, and the party we would have had. Can you not come and appear to me, and bless me, on your birthday? I will put some pretty flowers ("fowers") in your room tonight. I hope we are together soon, and never separate again. The love I feel for you is like no other, Jennifer. Happy birthday, my precious baby, my little angel! (Tears are coming now.) I *love* you!

I also had a birthday card for Jennifer the next day, her birthday.

Rosa

On July 11, I went to Malibu to pick up Jessica (then nine months old) for the weekend. When I got there, Nancy was on the telephone with Rosa, who was still in prison in Chowchilla, California. Nancy handed me the phone, and Rosa and I talked for several minutes. It was the first time that I had ever had any personal contact with her, and thereafter we would communicate by letter and by telephone for several months. As time passed, it would become apparent to me how lonely Rosa was in jail, and how much she missed her family. It was difficult to be of much help, but I always answered her letters faithfully and encouraged her to call us collect whenever she felt like talking, so she would have someone on the outside besides her family with whom she could communicate and express her feelings.

Journal Entry: July 15, 1992, Letter from Rosa Pivaral, written July 11, 1992, from a state prison for women, Chowchilla, California

Dear Gerald and Suzanne,

Hi, how are you doing? As for me, I'm doing O.K. It could be better if I was out, but in time I'll be home. I just want to say thank you for everything that you did for Jennifer. I know that you guys loved her a lot. I don't really want to talk about that because I also loved her, but God knows why that happened to my little girl. I'm very happy that you guys are the godparents of my daughter, Jessica. I really appreciate all that you've done for my girls. When I go to church, I pray for you guys all the time.

I would like for you guys to write to me if it is possible. I'm sending you two forms. They're for visiting. You have to fill them out and then send them back as soon as possible, so that you'll be able to come and visit me when my mom comes. I want you guys to send me some pictures when you have a chance. I'll be waiting for your letter, and may God bless you guys.

Love always,

Rosa

Journal Entry: July 17, 1992, Letter to Rosa Pivaral

Dear Rosa,

I received your letter and the two visitors applications on July 15. I filled out the applications for Suzanne and myself, and mailed them back on July 16. Please let us know if everything goes O.K. with them. I was very happy to hear from you. Please write as often as you wish, or call *collect.*

I want you to know that Jennifer was the greatest gift ever to come into my life. I loved her, and love her still, with an intensity beyond description. When I die, the first thing I want to see is Jenny, waiting for me. For me, her death was a terrible blow, but she has changed my life and shown me what *real* love is. She is in my heart and mind most of every day, and she is always at the center of my morning and evening meditations. Although Jenny had a lot of medical problems, I would not have traded her for anyone or anything in the world. I think of myself always as her father, and of her as my *true* daughter. Someday there are *many* things I want you to know about that beautiful, precious child. Life has seemed *very empty* without her, with one exception—Jessica. We love her very much. She gives me *so much happiness* when she comes to visit! Loving her really helps heal the pain. Of course we think very much of Graciela, Maria, and Nancy, and really enjoy getting together with your family. We are looking forward to visiting you soon. Jenny and Jessica are alike in many ways: both *very* smart, *very* beautiful, with similar mannerisms. I will be thinking of you often.

With love,

Gerald

On July 29, 1992, Suzanne and I received another letter from Rosa Pivaral, written from prison. Having realized that I understood Spanish pretty well, Rosa wrote this and all subsequent letters to us in Spanish, which was fine with me, although my letters to her continued to be in English. Rosa and I continued to write to each other fairly often until her final letter to me of September 26, 1992, which I received on October 1. She also telephoned us collect from time to time. Although Suzanne and I had planned on going to Chowchilla with Rosa's mother, Graciela, to visit her, it never worked out. At one point during our communications with Rosa, she became quite upset and angry because she felt that we were trying to steal Jessica from her. This was totally untrue, but I understood Rosa's anxiety and frustration, being confined to jail, and having no control over her own life or her daughter's. Rosa quickly got over this anxiety, but her emotional states seemed to fluctuate significantly, and after her initial flare-up with us she never encouraged us to come to visit her.

I sent Rosa a little money from time to time, so that she could buy a few things that would otherwise be unavailable. Rosa was generally appreciative of our interest and love for Jessica and Jenny. Rosa often expressed deep sadness and regret about Jennifer's death. She wanted to be the mother for Jessica that she had never been for Jennifer. Rosa was very unhappy that, on her twenty-fourth birthday, August 24, she could not be with her family. She had been in prison for fifteen months and was expecting to be released in three months. Rosa hoped that, upon her release, they could be reunited. I had some indication that her hope was in vain, since her family said that she might be deported to Guatemala, her home country, as a result of her multiple drug convictions.

In my August 1, 1992, letter to her, I asked Rosa if she would be coming to Los Angeles after her release from prison, or if she would be forced to return to Guatemala. As tactfully as possible, I told Rosa that, if she wished, Suzanne and I would raise Jessica—that we would love to. Despite my assertions that this was only an offer and that I sincerely respected the fact that she was Jessica's real mother, this was the match that ignited Rosa's anger toward Suzanne and me. Later, I was able to understand how terribly threatening my words must have been. I came to know that Graciela, Rosa's mother, who had legal guardianship of Jessica, would never let Rosa raise Jessica except under her close supervision and if Rosa stayed clean of drugs.

In a subsequent letter, Rosa responded vehemently that she intended to raise Jessica, that she would find a good man to take care of her and her daughter, and that my words had hurt her very much. However, in the same letter, she apologized for her tone, admitting her strong anxiety and distress. Her following letters were much more optimistic. In her last letter to us, Rosa sent a photo. Happy that she would be released within sixty days, although she did not know where she was going, she said again how much she looked forward to being with her daughter and family and to meeting Suzanne and me.

The First Anniversary

Sunday, August 9, 1992, was the first anniversary of Jenny's passing. Suzanne was away on a retreat at Gethsemani, and I was alone. The stage was set in a manner ironically similar to the previous year when Jenny had died. I was not afraid of being by myself; in fact, I had been anticipating the anniversary, in a way. Somehow, during the emotional buildup I had been experiencing for a week, I had grown to believe that, in some manner I could not say, something meaningful would happen. My expectations rose daily. But when the day arrived, I found, with much heartache and disappointment, that the only experience to offer itself was one of being alone, physically and spiritually. At home alone, I looked around the condo. It was empty and dead. There was nothing but walls, and carpeting, and furniture. No beautiful spiritual presence; no great revelation or feeling of oneness with Jenny. I could not feel her.

Late in the afternoon, I called Diane Keane from the Compassionate Friends, whom I had not seen in several months. In tears, I told her what had happened, and how empty and disappointed I felt. For whatever reason, it was just not a time to be uplifted. Once again, the stark reality that Jenny was gone had knocked the wind out of me.

Dreams, and a Strange Occurrence

Journal Entry: Saturday, September 26, 1992, 5:30 A.M. (I awake)

Dream!

- Gerald and Suzanne where?
- My not knowing about Jenny.
- *Pajama bottoms I am wearing.*
- *Finding girl (SCA?).*
- Suzanne and Gerald talk.
- Jenny still in *white, one-story house in Champaign-Urbana? (near Johnstons?)*
- Suzanne: Jenny dead (my denial).
- Suzanne: *Her bones burned.*
- My recollection of (and horror of forgetting) her death: June 11 (?!).

- After I awake, I feel like Jennifer has been in bedroom with Suzanne and me.
- Hear bedroom door creak?
- Old feeling like 3:35 a.m. awakenings.

Since Jenny's death, I have had dreams about her that I have not recorded in the Journal. However, of the dream entries included in the Journal, the one above is the only one that does not relate the dream in a narrative style. I only recorded it in outline form at the time, given the early hour of the morning. Later, I entered only the outline in the Journal. This particular dream was so disturbing that I could not bring myself to articulate all of the details. As I look at the notes now, some of the references are vague to me. However, I now narrate the dream as best as I can remember it, almost three years later.

In the dream, Suzanne and I were in a house somewhere, apparently in Champaign, Illinois, where, in real life, I had gone to college and worked from fall 1967 through spring 1976. In real life, I did not even meet Suzanne until 1980. Regarding the dream, I cannot remember if we were living in the house or just staying there temporarily. The scene took place in the morning; apparently, I had just recently gotten out of bed. It was strange that I was wearing pajama bottoms in the dream, because in real life I preferred to sleep in underwear and a T-shirt.

SCA was Suzanne's brother's engineering firm—Schimpeler Corradino Associates. I have a vague memory of recognizing some female friend in the office there; I cannot understand how that scene fit into the rest of the dream.

In the dream, I was looking for Jenny and could not find her. Then Suzanne and I were sitting at a breakfast table in a nook. I then thought that Jenny might still be at the white, one-story house in Champaign, mentioned above. In reality, this house was next to the Johnston's home, the residence of a university professor and his family where I had lived after my graduate study at the University of Illinois. I was never in the neighboring, white, one-story house and have no idea who lived there; however, I always liked that house. (This dream seems to be filled with disparate, unexplainable elements jumbled together illogically from many periods of my life. Although I am usually skilled at deciphering the unique logic and symbolism of the subconscious, many of the elements in this dream remain a mystery to me.)

While Suzanne and I sat at the breakfast table, I asked about Jenny.

Suzanne looked at me in shock and said, "Don't you remember? Jenny died!"

I seemed not to understand or remember this happening and even denied it. Then Suzanne said something that is indelibly imprinted in my memory, but which haunts me because I have never been able to decipher its meaning.

With deep emphasis, as if to jog my memory, Suzanne said, "Don't you remember? *Her bones burned!*" This statement caused me to be flooded with the realization that Jenny had indeed died. I was bewildered and horrified that I had forgotten! Then I recalled that she had died on June 11. (I have asked myself why June 11, which is wrong. Jenny died on August 9, 1991.)

I awoke feeling that Jennifer had been in the bedroom with us. Also, I had apparently heard the bedroom door creak, or thought that I had heard it creak, which reinforced the eerie feeling of Jenny's presence. I had that old feeling I used to get so many mornings the first few weeks after Jenny's death, when I would awaken at 3:35 A.M. with the odd feeling that she had been in the bedroom.

What puzzles me the most is the import and the cryptic nature of Suzanne's comment to me, "Her bones burned!" The symbolism has eluded me to this day! Months later, I had another odd dream in which Jennifer's body was going to be cremated. I recall a disturbing and bizarre scene of bodies on what appeared to be little railroad cars lined up on tracks that led to some kind of incinerator. Suzanne and I never discussed the idea of cremating Jenny. The dream left me quite shaken, and I felt troubled by it for some time.

Journal Entry: Thursday, November 26, 1992, Thanksgiving

Jenny, when I got out of the shower this morning, the cardboard dresser (one of three) in the *corner* (of your room) was overturned, and the animals on the floor! Did you do it? I am recalling about three weeks ago when I found the sock drawer to that same dresser pulled open! And today, Suzanne said that last night she heard a strange but friendly sound in the kitchen, and rapid breathing near her as she lay on the living room sofa. I'm also recalling several months ago when the rocking chair in your room creaked and squeaked so loudly during a couple of my meditations (same area of the room!). Suzanne has mentioned other signs, like the time she said you swung our bedroom door shut and open. I also recall the tiny, subtle lights floating near the ceiling of your room a few days after you died (and lights many other times). And not too long ago, Suzanne swears that you rushed past her down the stairs and into your room where I was meditating. Jenny, please give me a sign before my very eyes, even if it scares me, so that I can know absolutely that it's really you! I *love* you!

On November 30, 1992, Rosa was deported to Guatemala directly from the state facility to which she had been transferred after the completion of her prison term. I felt deeply sorry her—a person who had no control over her own life, a mother separated from her daughter, her mother, and her sisters. I must admit, however, that I also felt relief that Rosa was out of the picture, that the turmoil of her life would not impinge upon Jessica's life, and that she would not be able to come between Jessica and me. Some of my feelings were selfish, but that is how I felt.

A Desecration

In early January 1993, I had to dismantle Jenny's room. It was one of the darkest and saddest days since her death, and I felt so utterly rotten about it that I made no record anywhere as to the exact date. The reason that I know for certain that this event took place during the first few days of the year is that, in an entry in Jenny's journal, dated Wednesday, January 13, 1993, I make reference to "my having had to rearrange the house a week ago (to put our cars inside to protect them), take down your crib, and pack away many of your things."

The hill we lived on had always been a prime target for car theft and vandalism. Gangs from nearby El Sereno and other social parasites considered our hill their territory, and hardly a day passed when someone's car was not damaged or stolen unless it was parked in a private garage. Since parking outdoors was a risk during the evening hours, Suzanne and I were lucky to have escaped harm as long as we did, considering that we had been parking out-of-doors ever since preparing Jenny's room for her a couple of years earlier. Suzanne and I had the option of parking in certain outdoor areas within our complex, but only at night, and if the spaces were already filled, our only option was the street. Sometimes, at dark, I would go out and pull our cars into the complex if there were open spaces, but even that was not without risk. Prior to January 1993, Suzanne had in fact had a couple of tires on her car punctured by vandals one night as it sat on the street right at the entrance to our complex.

One morning, I went outside about 7:30, walked down the driveway of our complex, and crossed the street to go to where my car was parked and drive to work. I unlocked the door of my car and got in. Something seemed odd, but at first I could not figure out what it was. Then I noticed a cigarette butt on the floor and small pieces of metal on the passenger seat. At first, I thought I had forgotten to lock the car the previous night (something unheard of for me), and that some idiot had climbed inside of it to have a smoke and mess around. Vowing that I would never make that mistake again, I reached down to put my key in the ignition only to discover that it had been drilled or punched out. Someone had tried to steal my car. Why they were unable to, I will never know. Perhaps they bungled the job or were scared away. I got out and walked around to the passenger side. The door had been pried away from the frame with a crowbar, and that is how the would-be thief got in. Later, he had unlocked the driver's door to make his exit.

The car was not driveable, and it took time to repair, causing us considerable inconvenience. In addition, our concern about the safety of our cars had escalated into alarm. Suzanne also told me about some friends of hers who, like us, had a Volvo (we both had older model Volvos), which they had parked in a residential neighborhood while at a party. It had disappeared when they returned several hours later. Volvo parts—particularly from older models—were a prime target of car theft rings in Los Angeles. We painfully decided we would have to dismantle

Jenny's room, pack her things away, bring all of my furniture from the garage back into her room, and park our cars inside.

Thus I set about one of the most painful tasks I had undertaken since Jenny's death. Suzanne was gone for the day, so I worked alone. I began with the most difficult and heartbreaking thing—taking Jenny's crib apart. I got my tools and, like much of what I did that day, performed the job as quickly as I could—almost frantically, to keep my mind and hands so busy I could not think, or allow the terrible sickness I felt inside to overcome me. I felt that, if I were to pause in my work or even slacken my nearly hectic pace, I would go to pieces.

Physically, I was very careful about how I did things, but inwardly, I felt almost violent. I was ripped apart emotionally and angry that I had to destroy my daughter's beautiful room solely because I had to protect my property from the assholes who preyed upon hard-working people like myself. I had no plans for altering Jenny's room, and although I might have done so in the future, I had no way of knowing that at the time. If there had been plenty of space, I would have left Jenny's room untouched. And I liked having the extra living space in the garage. Rearranging everything would make us rather cramped.

After taking Jenny's beautiful bright red crib apart, I tied its parts together securely. I carried it upstairs, along with the mattress, and returned to finish the job. In order to get my furniture from the garage (except the empty terrariums, which would remain there) back inside, I had to take all Jenny's things out of her room except one set of shelves containing various toys, games, cassette tapes, and so on. I also kept out a few of her favorite dolls (especially Raggedy Ann and Ernie) and stuffed animals, which could be set on the back of the sofa bed and would remain in the room. The rest had to be packed away, including Jenny's clothing and shoes, since I would need to place my dresser in her closet to accommodate the rest of the furniture.

After Jenny's room had been emptied, I carried in all my furniture—the desk and chair, lamps, two filing cabinets, a chest, cabinet, end table, dresser—down to Jenny's room and, after experimenting with many arrangements, settled on the only one that seemed workable. The room looked hideous. Especially with the filing cabinets, it reminded me of an office. All the charm, beauty, light, and life it had sustained even after Jenny's death had been utterly destroyed. It was a desecration. The harmony and vibration of the room—its very essence—had been shattered and dispersed. What had once been a place filled with the deepest love and the joy of a little girl, and which had become a shrine, was now only a room, in the deadest and most utilitarian sense imaginable.

I died inwardly on that day—again—just as part of me had died with Jenny's passing. I was still adjusting to Jenny's death in phases, by degrees of admission and acknowledgement. That day, through an act that further testified, brutally, to Jenny's absence, I had reached another level of awareness—an agonizing milestone—in the long process of grieving. Although I always dreaded the day that would eventually come when I would have to change Jenny's room, and even though I knew that it would be deeply painful, I was not prepared for what it did to me. I was not emotionally ready to do what I had to do out of necessity. My soul felt gray and utterly empty. It was as if Jenny had left me only yesterday. An aching wound had been reopened.

The one thing I did that had a redeeming effect was to arrange an altar for my yoga meditations on top of the beautiful wooden chest that contained many articles of personal spiritual significance, and which I had placed in the spot that had been occupied by Jenny's crib. Ever since I had begun meditating after Jenny's death, I had sat on the floor on blankets with my back against the front of the sofa bed facing Jenny's crib, which happened to be east. I had placed a tray holding a candle, some incense, and so on on the floor in front of Jenny's crib. Now, the only difference was that the tray and other articles were arranged on top of the chest, so that, by coincidence, Jenny's former sleeping area became a focus for my meditations.

By late afternoon, I had finished the job. The den (formerly Jenny's room, and still so, in my mind) was arranged, the garage was reorganized, and Jenny's things were securely stored there. The only thing that remained was to load my car with junk that I had cleaned out of the garage and haul it somewhere. Among these discardable things was one possession of Jenny's that I had decided to throw away—the little three-piece, blue and white, cardboard chest of drawers she had brought home from the hospital. I am not sure why I decided to get rid of it, since I did not want to, and since to do so was extremely painful, except that I suppose I thought there was no room for it and that, in time, it would deteriorate and become broken anyway. I very much regret getting rid of that precious memento. If there was any way I could get it back, I would. Frankly, I think that, by the end of that day, I was so done in, physically, emotionally, and mentally, that I did not realize the import of what I was doing.

Around dinner time, Suzanne came home. The garage door was open, and I was standing outside, just looking at things, when she walked up. She spotted Jenny's cardboard chest of drawers, and I could tell from her face that there was a wrenching inside of her. She had known what I planned to do that day, but when she was directly confronted with the evidence that it was done, it was a great shock to her. We walked into the house and went downstairs to look at what had been Jenny's room. I knew that she was stunned almost beyond words. I went back outside, loaded everything into my car, including the chest of drawers, and drove away. I spotted an enormous dumpster in the parking lot of a church a couple of miles from our home. I parked next to it, quickly got rid of everything, and left. As I pulled back out onto the street, I looked back. In the fading gray light, I could see part of the little blue cardboard chest sticking up above the rim of the dumpster. In no way would it be trite to say that part of my heart was left behind forever in that dumpster. Feeling utterly empty, I drove back to a house totally different from the one it had been that morning, one from which the heart had been removed, and which was now less of a home.

My Journal entry of Wednesday, January 13, 1993, also references a very unpleasant dream that I do not remember very well but which obviously made a strong impression upon me at the time. Apparently, on the day that I dismantled Jenny's room, I had eventually gone to bed and had "the terrible nightmare that followed, in which you were alive but we returned you to the county," the reference to which is followed by the phrase, "(of course I would have *died* before doing that—you know this!)." It is clear that the act of "desecrating" Jenny's lovely room disturbed me so much that it caused me to have a dream the same night whose theme was abandoning her, a scenario which my subconscious mind had chosen to symbolize the demolition of her room and which, without doubt, was also a manifestation of the anxiety that I had felt during the few weeks before Jenny's death and which was still not entirely resolved.

Jenny Protects Me From a Fraud

On Wednesday, January 13, 1993, I arranged a reading with a man from England who represented himself as a medium and who used the title of "Reverend." Given that I can say nothing good about this person, I shall, for legal reasons, not use his real name. Instead, I will refer to him simply as "the Reverend." I had first heard about the Reverend on August 31, 1991, only about three weeks after Jenny's death, from my good friend, Gillian McKenna, who in turn had been told of him by some acquaintances who ran a nursery in Topanga Canyon, a mountainous area near the coast, north of Santa Monica, where Gillian lived.

I called the nursery in Topanga Canyon on Sunday, September 1, 1991 (the same day, in fact, that I first reached Nicki Mellette, the astrologer, and after which, over the next several weeks, I had readings with Freda Fell, Nicki Mellette, and Jach Pursel). The person with whom I spoke was by no means particularly friendly or helpful, but I was able to learn that the Reverend was not expected back in the United States until around May 1992. Thus, for the time being, it was evident that the Reverend would not be a candidate for providing me with any psychic information about Jenny.

Then, in the following spring of 1992, although my records are not completely clear as to how all of this came about, I obtained an appointment for a reading with the Reverend on Tuesday, May 19, 1992. However, the Reverend subsequently canceled my appointment, which was to have been in Santa Monica, and all of his other appointments, including one Gillian had made, due to "illness," and returned to England. I was told, however, that he would come to the United States again sometime between January and May 1993, that I was on a mailing list, and that I would be contacted for an appointment when they became available.

I now recall that Gillian, who was deeply interested in learning about several deceased persons who were quite dear to her, but who at the same time was skeptical of mediums and fearful of being duped, had stressed to the person making her appointment that she was most concerned about being dealt with in an honest and forthright fashion. When her reading was subsequently canceled, she was of course suspicious about the Reverend's "illness." However, given that I had also received a notice of cancellation, her suspicions were allayed.

Again, months passed, and then on December 2, 1992, I received a notice in the mail that the Reverend would be arriving in Los Angeles in January 1993 and that, beginning January 11, a limited number of private sittings would be available. (Interestingly enough, Gillian did not get a notice.) On December 3, I called the number provided and made an appointment for Wednesday, January 13, 1993, at 10:30 in the morning. The fee would be one hundred dollars, and I was to bring a ninety-minute cassette tape. The reading was at an address on the west side of Los Angeles in a private home.

On the thirteenth, I left work and drove to where I was to meet the Reverend. The weather was rainy and depressing. I was not at ease because of having to take time off from work, and it was difficult to forget the fact that work would be piling up. Nevertheless, I wanted to keep myself in a receptive state.

I arrived at a stylish private home featuring Spanish architecture in an affluent neighborhood in western Los Angeles. I was greeted by the Reverend, a middle-aged man with gray hair and of medium build, who had a kind of occult aura about him. He was dressed in black and wore some kind of medallion around his neck. He was the only one there, and I inferred that the residence was probably being loaned to him during the day while the owners were away, probably at work.

We sat facing each other in the large, well-lit, comfortable living room. The ambiance was colored by the gray, somber atmosphere outside. Between us was a small table upon which had been placed a cassette tape recorder. The Reverend and I chatted a bit, and he asked if I had ever consulted a medium before. I mentioned Freda Fell. Like Freda, the Reverend stated that, rather than asking specific questions, I was simply to let him speak about whatever came through to him.

Something that defies description happened at this time. The Reverend was doing a couple of last-minute things before getting into the reading. I am not sure if he was even seated across from me at the time; he may have gotten up for a minute or two. At any rate, he was totally unaware of what was taking place, and I never made it known to him. Suddenly, Jennifer's beautiful spirit was with me and all around me. I could sense some kind of aura or field of energy all about me created by Jenny's presence, and which was so distinct that I could unmistakably tell it was egg-shaped, except that it was very large. I could almost measure its dimensions—it was twice my size and completely engulfed me.

It was one of the most overwhelming spiritual presences I had ever experienced, and never since her death had Jenny come to me so directly and dramatically. I was not indulging in wishful thinking, nor was I the victim of any power of suggestion created by the setting, by the Reverend, or by myself. The beautiful, exquisite, light-filled soul of Jennifer Pivaral was saturating me with her love and protection. It almost took my breath away. Somehow, I suppressed the flow of tears. I did not know why, but I did not want the Reverend to know of my experience. As time passed, the manifestation faded away, but I was left with a permanent impression on my spirit from this wonderful experience. And I wondered what would happen during the reading, given that something so remarkable had taken place when it did.

The session began immediately thereafter. After turning on the recording machine, the Reverend told me that it was his custom to recite aloud the Lord's Prayer at the outset of each reading and asked me if I had any objection to his doing so. I said no. He settled into a receptive state, and then he began, slowly at first, to offer various remarks.

I will not reproduce anything the Reverend said to me over the next hour, because it was pure bullshit. Almost from the beginning, I sensed that, through his vague statements, which were often followed by questions of clarification to me, he was on one long fishing trip. This tendency manifested itself through the reading, and, once the Reverend felt he had an insight into my psyche—which he did not—his vague insinuations and information-hunting were padded liberally with half-baked attempts at psychoanalyzing me, which became so repetitious that I began to squirm and wish that the session was over so I could clear out and get back to work. It had become obvious that I was wasting my time.

Jennifer never came up at all. At one point toward the end of the reading, the Reverend finally made some tentative remark about the possibility of a dead child. But his mode of operation had become so obvious that it was clear that he was only fishing. Therefore, I did not respond to the bait he had thrown out.

Somehow, the Reverend inferred that my mother was also dead. She was very much alive at the time and still is today. Nevertheless, once he had gotten the idea that she, too, was on the other side, he proceeded to pass on to me many words of comfort and advice from her dear, departed spirit. I was too embarrassed to correct him.

For me, every minute dragged. I uttered my own Lord's Prayer—that this nonsense would be over with so that I could get back to work. I should have acted like a man and ended the reading myself. But I was just too uncomfortable. Finally, the reading ended and I paid the Reverend his hundred dollars! This sounds stupid, and it was. But given that I had not cut him off earlier, I felt that, since I had taken his hour, I should pay him. It was like going to a restaurant, ordering something that was badly prepared, eating all of it, and then complaining. I made a rapid exit and returned to work, thinking about the time I had wasted and the paperwork that would be waiting on my desk. I was so disgusted that I threw the tape recording of the reading out the car window. Later, I regretted that I had not saved it, at least to play for Gillian so that she could learn firsthand what I had been subjected to.

The experience was not really a loss, because, despite that fact that the Reverend was an unabashed, utter fraud, Jenny had touched my soul in an unprecedented way. The message that I got from it was very clear. Jenny loved me. She was looking out for me and had protected me from this man by demonstrating a presence that was impossible not to recognize. She was telling me that I did not need any more "Reverends" in my life to be near her.

However, the episode was not over. After I had arrived at my office and shoveled out from under some of my work, I telephoned Gillian to tell her what had happened. When I enlightened her about the credibility of the Reverend and what he had done, she was livid. Although she need not have felt personally responsible in any way, she was most apologetic, since it had been through her that I had learned of this man. And, we were both dumfounded that the Reverend had come so highly recommended by a couple of Gillian's acquaintances.

Gillian was not one to let anyone take advantage of her friends. In short order, she telephoned the Reverend, put him straight in no uncertain terms as to how she felt about him, made some well-worded threats to the tune that such unscrupulousness might bear looking into, and demanded that he return my hundred dollars. He readily consented. Gillian insisted on going with me to collect my money, so later that afternoon I left work and drove again over to the west side to meet Gillian. When I arrived, it was raining heavily and the intersection in question was heavily trafficked. I waited at least half an hour, but, somehow, we missed each other and never linked up.

Having come that far, I returned to see the Reverend on my own. When I arrived, I was agitated and eager to have the encounter behind me. I made a hasty U-turn in front of the house and parked against the curb, in order to make as quick a getaway as possible. Running up to the house in the rain, I pounded on the door. Finally, the Reverend answered and handed me an envelope. I did not pause to look inside, and we hardly spoke. I made some pretext about being in a terrible hurry, and darted back to my car, only to discover, to my horror, that, in parking against the curb, I had somehow put a gash in my right front tire. I could hear the air hissing out of it, and it was obvious that it would be completely flat within a few minutes.

Panicked, I jumped in the car and sped away. Arriving back at a main street, I searched frantically—in an unfamiliar neighborhood—for a place that sold tires. I knew that mine could not be repaired. After a couple of stops, I was directed to a tire store within a few blocks. I raced to my destination. All this time, the clock had been running out; the tire was getting lower and lower. There was a spare in my trunk, but I had no desire to get out in the drizzle in a strange locale with darkness coming on and get filthy. Besides, I would still have to replace the tire.

I pulled into the tire store in the nick of time. While I was waiting for the replacement to be put on, I checked the envelope the Reverend had given me. I was relieved to find five twenty-dollar bills. He had kept the hundred-dollar bill that I had given him, but at least I had the money. Of course, after I paid eighty dollars for the new tire, there was just enough left to pay for all the gas I had burned up that day and a bite to eat.

I was greatly relieved when I arrived safely home. I telephoned Gillian and told her all that had happened since our last conversation. Although she had waited for me at the agreed-upon intersection, as I had for her, we had mysteriously failed to find each other. I was convinced that my mishap with the tire was no accident. Gillian agreed. Had the Reverend deliberately caused it? No. But I had some psychic sensitivity of my own—more than he did—and I knew there was very negative energy around him. Whether this energy was conscious or not, or embodied in some kind of entity, and whether or not the Reverend had any occult talent at all, I do not know. I was just glad that he was behind me and chalked it up to experience.

Gillian, who had abandoned any intention of having a reading with the Reverend, received a couple of nasty and somewhat threatening, albeit clumsily staged, telephone messages from him over the next couple of days. After that, he disappeared from our lives.

With the Reverend, my psychic quest came to an end. I had had three very meaningful readings in the fall of 1991 with Freda Fell, Nicki Mellette, and Jach Pursel—all honest and credible people. That was enough. I have sought no more assistance in contacting Jenny. And, after my experience with the Reverend, Jenny would continue to manifest in various ways of her own choosing. Certainly, there would remain many unanswered questions about Jenny, or at least questions which could be answered in much greater detail—about the conditions which had created her short life, the actual physical cause of her death, the nature and extent of my past lives with her, what the future might hold, and so on. Perhaps someday I would know all of these things. For the time being, I had come to understand a great deal, and I was very grateful.

Journal Entry: Wednesday, January 13, 1993, 10:30 P.M.

Jenny, today I had my reading in Los Angeles with [name omitted for purposes of book] from England. Although I bear him no ill will, I believe him to be a very seedy fraud. The reading was a huge disappointment, with no mention of you. Gillian McKenna helped me rescue my $100.00, although I got a flat tire in the process. But I recall how, before the reading, as I sat in the chair, I felt myself surrounded, wonderfully engulfed, almost tangibly, with the presence, love, and light of your beautiful soul. I had to fight back the tears. The "force field" was actually egg-shaped that enveloped me. I believe that you were protecting me, and giving me a clear sign that I needed no medium to experience your presence and love. How tremendously pure and beautiful and powerful it was; and so in contrast to the barren, meandering, confused reading that followed.

The experience of you was especially meaningful to me because of my having had to rearrange the house a week ago (to put our cars inside to protect them), take down your crib, and pack away many of your things. How painful and killing that seemed—like the terrible nightmare that followed, in which you were alive but we returned you to the County (of course I would have *died* before doing that—you know this!). So thank you, Jennifer, for your beautiful, unmistakable presence today, which made me fight back tears of joy. What a great, big soul yours is! I love you, I love you, I love you, and always. I look forward to leaving here and being with you again in the Lord's light and bliss! Please protect and guide us! Mommy and me!

Dreams and Visions

Journal Entry: Monday, March 1, 1993, 10:22 P.M.

Jenny, tonight, in meditation, I felt more strongly than ever that, as you have been my daughter several times before (as well as other relationships), so also has Jessica been my daughter, my child, before. And I think that you and she have been sisters before, with me as your father. And I really wonder: is Jessica Wendy, the siamese twin who was born dead and attached to you at birth? I have a strong sense that this is true. And that you two fought to get here then (to me?)—and now she has found the opportunity to return. I love you both so much! Sometimes I almost see you and Jessica as the same person, and even wonder if you have come back as Jessica. I really don't think this is true, but I feel very strongly that Jessica was Wendy. Again, I love you both so very much! You are still, and always, the reigning Queen in my life, sitting on the center throne in my heart. And Jessica is there also, another star who, like you, lights up the dark firmament of my life.

On Wednesday, March 17, 1993, I awoke at 2:30 A.M. from an extraordinary dream in which I found myself in England (where I have never been). The first scene took place in a garden where I was with Paramahansa Yogananda, the great spiritual guru and founder of the Self-Realization Fellowship. There was really no dialogue, except that he said something to me—one brief, succinct comment that carried profound meaning and which summarized the state of my life. Then the scene changed, and I was somewhere else in England, in a large and friendly private home, the guest of some people I did not know. Apparently, I was there to enroll in some kind of school, like a university or something.

The remarkable thing about the dream, in addition to encountering Yogananda, which was highly significant, was an unprecedented and intense feeling of freedom and joy. It was one of the sweetest, purest, most ecstatic sensations I have ever experienced. Then I realized that I had brought absolutely nothing with me, and that, before coming, I had not brought to closure any of the day-to-day matters of my life—my mortgage, my bills, my work, nothing. I realized with terrible sadness and disappointment that I would have to return, and I awakened.

I looked at the clock. It was 2:30 in the morning. That feeling of inexpressible freedom and happiness was still with me; I ached from it. But in time, sadly, it would slip away. I realized immediately what the dream symbolized. The matchless spiritual freedom was death. I had known the unbounded joy of release from the body, from physical existence, and from its worries, concerns, and limitations. Then, heartbreakingly, I was called back.

Why England? I do not know, except that England had figured in another dream of great spiritual import many years earlier. England was, after all, our "mother" country. Did my psyche associate this with the goddess aspect of the deity, or with the source from which we have all come and to which we shall all return? Possibly. And, hopefully, was this great joy and release what my beloved Jenny had found when she left me? Finally, and oddly, if I remembered it at all upon awakening, whatever Yogananda said to me was immediately forgotten, at least consciously, and to this day I have never been able to remember his words. Yet the unalterable impression remains that whatever he said was deeply insightful.

In March 1993, Suzanne and I received a visit from a licensing program analyst from the State of California Department of Social Services, Community Care Licensing Agency. He had come on a licensing renewal visit, since our foster family home license was due for renewal. Before the end of our initial licensing period, Suzanne and I had opted to renew our license for an additional year, even though there were no foster children in our home. Each year that we renewed meant extra time and work, including filling out some additional paperwork, receiving periodic home inspection visits, possibly going to classes, and at least one of us maintaining certification in first aid and CPR (something Suzanne, as a nurse, had to do anyway, but the agency kept reminding us about it).

In addition to the bureaucratic hassles, there were other things to consider. Our experiences with the County of Los Angeles Department of Children's Services had left a sufficiently bad taste in our mouths to discourage us strongly from becoming involved with them again. The other thing was that most foster children were not usually placed deliberately in foster homes for an extended period of time (more or less permanently) as had been the case with Jenny. The real goal of the county was to get children home with their real parents, if possible. For us, this meant the likelihood of getting attached to a child who would be taken away at some point. Although we admired other foster parents who could deal with this, we did not wish to. Neither of us could face further heartbreak. And I had heard some troubling stories about children being yanked out of foster homes and placed in others for very whimsical reasons, such as cutting down on driving time for the social worker. Suzanne and I were not willing to deal with this kind of thing.

Thus, on March 26, we announced to the licensing program analyst that we did not wish to renew our license. Although I saw no reason to do otherwise, I was sad, because it made our decision official not to have any more children in our home, at least through the county foster care program. It was like dying inside just a little bit more. On April 20, we received notification that our file had been closed. This did not restrict us from applying to the program at a future time, but I knew it was the end, and it was painful.

On April 21 in the early morning, I had a second dream of unmistakable spiritual import. Over the years, both before this dream and after it, I have had many recurring dreams involving homes and mansions of overwhelming beauty and proportions. These edifices, into which I have moved, have taken on every architectural style imaginable. They are often strikingly opulent and always of palatial size, containing uncounted rooms, many stories, and frequently, complex and endless subterranean labyrinths and rooms. Clearly, these dreams have nothing to do with material ambition. They represent the architecture of the soul in all its richness, diversity, and mystery. And always, each dream of this type is tied to the others by the same inexpressible joy, fulfillment, and spiritual revelation that come from contact with the innermost living self.

In the dream, the edifice I encountered, and which was now mine, was surrounded by vast, gently rolling lawns. Their richness and verdancy was powerfully enhanced by the softly glowing blue and orange sky which indicated evening twilight (always, in my mind, a time of special power and significance). Somewhere behind the house, I discovered a beautiful, deep pond filled with large goldfish and bordered by lush vegetation and trees.

I returned to the house and stood before it. It was magnificent. Several stories tall and circular in form with a flat roof, it was built almost entirely of glass. Around its entire perimeter, at ground level, was a spacious terrace, with a rich, polished black floor of terrazzo or marble. I stood in silence, contemplating the structure. Glistening softly in the evening twilight, it was so incomparably beautiful, and its form was so pregnant with meaning, that, at one moment, I was overcome with emotion. I put my face in my hands and wept with uncontrollable joy.

I awoke. It was early morning and still dark outside. I lay in my bed, filled with an unbounded happiness and peace that I had experienced only a few times in my life. I had communed with a deep, eternal aspect of my highest self. There was a feeling—which the house had represented—of new spiritual life, and although it was even more glorious, it was very close to the exquisite feeling of release and joy I had encountered in my England dream only a month earlier. Never before in my life had I wept with joy in a dream!

After I awoke and lay in the darkness, the intense feeling stayed with me. For the next few days, the emotions of the dream stayed with me, diminishing over time but leaving a permanent impression in my being which has never gone away.

Journal Entry: Saturday, May 1, 1993, 11:00 A.m.

Jenny, for some reason, I now wish to record a dream I had in Jim Roggenkamp's office in Louisville when Suzie and I went there to bury you at Gethsemani. [Trip: Saturday, August 17, 1991 through Saturday, August 24, 1991; burial: Monday, August 19, 1991.] I *think* the dream was *before* your burial, but I'm not sure. I had fallen asleep on Jim's office couch. In the dream, I was by the ocean, on a beach. I sat on a large wooden chair, like my red baby chair that I gave to you, except this chair was much bigger, and unpainted. The waves advanced and receded through the chair legs, and the water carried you in and out, floating on the surface. You were the size of a little starfish, but I could see you very clearly, and you looked and smiled at me calmly. Finally, after going out on a little wave, you returned no more.

I awoke, and knew this symbolized your passing; and I recall so clearly that you wore (in the dream) that pretty blue and red plaid dress that you wore on June 30, 1991, when Suzie and I took you to Rancho Calamigos. You loved the swimming pool there so much! I bought you a swimsuit immediately after that. Today, I am looking at the photos of you at Rancho Calamigos, sitting by the pool in that plaid dress, and the photo of you and Sue Collins at the 694 Vallejo Villas pool on July 4, 1991, your first time at our pool, and in your new swimsuit. And right now I have tears in my eyes, because I miss you so much, and because I know that my life on this planet will never be again like it was when I had *you,* my love!

Journal Entry: Wednesday, June 23, 1993, 6:30 P.M.

Jenny, tomorrow—Thursday, June 24, 1993, is your fifth birthday! (You were born June 24, 1988.) Since you left this world on August 9, 1991, time has lost all meaning for me. I feel sad and at a loss for words. I love Jessica *very* much—but *you* can never be replaced. I rededicate my love, my yoga, my soul, to *you.* However long it takes, I'll find you, and be with you forever; I promise this. I'll think of you all day tomorrow—but I always think of you, my precious little love! You are eternally in my heart!

On July 12, the body of Self-Realization Fellowship teachings I had resumed in January 1992 came to an end. I applied immediately to receive instruction in the second, third, and fourth levels of kriya yoga that remained (the first of which, itself an advanced level, I had practiced since 1967). It was required that I practice the second level for a year, which I did. Then, during the last two months of 1994, I acquired the final two techniques, ending a quest I had begun in January 1979, when I first made contact with SRF. It was my intention to practice these powerful meditations for the rest of my life.

On July 20, 1993, Nancy Pivaral told me that Rosa, still living in Guatemala, was pregnant.

For October 1 through 12, I went back to Illinois to visit my mother. During the last few days, I went to Chicago to see my lifelong friend and spiritual brother, Jerry Alber. It was not unusual for odd things to happen when we were in each other's presence. Our spiritual chemistries seemed to be awakened when we were in close proximity to each other, including our dreams when we stayed with each other from time to time. Thus, early in the morning of October 10, while at his apartment, I had the most extraordinary dream about Jennifer that I have ever had. I had to awaken Jerry in the middle of the night to tell him about it. Jerry and I canceled our plans to go to Lake Geneva, Wisconsin, that day—a place that in both our minds was one of great spiritual power and which had played a spiritually significant role in my life, ever since I had first gone there in August 1964. We agreed that to go at that time would just be too much for me, so soon after my powerful vision of Jenny.

Journal Entry: Sunday, October 10, 1993, 10:00 A.M., during a stay with Jerry Alber in Chicago, Illinois

Jenny, at 2:00 A.M., I awakened from the most profound dream/vision I have had of you since you left this earth! In the dream, you were dead, but there was not really any grief or mourning in my heart. I cannot really translate into words what it was really like or how I felt, because there is nothing in everyday waking experience with which to compare it. Your body was small, like that of a large doll, and very light, weighing almost nothing. You were laid out very beautifully and perfectly on a kind of "tray," by means of which I carried your body from place to place. You were clothed in a beautiful, pristine, white dress, decorated (I believe) with subtle touches of pink around the borders and seams. This dress was a kind of "marriage gown," and I was preparing you for some kind of "marriage ceremony" in which you were the "bride." (For some reason, I have a strong intuitive preference in this case for using the term "marriage" rather than "wedding.")

In the first scene, you were in your gown/dress, lying on the "tray" which was on the ground at the edge of a bank covered with wet green and yellow autumn leaves. The bank sloped steeply down to a body of water which, because I saw only a narrow strip of it in the dream, I thought at the time was perhaps a river. However, in retrospect, it was very possibly a lake, because the steep bank reminds me strongly of the bank which slopes steeply down to the waters along the eastern perimeter of Conference Point Camp on Lake Geneva. In my mind's eye I could visualize the "house" of the "family" into which you were to be married. It was to the left, down the shore, and was a large, brick house with several columns in front. I saw the house only in my mind, however, and not in actuality. I was doing something (I do not know what) to "prepare" you for this "marriage," something in the way of arranging you perfectly for this "event," for this "family," down to the smallest detail, because I wanted you to be "perfect" for whatever was to take place.

Then the second scene occurred, in which I carried you on your "tray" into a room which was actually like the den in my mother's home in Bloomington. But instead of the bed which is really there, the sofa bed from the living room was in the den. It was unfolded, so that I could sit on it, and your body (no longer on the "tray") was placed very carefully on the arm of the sofa bed. The closet actually in that room was now a "doorway" to the kitchen. The door was slightly ajar, so that some light came through into the den, and there were two people talking quietly in the kitchen (I sensed that they seemed to be my mother and father, but I am not sure). The den itself was rather dark, and as I looked at your body laid out on the arm of the sofa bed, I could see that your eyes were slightly open. I wanted to close them gently, but as I shifted positions slightly from side to side, I noticed that some small amount of light was reflected in your eyes (which thus far were exactly like the clear eyes of a baby doll). This reflected light and my movements gave me the distinct perception (although I assumed it to be an illusion) that your eyes were moving.

At this moment, Suzanne entered the room through the doorway from the kitchen, and, since it was still rather dark in the room, I cautioned her to move very carefully, telling her that your body was poised there on the arm of the sofa bed. I was concerned that she might accidentally bump it and knock it off. Then, somehow, there was much more light in the room. Also, your little body was now in more of a sitting position. As I looked intently at your face, I saw that your eyes were indeed open and really moving. I could not believe it at first, but I quickly realized that you were truly, miraculously alive again, come back to me, returned from the dead, "resurrected."

As I fully realized this, I was filled with an indescribable joy, much like the inexpressible happiness I have felt in two other spiritual dreams I have had during the last few months. I saw your beautiful face with an astonishing vividness and clarity, filled with light, and the clear, profound realization filled my mind of your utter flawlessness and perfection. For although your face and eyes were always absolutely beautiful in earthly life, there was at this moment in the dream my crystalline perception of your perfect beauty, and in your "resurrected" state your face and whole being had a radiant, shining, "transfigured" quality. Your eyes moved and sparkled, and I saw in them that purity, innocence, and perfection which you always manifested to me in life, and, above all, that indescribable knowing, intelligence, and wisdom which poured out of your radiant, ancient soul. And you looked at me with those deep eyes and smiled so simply and beautifully, as if to say, "Yes, of course, I am really alive. I am resurrected. I have come back to you." And I said, "Oh, Jenny, you're really alive," and I was filled with inexpressible joy as I leaned forward and rested my head on your breast and you put your little arms around me.

It was at that moment that I awoke, and I knew with absolute knowing that I had been with you, that you had come to me, that we had been together. I experienced once again, as I have on certain past occasions after waking in the night, that very pleasant but slightly "spooky" feeling that you had been there with me. Never, since your death, in waking or in dreaming, have I seen you, and especially your face and eyes, with such astonishing, "unearthly" clarity. I "know" now that my dream/vision of you was astral in nature, that we were together on a higher plane. And somehow I know intuitively that your "marriage" was not in any way a physical or carnal one, and indeed not even a marriage to another being, but a "marriage," or "graduation," or "transition" to a higher, more perfected, more spiritual level of existence or state of being.

This dream/vision is the only one since your death in which I have had such joy with respect to you, and freedom from the sorrow of your leaving me here, although at this moment I recall also the beautiful dream I had of you coming to me as a young woman, a dream which took place during the night after my formal initiation into kriya yoga at Self-Realization Fellowship earlier that same evening.

When I went back to sleep that night, I had several more unusually intense and vivid dreams which, I am sure, were a kind of overflow and release of the powerful psychic energy generated from my encounter with you. All three other dreams involved water, as did my dream of you, one of the dreams being in California along the beautiful Pacific ocean, another of Lake Geneva. In both the Lake Geneva dream and the third dream I was a lifeguard, which I feel strongly symbolized my "guarding your life" while you were with me on this earth.

I awoke this morning in a state of profound psychic and spiritual stimulation, a state which still persists, and my meditation this morning with Jerry was very unique in its depth and intensity of concentration. As Jerry said this morning, this dream/vision I had of you last night is one of those rare and precious experiences which give us the hope and strength we need to continue in this life and which enable us to have the faith and determination necessary to persist on our path, the only real and worthwhile path, toward self-realization.

After so many recent months of emptiness and wondering where you are and who you are, I am now deeply reassured about your continued and eternal presence in my life, your love for me, and your greatness in the hierarchy of spiritual beings who guide us and offer us their help.

Since this dream/vision possibly seemed to represent a kind of spiritual advancement or progression in your spiritual journey, I am wondering if (and hoping that) the kriya I have done daily for you for the past couple of years has helped you in some way. I have faith that it has, and I will continue to do it faithfully for you every day.

The End of a Marriage

On November 30, 1993, Suzanne and I began counseling with Rona Schwartz, a Ph.D. psychologist. This was at Suzanne's initiative, and stemmed from the fact that, as she had done periodically over the years, Suzanne once again had expressed her unhappiness and her desire to end our marriage. I tried to view this as Suzanne's desire to work on the marriage, because looking at it any other way was terribly painful and frightening. However, the truth was that Suzanne was really looking for a graceful way to end the marriage (perhaps a Southern tradition, since my first wife's mother—also from Kentucky—had said something similar).

Suzanne's medical insurance paid more than mine for counseling, and since Rona had come highly recommended by a friend of Suzanne's and because she also accepted Suzanne's insurance, we opted to work with her. After the first session, which Suzanne and I attended together, we went to see her separately so she could understand each of our perspectives before bringing us together.

I liked Rona. She was empathetic and caring, she reacted perceptibly and humanly to what I had to say, and she offered many insights. She felt I had many personal issues that had to be looked at before my side of things could be integrated with Suzanne's. In my sessions with Rona, I found myself pouring out rivers of thoughts, feelings, and long pent-up emotions. Besides sharing my background and feelings about the marriage, I talked at length about Jenny.

By early 1994, it had become apparent that Suzanne would be leaving Huntington Memorial Hospital in Pasadena and accepting another position that had been offered to her by her friend, Zippy, at a hospital on the west side of Los Angeles. The new job would mean a promotion and a sizable increase in earnings.

When Suzanne asked me one night if I was not happy for her, I had to be truthful and said something like, "I suppose I should be, and I guess I'm happy for you, but the truth is that I see this as another obstacle to resolving our problems. One of our chief sources of contention has always been money and how it should be used, and I had hoped that in time I would become more your financial equal, that the playing field would be more level, and that we would be in a better position to work on our differences." (Suzanne was more than eight years older than I was. She had always had good jobs and had for a long time earned more money than I had.) "With this large raise of yours, frankly, I see no hope of ever catching up with you or being your financial equal, and in addition, the more you earn, the less I feel like a real person and a valid partner in this marriage."

With that, I had said it all, and as the days passed, Suzanne's raise became in my mind more and more of a death knell to my hopes. I knew from years of bitter experience that more money simply meant more struggle for control and power.

In January 1994, in addition to our seeing Rona individually, I went through the most honest, painful, and awesomely frightening process of soul-searching I had ever experienced. For the first time in my life, I allowed myself to open the Pandora's box that had lain undisturbed—but which had caused me intense suffering—since my adolescence: my overwhelming fear of being alone. I admitted that, in my own mind, being alone was death. Therefore, rather than reconciling myself to being alone, I resigned myself to death. Not to physical death, but to something perhaps equally daunting—the death of my self, or at least part of my self.

I finally realized that I would not die if I were alone. My ability to face this issue and survive it was due in large part to the hundreds of hours of kriya yoga meditation that I had practiced. On January 24, I went to Suzanne's counseling session with Rona. I had told Rona of my intention to come and why, and although she had suggested that I might wish to reconsider, I insisted. I had made up my mind, and any postponement was unendurable.

As Suzanne, Rona, and I sat talking about this and that, I turned to Suzanne and brought the conversation back to the reason she had wanted to start counseling, which was to look at our marriage and consider the possibility of ending it.

When Suzanne responded by saying that it was not the most opportune time for her to make such a decision, given her focus on getting settled in her new position, I became incensed and said, evenly but with much emotion, "So what am I supposed to do? Just sit around until it's more convenient for you to get rid of me?" I thought to myself angrily, "Since it suits your schedule, you'll keep me dangling until you're ready to make a decision, like you did before Jenny died!"

I was tired of feeling like I was on trial and waiting for the jury to return with a verdict. I took a deep breath and prepared myself. Evenly and kindly, I said, "Since you've wanted out of this marriage for so long, I've decided it's time to let you have your wish. You have a new job now, with a very good income, and I think that you should have the opportunity to succeed or fail on your own efforts, without what you view as my interference and attempts at control. I don't want you to resent me any more. Therefore, I think the time has come for us to end our marriage. Rona has said in the past that she felt that there was a volcano of emotion and resentment waiting to erupt between us. Honestly, for myself, I do not feel that way. It's time for you to have the freedom you seem to want so much. And I want you to know that this has been the most difficult and painful decision I have ever had to make."

Rona and Suzanne were silent. To say the least, Suzanne was stunned. After a bit, we talked further. I felt as if a tremendous weight had been removed from me. Suzanne was tearful, but she accepted my decision without argument. Rona supported it and made no attempt to alter what was taking place. I explained that I had already done a considerable amount of research and that, if Suzanne was willing, I could do all of the legal work on the divorce myself. She readily agreed. After the session, Suzanne and walked out together.

We were both a little tearful, and I said, "If, for any reason, we should want to change our minds about this, there will be time."

I meant what I said; I was not just trying to get out of the course of action to which I had committed. Suzanne said that she needed a little time alone and went off on her own for an hour or so. We had come in separate cars, so I drove home alone.

I did not return to see Rona. I saw no need. Suzanne continued her sessions for a short time, but within a few weeks ended her counseling also, given the heavy demands of her new job and her difficult schedule. The hostility and venom that I had feared might surface never came. I was astonished to realize that, rather than augment any bitterness, the decision to divorce did a great deal to clear the air between us. Both of us, without question, felt released from a heavy and painful burden. For the most part, from the day of my announcement forth, we were much kinder to each other. Many of the sources of our contention and friction would now cease to exist; and, since we would have to continue living together for perhaps some time, we both realized the deep importance of getting along, respecting each other, and not injuring the other with ugly words and actions.

A Birth

Journal Entry: Saturday, February 26, 1994, 11:00 P.M.

This afternoon, Nancy Pivaral told me that Rosa Pivaral (Guatemala) had a baby boy, Jonathan, two to three weeks ago.

I Am Alone

On April 9, 1994, I received notice from the Los Angeles County Superior Court that all of my paperwork for the dissolution of marriage had been approved on April 6, and that my marriage to Suzanne would legally end on August 16. Since January, I had worked day and night and on weekends without a lawyer in researching, preparing, and filing the reams of documents required to end a marriage in California. It was without any exaggeration a difficult and formidable task, and despite the circumstances I had reason to feel not a little pride at having successfully negotiated our course through the complex legal system and sluggish bureaucracy without a hitch.

Suzanne and I had settled our marital affairs fairly and without contention, and in May I bought her interest in our home. She had little desire to remain there and did not want to be tied to a mortgage, but for me it was very important, both emotionally and financially, to stay. I wanted to be where Jenny and I had lived together. On May 28, Suzanne moved out. It was a sad time, but we made the best of it. I helped her supervise the move and did everything I could to assist her getting settled in her new apartment in Alhambra, in a quiet and extremely pleasant neighborhood next door to a Catholic convent.

Journal Entry: Thursday, June 23, 1994, 7:00 P.M.

Jenny, tomorrow, Friday, June 24, 1994, is your sixth birthday (born June 24, 1988). Now it is just Sarada and me. Suzie moved out on May 28, 1994, a few weeks ago. I am so glad I have Jessica. I love her so much. But no one can *ever* replace you, my wonderful, sweet baby, and I am not looking! I wonder what your half brother is like? Tears fill my eyes, because briefly I feel you close, but want you closer. You are my *one truest love*. Pray for, protect, and guide our Suzie. I love her and miss her. May your precious spirit be near me until we are face to face again.

Love,

Daddy

Jerry Alber Arrives—and Leaves

On August 6, Jerry Alber arrived from Chicago to move in with me. He had packed his things into a rental truck and come out with a friend who would then fly back to Chicago. Over the past few months, Jerry and I had been talking about the possibility of his moving to Los Angeles, for several reasons. First, we felt that, given our friendship of so many years, and since we both had similar world views and serious commitments to meditation, living together might make a good arrangement. Second, it seemed then like an especially opportune time, since I was living alone after my divorce, and he had for several years been growing more and more weary of the bitter Chicago winters.

After Suzanne had moved out, I had made changes in the house in preparation for Jerry's arrival. Jenny's room, which had later become my den and meditation room, was made ready for Jerry. I cleared everything out, put on a fresh coat of paint (the same color, a sort of light, pinkish sandstone), and left it empty. Truly and sadly, that was the end of any connection, at least physically, between that room and Jenny, although to this day I think of it as her room, and I always will. And only during the time that she lived there did it seem other than just a room.

Besides relocating the furniture, I was faced with the dilemma of where to place a proper meditation area. I allocated a portion of the small upstairs den for that purpose, since it had good ventilation and was not likely to get a lot of foot traffic. Ideally, of course, one should have a room, or perhaps even a large closet, dedicated exclusively to the activity of meditation; but the condo was not large, and such an arrangement was impossible. A portion of the shelving on the east wall of the den became an altar that meditators would face. Finally, I hung my icons and other pictures of personal significance, including some photos of Jennifer, on the walls of the den and arranged things so the chest that had formerly served as my altar and which was filled with various objects of metaphysical significance was also in the room.

August 16, 1994, came—the dissolution of my marriage to Suzanne became final. Many emotions in regard to Suzanne and our divorce were still new and tender. Given what I had worked through and experienced, there was little I had not already felt.

Jerry Alber moved back to Chicago October 30. Although not finding the right job after moving was an issue, his primary difficulty was adjusting to the relatively chaotic vibrations of Los Angeles (something I could identify with, since living in L.A. was like living on another planet). Despite having to face the cold winters and humid summers again, he felt that going back was the right choice. Fortunately, he was able to secure a position with the firm he had worked for before coming to live with me. Thus, I was alone again except for Sarada, my cat, who had been with me through many experiences—in fact, since before I had met Suzanne.

Meditation for Jessica, Jenny's Footprints, an Odd Occurrence, and an Insight

On November 21, I began doing a portion of my kriya yoga meditation for Jessica Christina Pivaral just as I had been doing for more than three years for Jenny. It came to me to do so, and I have continued the practice ever since. As I have performed a specific number of exercises, I have done so in such a way, hopefully, that both Jennifer and Jessica, wherever their souls are (Jennifer's, in another world, Jessica's, here with me on Earth), might also derive spiritual benefits from the practice. Such a decision seemed entirely appropriate, given my strong conviction that the three of us were intimately bound together, karmically and spiritually. Even the possibility that such practice on my part might help them was reason enough to do it faithfully.

Early in 1995, I decided it was finally time to frame the beautiful gift of Jenny's footprints that had been given to me by All Saints Children's Center after her death. I had the entire sheet of paper with several children's footprints professionally mounted and placed in a beautiful red frame. The piece now hangs on a wall in my living room, directly above my grand piano, where it catches my eye every day and serves as a testament of my love for Jenny to anyone who comes to my home.

One evening after work, I felt an urge to do something I had not had the courage to do since a few weeks after Jenny's death. Without pausing to reflect for fear I would change my mind, I got out a copy of the videotape that All Saints Children's Center had made of Suzanne and Jenny just before Jenny started going to day care there in late February 1991. The tape showed Suzanne discussing Jenny's Broviac catheter, her gastrostomy tube and bag, and her colostomy, and demonstrating how to change the various dressings.

I went downstairs, got the tape, came back up to the living room, pushed the tape into the VCR, and sat on the floor to watch it. I wondered how I would react, but when the tape started to play and I saw Jenny and Suzanne, I did not feel much of anything—certainly not happy, perhaps sad, and kind of numb. As I watched the first few minutes, I began to feel as if perhaps it was not the right time to be viewing the tape. After all, I thought, I had acted very impulsively.

It was dark outside, and probably around 8:30 or 9:00 o'clock. Since it was a pleasant night, all of the windows and the sliding door were wide open. However, everything was extremely still, and there had been virtually no air movement through the house all night, in spite of the cross ventilation.

Several minutes into the tape, just as I began to feel I should wait until another time to see it, a sudden, violent wind blew literally out of nowhere. The rush of air that came in through the balcony door was so powerful that it blew the screen out of the den window on the other side of the house, thirty feet away. Since December 1988, I had never experienced such a wind on our hilltop, not even during the occasional winter rainstorms; and none of the screens, which were securely in place, had ever been blown out.

At the same moment, I felt strongly Jenny was there. I shut off the videotape and rushed outside to replace the window screen, taking precautions so that such a thing could never happen again. After I went back inside, I rewound the tape without hesitation and put it away. The timing was just not right.

Wind has figured prominently in several major psychic-spiritual experiences of mine over a period of thirty years. It manifested itself to me in a peculiar but dramatic and unmistakable way in 1964, when I was fifteen years old and had a series of mystical experiences on the shores of Lake Geneva, Wisconsin, that would forever change my life.

I sensed very clearly an underlying, noumenal connection and a link to my own inner feeling that, for whatever reason, I had not picked an appropriate time to view the video. Am I saying that Jenny made the wind come up? No. I am not arguing a causal connection, but rather an acausal one, one more mysterious, but nevertheless real. Jung attributed such mysterious, acausal connections between certain events to synchronicity—and rightly so—although I do not believe that he really understood the principle in its deepest, occult sense. I find his treatise on the subject almost unintelligible.

Be that as it may, there is no doubt in my mind that, on some level, my feelings, the wind, and my clear perception of Jenny's presence were irrefutably linked as part of the same event.

I went to visit my mother for ten days in early June. I mention this briefly, and only because I had a great insight into my childhood and early life while I was there. In addition to seeing some relatives from Tennessee whom I had not seen since the mid 1970s, we drove to nearby Toluca, Illinois, to see members of my mother's family, one of whom I had not seen since I was a child. These meetings were a revelation to me because I realized how much of my loneliness I had buried over the years, how much contact I had lost with my relatives, how much I really cared about them, and how there were certain times during my childhood, especially when I had been with them, that I had been truly happy. When I saw my cousin Carolyn Divan again, I cried. We have since become friends again, and I promised her and others that I would not let the relationships lapse. My experiences in Illinois that June touched powerfully upon the theme of loneliness which has threaded throughout much of my life, the pain of which had been transformed most dramatically during the time that my beautiful Jenny had been with me.

Journal Entry: Friday, June 23, 1995, 6:00 P.M.

Jenny, tomorrow is your birthday again (born June 24, 1988)! Saturday, June 24, 1995—*seven* years old! I can't believe it has been a whole year since I've written anything in our Journal! I know it is because I feel numb a lot of times, don't know just what to say, and am kind of afraid of the hurt. I remember so clearly the morning you died... When you left me... Yes, I would like to leave here *now* to be with you! I mean it! Life is so fast—mine will be gone soon—you know, angel, I am *counting* on you greeting me, on seeing your shining face, on being reunited with you. Please help and guide me in *all* things—in work, in meditation, in *Darkness Is Light Enough* and books to come. Carolyn Divan, my wonderful just-rediscovered cousin, would love you so much. I wish I could take you with me to visit her. If my mom could see you too, maybe she could realize what you mean to me. My devotion to you is forever.

All my love,

Daddy

I Begin Writing Jenny's Story

I began this book on July 11, 1995. Like most of the other major events and decisions in my life, the ones of real and lasting significance, like Jenny herself, writing her story was more like a revelation, or command from some inner voice that I feel I must obey, rather than a conscious, logical decision. In addition to manifesting suddenly and unexpectedly, the "decisions" come with an ominous inner sense that I am destined for such-and-such an experience, or that I am fated to take such-and-such a path. I feel I have no choice in the matter unless I want to buck the "Yod," the "finger of God"—which, in my mind, is running away from God and the self and courting disaster.

Some of my most profound insights, inspirations, and revelations come in the bathtub. I soak in a very hot bath almost every night after I have finished all my household chores, and then I do some simple hatha yoga exercises in front of the TV before going to bed. Apparently, relaxing in the hot water up to my neck in the quiet, softly illumined master bathroom, sometimes brings on a profound state of receptivity to various ideas and intuitional promptings.

The evening of Monday, February 27, 1995, I found myself soaking in just such a steaming bath, letting go of my tensions, and trying to think of nothing at all. I had been lying there motionless for about ten minutes when, out of nowhere, I realized in the briefest moment that it was time to market the unsold manuscript of *Darkness Is Light Enough* again—after it had lain dormant for years. I also recognized that I had to begin immediately putting the material (which had originally been typewritten) into a word-processing progam. Finally, that quiet but unmistakable voice of destiny came, telling me that there was something else I needed to do—something, in fact, I had said several times during the last three and a half years that I had no intention of ever doing. Writing Jenny's story.

Beginning almost right after Jenny's burial and from time to time thereafter, a number of people, including Suzanne, had brought up the idea of my writing the story of Jennifer's life. I had said no every time, gently, but immediately and unequivocally. I felt it would be much too painful, especially during the first years after Jenny's death; the pain was too fresh and too intense. I could not add more to it. And, I was drained and empty from the grief and loss. After I had poured my soul into a manuscript that had not been published, I had decided that my writing days were over. I was not going to undertake any more such projects that would not find fulfillment through publication, for in my mind this was very important in terms of feeling validated and fulfilled. I was not going to write another manuscript-sized diary. The matter was closed.

When I heard that fateful voice in my head, I moaned inside and responded with, "No! Please! I don't want to do this! I don't want to drag that manuscript out again, and I can't write Jenny's story. I just can't face it, and I can't bear the thought of another herculean writing project that might not come to anything, especially after the last failure."

But the voice persisted. Not only was it unrelenting, but it took on the tone of a command. I was being told that I must do these things.

I could not escape the voice or its promptings. I almost felt in the grip of some thing; my solar plexus seemed like it was about to explode with nervous energy. An intense struggle went on inside me for several minutes. Then I made a clear decision, one from which I would not back down.

"All right," I responded mentally, as if I were negotiating with someone. "I will try again to find a publisher for my book, and I will undertake word-processing it. But I will not write the story of Jenny's life unless the other manuscript is published. It just isn't fair. But if the earlier manuscript does find a publisher, then I vow to write Jenny's story."

On March 3, I began word-processing the old manuscript. By working at it intensely and continuously, I had completed the task by mid-June. I had a finished product that had been word-processed, edited, and reprinted to yield a beautiful, professional-looking new edition. While doing the word processing, I had also been conducting a new marketing effort with a refined strategy. The gods led me to Galde Press in Lakeville, Minnesota, a small but successful publisher that specialized in works of a metaphysical nature. On July 7, I was offered a contract for the publication of *Darkness Is Light Enough,* which I signed. The goal would be to have the book on the market by the end of the year. An issue of many years had finally been resolved.

I began to wonder when I should start on Jenny's book. Perhaps at the end of the year, after the other manuscript came out, I thought to myself. But then I thought, "What am I waiting for?" So, on July 11, 1995, I set about writing the story of my beloved daughter so that many people would know about the glorious love she had brought into my life and the lives of others. I worked relentlessly, almost without pause, and, on October 14, 1995, I had a finished manuscript. And that is how I came to write Jennifer's story.

Journal Entry: Tuesday, August 8, 1995, 7:00 P.M.

My sweet Jenny, tomorrow, Wednesday, August, 9, 1995 is the four-year anniversary of your passing (August 9, 1991). I have been thinking about you so *very* much every day, because, as I hope you know, I started writing a book about your life story this July. I want many, many people to know of you, to remember you; to know how I love you!

Suzie and I took your sister, Jessica, to Disneyland at the end of July, and she really loved it. One of your favorites is hers too—Mickey Mouse—and Minnie, and Goofy! I have some new photos of Jessica, which I had framed, and I'm going to hang them on the wall tonight.

Jenny, please guide me in all things! Your presence in my thoughts and heart is moment-to-moment, unending. Bless and protect me, my yoga, my life, *your new book.* Love to you, my Angel.

Daddy

Mementos—A Last Look

During September 1995, as I started to glimpse the end of this manuscript, I began a final sweep through my mementos of Jennifer's life. Although before that I had sifted extensively through my memories and carefully reviewed numerous documents, asking Suzanne many questions, I wanted to expose myself to anything that remained unexamined. During this process, I was in touch again with a number of people, including Dr. Laurance, Jenny's pediatrician, and some of the staff of the pediatric ward at Huntington who remained from the days of Jenny's residence there. On September 18, during a visit to Huntington, I was given a photo album of Jenny's that I had never seen before. It contained more than two hundred photos that began in fall 1988, when Jenny was only a few months old, and ended with pictures from her going-home party on February 22, 1991. I was deeply moved, and although I shed some tears, it was not a severe shock to see, since it closely paralleled the videotape of Jenny's life at Huntington that I had first acquired in April 1992. I spent many hours poring over and chronologically rearranging the photos in the album, some of which I had mounted and framed.

There was also another photo album I had compiled while Jenny was alive, starting in November 1990 with many snapshots I took of her at Huntington. My heart aches both with joy and sadness when I look at the images of her at Huntington: in the playroom; riding in her wagon around the halls and outside in the fresh air; modeling Suzanne's sunglasses; standing by the vending machines in the cafeteria; sitting in her hospital crib, posing like a queen while being attended to by one of the nurses; sitting on a blanket in the hallway of the pediatric ward; lounging around outside the hospital in the warm sunshine with Suzanne, Sue Collins, and me; and, a photo on Santa's lap, who visited the hospital a few days before Christmas.

Then, the photos of her first visit home on December 15, playing in our living room and standing in what would be her own room in a couple of months, beaming up radiantly at the camera; her visits to a park in January; her going-home party at Huntington on February 22; the many images of her while she lived at home with us; two beautiful photos of her taken in May at All Saints Children's Center; Maggie Rascoe's birthday party (her friend from All Saints), which Jenny attended on June 8; and, Jenny's own third birthday (June 24) party at Vallejo Villas on Sunday, June 23rd. And, the final image in the album, my snapshot of her and Sue Collins sitting side-by-side by our pool at Vallejo Villas on July 4, 1991, the last photo I ever took of Jenny.

Also included was a sunflower petal and clover leaf from Jenny's grave. Suzanne had returned to Gethsemani for a retreat the August after Jenny's death. After her return to Los Angeles, she told me that one of the brothers had planted a sunflower on Jenny's grave that had grown quite tall but had not bloomed. On the last day of her visit, the flower had opened to display its full magnificence, and she had brought back one of its petals to me as a keepsake.

When I looked through these and many other things, such as the register book from Jenny's funeral mass and an album of bereavement cards, I remembered how I used to love doing things that involved getting Jenny's life in order. I recalled going to the county in March 1991, after Jenny had come home, and getting a copy of her birth certificate. And I remembered the pleasure I felt in making Jenny's identity "official" (something that turned out to be important and which no one else had ever thought to do) by applying for a social security number for her the same month. Her card arrived in April.

Suzanne, of course, had mementos also: photos of Jenny; a little piece of towel stained with bile from Jenny's stomach; and a lovely piece of art entitled the "Fish Painting," something Jenny had done only a few days before she died, and which I had framed for Suzanne.

On September 28, 1995, I again viewed my videotapes of Jennifer, that is, the one comprising almost two years of her life at Huntington, and the other of her and Suzanne on February 21, 1991, at All Saints Children's Center, the day before Jenny came to live with us. I had not watched either of the tapes since May 1992, except for the first few minutes of the All Saints video, which I had seen during the first part of 1995 when I had turned it off after the strange occurrence with the wind. My abstinence from watching them—nearly three and a half years—was due solely to my fear that they would be too painful to see. However, although they were deeply moving and meaningful when I finally looked at them again, I was relieved that the experience was not so gut-wrenching as I had feared. This was due solely to the fact that, before confronting them once more on September 28, I had written most of this book, which meant I had already done much soul-searching. Since July 11, 1995, when I first began this manuscript, I had lived immersed in the memories of my experiences with Jenny, which ranged from times of exquisite beauty to those of indescribable emotional pain. Almost the very first thing that I wrote about was the morning I had awakened to find Jenny dead. For although I knew that many other difficult and painful episodes would need to be relived and articulated, I thought to myself, "There. Now that's done. Nothing can be more painful than that."

As I watched the All Saints tape, one of the first things I noticed was how vocal Jenny was and how much she interacted with Suzanne. Over time, it had been difficult to remember exactly what Jenny's voice had sounded like, and hearing her again stirred to life a whole world of feelings and associations. Jenny had always gotten very involved in the changing of her dressings, the setting up of her pumps at night, and so on, and in the tape, she did something she used to do all the time that I had not thought about for a long while. As Suzanne was working on her dressings, Jenny would look at her questioningly from time to time and say, "Almost?"—meaning that she was wondering if things were just about finished up so that she could get dressed and go about her business. And, during the time that I had known Jenny, she would, under the same circumstances, also often say, "All done?" And Suzanne and I would answer, saying "Almost, almost done," or, "Yes, all done." Since Jenny's death, I have often wondered what she was referring to when she lay in her crib, asleep, on her final night on earth, after many hours of turmoil, saying "All done, all done." What had been "all done" in her mind that night? A change of dressings in a dream? Her life itself?

Sometimes, during the tape with Suzanne, Jenny would say, "Ow," or "Owie," which probably indicated that she was simply getting impatient or just "cautioning" Suzanne to be careful. When we had known her, Jenny would usually say "owie" when she had a stomach cramp. At such times, she would have Suzanne or me gently pat her tummy with the palm of our hand while saying, very softly, "All better." And it usually worked. I was reminded of how brave and stoic Jenny used to be about physical inconvenience and pain, of how very little and how rarely she complained, even when there was good reason, and of how strong her wonderful little spirit had been.

As Suzanne demonstrated Jenny's dressings to the staff, Jenny would make reference to the "tapes" (which always came out in a cute sort of punctuated way and sounded like "tapsh"), and the "wipes" (baby wipes). Jenny was almost always manageable during these procedures if she was given a piece of surgical tape to play with, and if she did not get it, one would be reminded until it was forthcoming. Several times during the demonstration, she admonished Suzanne in a clear voice, in her typical adult fashion, about her gastrostomy tube, saying, "Don't touch. Don't touch." Finally, when Suzanne had finished all the procedures and produced a fresh diaper, she said to Jenny, "Buns up!" (a little command I had forgotten about). And, responding immediately, Jenny arched herself up, hoisting her bottom off the table so that Suzanne could put on the diaper.

At the end of the tape, Suzanne stood Jenny up and arranged her little top and her shorts. During the last few seconds of the video, I stared into the beautiful, bottomless depths of Jenny's wide eyes, remembering what an ancient, wise, incomparable soul she was.

During the period I watched these videotapes and reflected on the powerful memories they aroused, I paused one evening to take stock of the various mementos of Jenny's life around my house. On the bookshelf was the block of wood that she had brought home from All Saints in July 1991, to which she had glued various little pegs and knobs. Next to it was the glass jar filled with the flowers that I had allowed to dry after placing them in her room on June 24, 1992, which would have been her fourth birthday. Then, there was the crucifix above the front door in the foyer, which at one time had rested on the top of her little coffin before she was buried. Downstairs, nailed to the wall on the right side of the door frame of Jenny's former room (still her room, in my mind), and at what would have been about eye level for her, was the Jewish good-luck charm that had been given to us by Suzanne's friend, Zippy, while Jenny was alive and living with us.

Finally, in the center of my altar was a beautiful soapstone box with a hinged lid and three inner chambers that I had only recently placed there. Inside each chamber was a smaller container. In the left one was a small piece of towel stained with bile from Jenny's stomach. In the center one, a small soapstone box upon which I had permanently sealed the lid, were the cuttings of Jenny's hair and fingernails that had been given to us at the time of her funeral mass at Holy Family Church in South Pasadena. In the right one was a delicate little gold bracelet Jenny had worn and a tiny dried flower she had once picked outside our home and given to me. Among all of Jenny's things which I had, and all of which I cherished, these were especially sacred. They belonged, I felt, in the company of the various objects of spiritual import that comprised my place of meditation, such as the pictures of Krishna, Christ, Yogananda, and others, and the lovely, much treasured, small white statue of the meditating Buddha that Suzanne had given me one Christmas. When I think of God, I think of Jenny. One cannot be in my heart without the other.

Jessica

Jessica Christina Pivaral, Jennifer's half-sister, was born on October 8, 1991, almost exactly two months after Jenny's death. Although as I have said, Rosa Pivaral, whose family was from Guatemala, was the mother of both children, they had different fathers. And whereas I have some information on Jennifer's father, that is, at least his name, country of birth (El Salvador), character, and general whereabouts, I have no information whatsoever on Jessica's father except that he was Hispanic and that he was in prison at the time Jessica was born. No father's name appears on Jessica's certificate of baptism, and I have never seen any of her other birth records. Rosa was also serving a prison term when Jessica was born. Just prior to giving birth, she was moved temporarily to a medical facility outside the prison and then returned shortly afterward. Emotionally, this must have been very painful for her—to bear a child and then to have it immediately taken away. Fortunately, Jessica was transferred almost immediately and permanently to Graciela, her maternal grandmother.

Jessica was loved and well cared for in her new Malibu home. Graciela, her maternal grandmother, was now her legal guardian. Rosa's two teenage sisters, Maria and Nancy, who lived with Graciela, their mother, also provided much care; in fact, from a fairly early age, Jessica came to regard Maria, the youngest sister, as a central mother figure, although she reserved the term "mommy" for Graciela.

In addition, especially at an early age, Jessica was surrounded by other family members—aunts, uncles, and cousins.

Jessica's physical surroundings are, in my opinion, about as close to paradise on earth as one can get. For many years, Graciela has held the position of a live-in housekeeper for an elderly, well-to-do widow in Malibu whose beautiful ranch-style home is situated at the end of a quiet road in a very natural, immaculately groomed upper-class neighborhood. The house, which sits on a small, gated estate, is surrounded by exquisite gardens filled with flowers, herbs, and fruit trees, and it is criss-crossed by winding foot paths. The most breathtaking feature of the property is the front of the house, which has a roofed patio the length of the structure, and is about sixty or seventy feet back from a cliff that drops off steeply to a narrow, private beach on the Pacific. From the patio of the house, one looks past a lawn of ivy and low shrubbery to a magnificent, totally unobstructed view of ocean, sky, and an occasional sailboat. Since the front of the house faces west, the sunsets are beyond description. When I visit there, the word that always comes to my mind is "Eden." Since I am a fanatic about quiet and privacy (and do not have nearly enough of either in Los Angeles), the setting is almost heartbreakingly beautiful. The only sounds to be heard are waves, wind, and distant sea gulls.

One of Jessica's playmates is Patty (an odd name for a male dog, but true, nevertheless), the enormous Irish wolfhound that lives on the property and belongs to the elderly lady who resides there. Despite the fact that Patty outweighs Jessica by a factor of five to one, he is literally afraid of his own shadow and is quite a docile companion for her. And even though I am an ardent animal lover who is usually able to make friends with even the most savage beasts, and although I have been around Patty for almost four years, he still will not come near me or Suzanne, or practically anyone but his owner, Jessica, and maybe a couple of others. It is also a little strange, but true, that the owner's deceased husband and a former canine pet lie buried somewhere beneath the beautiful flower beds between the house and the road.

Just a few blocks away is a large community park with many play facilities for children. The residential streets there are quiet and relatively safe and are frequented by people with strollers, those walking their dogs, and even people on horseback, since many residents in the area keep horses.

After seeing Jessica for the first time in October 1991, when she was two and a half weeks old, my feelings about her were tentative. After the Pivarals came for dinner on Thanksgiving, Suzanne and I became Jessica's godparents and had her baptism at Holy Family Church in December. We did not see the baby again until May 1992, when we drove to Malibu to visit her when she was a little over seven months old. Then my heart had opened up to her like a flower, and I loved her very much. The following weekend, May 23 and 24, Suzanne and I brought Jessica home with us to stay overnight, and she has been coming ever since, every three or four weeks. Since Suzanne and I no longer live together, Jessica sleeps at my house, and Suzanne comes over to visit.

When Jennifer came into my life, she was in many ways a savior to me. Her love and the love I was able to give her transformed me, and her passing has not changed that, despite the long and difficult grieving process that continues even today. More than four years after her death, her spirit continues to exert a powerful and positive influence on my life.

However, my life would not be what it is today unless another little savior had appeared on the scene to help ameliorate and transform the devastating emotional consequences that Jennifer's passing had for me. In my mind, the presence of Jessica Christina in my life is no accident, but part of some Design. Is she the "Tina" that Nicki Mellette, the astrologer, kept naming inadvertently a couple of weeks prior to her birth? And is she one of the children that Lazaris said would come into my life in conjunction with Jennifer's influence and guidance? (One reference he made during a reading on October 12, 1991, only a few hours before Nancy Pivaral had called to tell me that Rosa had given birth to Jessica on October 8.) In my mind, the answer is "yes" to both questions.

I wondered many times during the first years after Jessica's arrival if she was Jennifer reincarnated. Today I do not believe this. It is my conviction that Jennifer's spirit is on another, higher plane of existence, nevertheless still in touch with my own heart, and that she shall remain there until I see her again after I too am gone. I also believe that Jessica and I (as father and daughter), and Jessica and Jennifer (as sisters), and probably all three of us together, are strongly connected through past-life relationships. I am open to the possibility that Jessica is the reincarnation of Wendy, Jennifer's dead Siamese twin who did not make it into the physical world.

But whatever the past may be, Jessica's presence in my life has been a priceless and exquisitely timed gift. When Suzanne and I first brought her home, she was still a helpless little baby. Fortunately, Jessica has always been very healthy physically. Nevertheless, I remember how, for at least the first year that she came to stay with Suzanne and me on weekends, I would cautiously and nervously approach her as she slept and place the palm of my hand on her back or chest to make sure that she was breathing. Sometimes, I became very frightened that she would die because of the way I had found Jenny dead. Over the years (I cannot believe how quickly they have passed!), we have been able to watch her grow and begin to crawl, to get about first in her little walker and later to struggle to her feet and walk by holding onto furniture, to begin to talk, and to become a personality.

Thus, although I feel that there is definitely something in my karma and in the plan for my life that has been drafted in the interior of my soul which seems to steer me away time and time again from the long-term stability and the commitments of a traditional family (I think, perhaps, in order to drive me, sometimes painfully, to seek self-realization), there has been a wisdom in all of this that has provided my life with a critical balance between my metaphysical world of perceptions and experiences and the beautiful knowledge and experience, through Jennifer and Jessica, of real human love and intimacy.

The Pivarals began to refer to me as Daddy, or as Graciela used to say some-times, Poppie, when speaking to Jessica. I have always been happy and proud that, since learning to speak, Jessica has called me Daddy. Anyone seeing Suzanne, Jessica, and me eating in a restaurant—one of our favorite activities—would think that we were a family. (Jessica has become quite a gourmet, although it seems that her favorite food will always be french fries and ketchup.) However, Jessica has always referred to Suzanne as "Suzie," since "Mommy" is reserved for Graciela.

In the coming years, Jessica will have many questions about the people in her life. One day in early 1995, Jessica asked Nancy, "Why doesn't Daddy live with us?" When she comes to Vallejo Villas to visit, she still seems to think that the photos of Jennifer are of her, and that all of Jennifer's artwork is hers. One day when I was standing in the living room with Jessica in my arms, I pointed to the "Pitter Patter of Little Feet" hanging on the wall over the piano and said to her, "Who did that?" Jessica smiled, and said "Me!" I hope that someday Jessica will read this book and know what Jenny meant to me, and what a lovely gift she her-self has been in my life.

During early 1994, after it had become definite that Suzanne and I would be getting divorced and that Suzanne would be getting her own place, I began to feel some concern about how Jessica would take to it. The first time she came to visit me for the weekend when I was living alone, not too long after Suzanne had moved out in late May, the condo probably did not look all that different to her, since there was still plenty of furniture that was familiar to her, including the grand piano. When Jessica asked where Suzie was, I simply answered that she would be coming over in a little bit. Later that evening, after we had spent most of the day together, it became time for Suzanne to go home to her own apartment. At first, Jessica seemed somewhat concerned, but I said, "Don't worry; she'll come back to see us in the morning," and we had little difficulty over it.

Soon we began taking Jessica over to "Suzie's place," and Jessica seemed to have no problem that Daddy and Suzie each had a place of their own. After all, the three of us were together most of the time anyway, and little had changed. And, over the most recent months, after spending Saturday with us, Suzanne has come by every Sunday morning, by which time I have gotten Jessica bathed and fed, and taken her to church. Getting Jessica out of bed on Sunday morning has never been a problem, regardless of how exhausting the day before has been. Usually, by 7:00 o'clock in the morning (what a horrible time to have to get up on a Sun-day!), Jessica is tapping me on the shoulder, making sure that I am awake, and telling me that she wants to go upstairs and watch TV.

I must relate one incident that took place when Suzanne and Jessica were in church, and which, for a time, put a moratorium on that activity. According to Suzanne, Jessica had been very fidgety and was becoming annoying to the man in the pew next to her. When Suzanne quietly reprimanded her and asked her to be still, at a moment which, unfortunately, happened to be one of dead silence in the service, Jessica yelled out something like "fut," as Jenny used to say. Jessica's pronunciation of the word was much better. Then, she yelled it a second time. The whole congregation heard it, and Suzanne was so mortified that she was almost paralyzed. What could she do? Pick Jessica up and walk out, drawing more attention to herself and possibly increasing the likelihood that the choice word might find expression again? Fortunately, there were no repeats that day, and when Suzanne began taking Jessica to church on Sunday regularly a few months later, the word seemed to have been forgotten, or at least reserved for other occasions. On one hand, one is not supposed to laugh at such things. And, certainly, such behavior must be corrected. Nevertheless, when Suzanne told me the story, I thought it was one of the funniest things I had heard in ages (and I am still amused by it).

From time to time, I have heard Jessica come out with some other interesting words and expressions (which she has undoubtedly heard from her little friends at day care). Unfortunately, my cat, Sarada, who is really unpleasant to anyone but Suzanne and me, and who never made up to Jenny, has never been nice to Jessica, either. She is declawed and therefore cannot scratch Jessica, and she would not bite her. But Jessica's repeated attempts over the years to become friends have been met only with nasty hisses and intimidating charges. Jessica has given up and has become unfriendly to Sarada, sometimes throwing a stuffed animal at her and the like. Nevertheless, she still tries to make friends. Occasionally, I will hear Jessica tearfully calling my name, only to discover that she is trying to go downstairs to get a toy, but Sarada is sitting in the hallway blocking Jessica's path and refusing to move. Jessica is afraid to go around her, and thus Sarada gets her revenge.

Only a couple of weeks ago, Jessica and Sarada were having an unpleasant encounter, and I heard Jessica address her spitefully as "Butt-Head." Later that same day, I was cleaning Sarada's litter box, and Jessica was watching (she was always interested in how I disposed of the "kittie poopies"). When she inquired what I was doing, I said, "Changing Sarada's litter box." Jessica responded, "You mean, Butt-Head's litter box." I could not restrain myself from laughing out loud. The name was well-deserved.

Jessica's favorites activities are playing with building blocks and doing jigsaw puzzles (always insisting on my help), watching videos, going to the swimming pool, playing in the park in South Pasadena (where Suzanne and I used to go with Jenny), and, most recently, shopping (not a favorite of mine). Finally, after many promises, Suzanne and I took Jessica to Disneyland at the end of July. Despite the brutal heat and incredible crowds, it was one of the most wonderful days I have had in a long time, seeing how happy and excited she was by everything. After every ride, she would look at me and say, "I want to go on that one again!"

During the warmest months, I take Jessica to our swimming pool. She loves the water, and I hope she will be able to take swimming lessons soon. I am an expert swimmer and used to be a lifeguard and swimming instructor. However, it is difficult to teach Jessica much when I only have her in the water a few times each year. One thing that has always amazed me is her total trust in me. She will throw herself without hesitation into water over her head, with me standing there to fish her out. In fact, this is one of her favorite things. As a child, I never would have trusted my parents in such a way.

Because of my relationships with Jennifer and Jessica, I have been fortunate enough to learn that loving a child and being the object of a child's love is one of the most sacred and beautiful things that one can ever experience. I realize that we feel differently about every single person in our lives. No two relationships are the same; each love is unique. I am sure that I love and adore Jessica as much as any parent loves their own biological child. I always want to be a part of her life, and for her to think of me as her "Daddy." I want to watch her grow up, and I want to be there for her. Ours is a beautiful, precious relationship.

The love I have for Jenny is a fire that burns eternally, one which has changed my soul through an intense and extraordinary alchemy, and which may truly be called "soul-searing." And although the love I had for Jenny was in every way parental and father-child in nature, there was another element to it that was pure, soul-to-soul communication of indescribable intensity and power.

The love I feel for Jessica is total, protective, parental, adoring, and faithful. She is now the most special thing in my life. When she first started coming to Vallejo Villas to visit, it almost broke my heart to take her back to Malibu. I felt like she belonged with me. Over time, I have become much more accepting and comfortable with the arrangement, especially because I know that she gets so much love and care at home and that she loves Graciela, Nancy, and Maria with all her heart. In fact, knowing this helps me to keep the true perspective that, after all, even though she loves Suzanne and me a great deal, in her mind and heart, Malibu is her real home. And that is how it should be.

In September 1995, when I was looking around the house at mementos of Jennifer, examining many of her records, and watching the videotapes of her, I also reflected with pleasure upon those things which spoke of Jessica: the numerous photographs of her that I had mounted and framed, including an earlier one of her taking a bath in the kitchen sink, and the recent shot of her, sitting in the living room and watching her video of *The Wizard of Oz* (I know it all by heart now); the plaque of baked clay on my shelf, with her handprint made at day care in May 1994 at two years and seven months; and, the georgeous 1995 wall calendar hanging in my kitchen, also made by Jessica at day care and given to me by her during the Christmas 1994 holidays, each month of which features a painting she herself did. There was also the portfolio that I had made for Jessica's artwork, just as I had done for Jenny. I had Jessica's Certificate of Baptism, and the candle which came with it; and, I had the extensive photo album which I had been compiling ever since the first snapshots were taken when I saw her for the first time in Malibu in October 1991. Finally, there was a lovely little book of snapshots and captions which Nancy Pivaral had made and given to me, featuring Jessica, but including Jennifer.

On Sunday, October 8, 1995, in the early afternoon, Suzanne and I drove together to Graciela's church to attend Jessica's fourth birthday party. On the way, I had asked Suzanne if she thought that Jessica would pay much attention to us, since she became very enthusiastic and gregarious on social occasions and tended to run around a lot. On similar past occasions, she had not spent much time with me, except when I had taken her to my annual company picnics where she did not know anyone else (and even there she had quickly made friends with other children). At one point during the drive, I even said, "I wonder if Jessica really loves me?"

After Suzanne and I arrived, and Jessica had played and run about, she charged up to the huge birthday cake and, in her excitement, accidentally stuck her entire arm into it. The room was full of Jessica's friends and relatives, and I was very touched when, without thinking, she ran immediately to me to clean her up. Later on, while playing and running outside, she skinned her knee on the sidewalk. Coming back inside in tears, she came straight to Suzanne and me and sat on Suzanne's lap for a while. When she wanted to go the bathroom to get a cool, wet paper towel for her knee, she would not let anyone but Daddy take her. And afterward, she happily spent much of her time in my arms. Her demonstration to me of her love and trust that day was a beautiful gift, and a direct and unmistakable answer to my question. The way she had looked to me when she needed help and comfort had made me deeply happy.

During the drive to the birthday party, Suzanne brought up the possibility that she would be moving back to Kentucky as early as the end of February 1996. After our divorce, she had mentioned from time to time her intention to go back eventually, but I had always tried to put it out of my mind. I did not even want to think about the possibility. In fact, several months earlier, I had had one of the saddest dreams of my life, in which I was saying goodbye to her. I have known for many years, of course, that Suzanne never really got "settled" in L. A., and I cannot say that I blame her. Throughout the part of our lives spent together on the West Coast, Suzanne has talked constantly of her homesickness (another problem in the marriage). But even now, when we are no longer husband and wife, the thought of her moving away is terribly painful.

I still love Suzanne very much, and I always will. Above all others, she is the one with whom I have shared the beauty of Jennifer and the sadness of losing her. That bond will always remain between Suzanne and me, and I feel a deep soul connection with her. In fact, since the end of our marriage, I have in some ways felt that love even more strongly, because the sources of friction that eroded our marriage are not there any more, or at least they have become irrelevant.

When Suzanne brought up the subject of returning to Kentucky again on the 8th of October, I felt as if I had been hit with a sledgehammer. The following day, I even experienced the same hypersensitivity to light, heat, and noise that I had felt in the days following Jenny's passing. There was a terrible, familiar ache inside of me, a grieving, a sense, once again, of death. I had once lost Jenny; now, the person with whom I had shared her was talking about going away. I was very shaken for a couple of days, and I called Suzanne on the night after Jessica's party to tell her that I still loved her very much and that I hoped she would give moving away a great deal of thought before making a decision. The choice, of course, would be hers, but I wanted her to know how I felt.

Suzanne and Jessica love each other very much. I have tried to imagine Jessica and me spending weekends without Suzanne, and the large hole that Jessica and I would feel with her gone. A day or two after the birthday party, I found myself wondering how I would explain Suzanne going away to Jessica, and how she would take it. I suddenly realized that I had never thought about how I would have explained Suzanne going away to Jenny, if that had come to pass. I had been so caught up with other concerns that I had failed to consider it. As far as Jenny is concerned, it does not matter anymore. But if Suzanne leaves, Jessica will miss her Suzie very much. And Suzanne will want to continue to be part of Jessica's life as much as geographical separation will permit. But the distance will inevitably weaken the bond.

Just as I still get melancholy when Jessica goes home after each visit, I am also usually sad because the temporary family that Suzanne, Jessica, and I become on those weekends has disbanded once again. And somewhere, deep inside myself, I feel a longing for what might have been—a lasting marriage and the possibility that a little girl who came home from a hospital to live with us might grow up and have a long life. Nevertheless, I accept that it is not that way, that it was never meant to be that way, and that, in spite of the sadness, life is ever offering new experiences and opportunities for growth and transformation. And, possibly the most important thing, there is my belief that my relationship with Jenny is eternal.

The Pivarals know that, God forbid, if anything should ever happen to them, I will take Jessica and raise her as my own daughter. But whatever comes to pass, I will cherish her always, not only because she is the sister of my precious Jenny, but simply because she is who she is, for which I love her totally.

Advice to
Bereaved Parents

At that time the disciples came to Jesus, saying, "Who then is greatest in the kingdom of heaven?"

And He called a child to Himself and stood him in their midst, and said, "Truly I say to you, unless you are converted and become like children, you shall not enter the kingdom of heaven. Whoever then humbles himself as this child, he is the greatest in the kingdom of heaven. And whoever receives one such child in My name receives Me; but whoever causes one of these little ones who believe in Me to stumble, it is better for him that a heavy millstone be hung around his neck, and that he be drowned in the depth of the sea."

—Matthew 18: 1-6

The Sufis say, "Let God kill him who does not know, yet presumes to show others the way." Experience is the best teacher, although not always a gentle one. I believe also that people should carefully heed the guidance of their own hearts. One must be receptive, willing to learn, and discriminating. The same is true of advice, if it comes from someone qualified to give it. I have often sought guidance from others. Yet I make my own decisions, right or wrong, since I am responsible for my own evolution.

Perhaps I have already given advice indirectly by recounting the story of Jenny's life. But I feel I should focus on some of the things I have recognized from my own experiences and offer some suggestions to others who have lost children.

Everyone is different. There is something unique in each human being's perspective on life, his personal religious ideas, ethics, morals, habits, and so on. Although there are millions of Christians, Hindus, Buddhists, Moslems, and more, each person within a tradition has his own religious concepts, even if they vary only minutely from the ideas of those around him. It can be no other way, for each individual perceives and experiences life through the personal filter of his own consciousness. And of course, one's viewpoint of life changes dramatically as he grows older. So each person views death and the loss of a loved one differently.

In my experience, no other loss of a loved one is as terrible as the loss of a child. Generally, this seems to hold true regardless of the age of the child or the manner of death. Whether the loss was an adult child killed on the highway or in a hunting accident, a teenage suicide or drive-by shooting victim, a child with cancer, a newborn, or even a fetus lost through miscarriage, the impact on the parents is often the same.

Parents who have lost a child often imagine that losing a child in some other manner would be even worse. For example, I have heard parents who have lost children to cancer say that they could never imagine the horror of having a child murdered. I am immediately reminded of a grief support meeting for bereaved parents in a private home I attended one evening. The leader opened the meeting with a short introduction and then provided an opportunity for each person to introduce themselves and say whatever they wished about why they were there. This part of the meeting, although often painful, served to dispel the tension felt at the outset of a meeting. As each person's turn came, the others listened attentively and compassionately to the painful but familiar stories being recounted—deaths of children through diseases, accidents, drug overdoses, and the like.

Finally, a couple who had come to the group for the first time told their story. After entrusting their baby to a sitter they had hired through an agency they had researched and found to have a solid reputation in the community, they went out for the evening. They returned to find that the sitter had killed their baby by shaking it repeatedly, causing a fatal intracranial hemorrhage. There was absolute silence. For a few moments, the group was so stunned at the horror of this that they were speechless. Despite the pain that each person there had felt as a result of the death of their own child, they could not imagine the agony and outrage that this couple must have felt. Although I personally feel this way also—that the death of a child through the cruelty, evil, or simple stupidity of someone else seems the worst horror of all—I have been quite surprised to hear, many times, that parents of murdered children feel that losing a child through disease would be even worse.

Parents who have not lost a child through suicide often have the idea that this would be the worst of all. Again, despite the terrible pain that the parents of suicide victims feel, they often disagree. Possibly this is because it is viewed that, however undeniably tragic and painful the aftermath for the survivors, the person who takes his own life has at least some control over his own death. Seeing this on the page in front of me does not do much to convince me. Parents of children who have taken their own lives face special problems. They have to wrestle with their own moral convictions and religious attitudes about suicide, and the attitudes of those around them—their relatives, friends, business colleagues, and the clergy. In addition, although parents always try to blame themselves for their child's death, regardless of the circumstances, parents of suicide victims have the burden of asking themselves if there was not something they could have done to prevent it. Did they miss something? Were they not paying attention? Did they fail to see the critical signs, the calls for help? Or even worse, did their child commit suicide because of them? Did they drive their child to it? I cite these questions not to cast doubt upon the parents of suicide victims, but to articulate the pain and self-doubt they suffer. Additionally, some of the people around these parents may wrongly blame them for their child's suicide.

Each situation has its own tragic circumstances, its own ironies, problems, and pain. A child has died. And regardless of how it happened, deep in the hearts of the mother and father, and others who loved the child, the loss is unimaginably painful, shattering, and unacceptable. With the death of any loved one comes grief and the re-examination of one's values and philosophy. Even though we know that death is inevitable, we push the reality aside most of the time—until another death touches us and forces us to think about what awaits us and every person we love and cherish.

If someone dies of old age, or if an adult dies of a heart attack because of smoking, drinking, undisciplined eating habits, or other forms of self-abuse, one is able at least to see an inevitability there that mitigates the loss to some degree. But when a child dies, it seems so senseless. What did the child do to deserve this? What kind of god could allow this to happen or justify it? One asks such questions in the face of many of the actual and potential horrors of life.

Regardless of the circumstances, parents often blame themselves for the death of their child, even if they are completely free of culpability. And if they do not blame the child's death directly upon themselves, they ask themselves and others if there was something they did or did not do to contribute to it. Surely there was something they could or should have done, or some warning sign that they failed to see or react to appropriately. Surely, they failed somehow as parents. How could they not have failed? Their child is dead. Perhaps its death is punishment for some sin or moral transgression that they themselves committed. This kind of self-doubt is natural and understandable. The strange thing would be its absence. The health, happiness, and every other aspect of that child's welfare was the parents' responsibility. The heart of the parent, in its own touching but sometimes strange logic, blames itself. The child sees its parents as omnipotent. Mistakenly, the parent also sees himself as omnipotent, and is then overcome with guilt and self-blame when he fails in that task—when he is unable to protect from harm the child who he loved so deeply and who trusted him and looked to him for everything.

From the day Jenny died, I asked myself if I could have prevented her death. Even today, I wonder if I made some fatal error in judgement the night she died. I will wonder as long as I live. A nagging voice inside asks disturbing questions. Should I have been more concerned that afternoon prior to her death, when we were coming home in the car from day care and she fell into that strange, deep sleep? That night, after she went to bed, when she was so fitful, should I have ignored the opinions of Zippy, Dr. Laurance, and Sue Collins and taken her to the hospital? Would she still be alive and with me today if I had done this? And finally, that night in the midst of my uncertainty and emotional turmoil, when that alarm went off inside me, seeming to tell me to turn off the pumps, and I dismissed it, though reluctantly—was that the fatal error? Was that the decisive act, a stupid insensitivity to my own intuition, that killed her?

Up until that night, I had been so vigilant with Jenny, trying so hard not to make any mistakes in caring for her. My failure to act on that final intuition bothers me more than anything else. Did I fail to respond to guidance that could have saved her life? Or, did fate or some personal destiny trick me or blind me to that prompting because it was really Jenny's time to leave? I must accept that I will probably never know for sure—at least in this lifetime. But I know this: If I could go back in time, with the experience and insight I have now, and make that decision over again, I would have disconnected Jennifer from her pumps and taken her straight to the pediatric unit at Huntington despite what anyone told me, medical authority or not. Therefore, my advice to parents is this: If you suspect that your child is seriously ill or that there is something wrong, get medical attention immediately and to hell with the doctor's advice. Do not take a chance with your child's life. It will be much easier to live with being viewed as overprotective than with the death of your child and the haunting fear that you could have saved their life.

One may also blame others for a child's death. Justifiable or not, this tendency is also natural, if not irresistible. Obviously, in cases where negligence or incompetence, medical and otherwise, on the part of others, is likely or even suspected, various avenues of investigation and legal action are open and should be pursued, both for the peace of mind of the parents and in the interests of justice being done and irresponsibility punished. I know next to nothing about such courses of action, however, because I never saw any reason to pursue them. In Jenny's case, neither Suzanne nor I were ever inclined to point a finger at anyone.

Many people gave Jenny every chance they knew how to give her, according to their experience and abilities. And they loved her. They were mothers and fathers to her for almost two and a half years. They bought her clothes and toys, and made Huntington as much of a home for her as anyone could have. They took her clothes home and washed them, gave her birthday parties, read her stories, and agonized when she was sick. And when it came time to let go of her and send her home with Suzanne and me, they gave us their blessing and total support.

In providing medical treatment and a room for Jenny, Huntington incurred astronomical medical expenses—in the millions of dollars—which they wrote off. From the president and C.E.O. to the maids, everyone knew and loved her. With respect to Dr. Laurance, I doubt that he ever came anywhere close to breaking even financially for the care he provided for Jenny, given what I know about the Medicare rules, restrictions, bureaucracy, and paperwork with which physicians have to deal. This is not even to mention Dr. Laurance's personal interest and commitment to her. I have been told about one episode with Jenny that occurred before I ever came to know her, during which she was in the pediatric intensive care unit and so sick that everyone had given up on her—except Dr. Laurance, who refused to stop trying. As far as I know, it was Dr. Laurance's determination and unwillingness to throw in the towel that enabled her to live and eventually provided me with the life-altering experience of being her father.

I have some regrets and feelings that maybe if someone had done this or that, things would have turned out differently. Maybe they should have kept Jenny in the hospital longer, for more observation, that week prior to her death. Maybe they should have been more thorough in testing her. Maybe Dr. Laurance should have been more cautious and admitted Jenny to the hospital when I called him the night she died. There are lots of maybes and no concrete answers.

There is one other thing about which I have concern and some regret, although the outcome for Jenny would have been the same. I regret that I did not prevent the swift removal of Jenny's pumps and her TPN—both the TPN which she took the night she died and what was left unused in the refrigerator. I feel strongly that the pumps and the TPN should have been tested by independent technicians and laboratories to determine possibly if there had been an equipment malfunction or a bad batch of TPN. In yielding to the wishes of others, I lost this opportunity. True, Jenny was gone and nothing could change that. But any parent would want to know why their child died—and if someone was to blame. Jenny's pumps and TPN were two possible explanations that were never explored. I would like to know the truth, even if it is painful, and to have no doubts. To me, knowing that Jenny died of natural causes would be better than discovering that someone had carelessly mixed up a lethal batch of TPN.

Regarding self-blame and placing blame on others, I thank Suzanne here, openly and deeply, for the support that she offered me after Jenny's death. If Suzanne ever harbored any feelings whatsoever that I had contributed in any way to Jenny's death, I never suspected it. When I questioned and doubted myself, Suzanne always reassured me, telling me that I had been a wonderful father and that my self-examination was entirely natural and a universal phenomenon among parents who have lost children. Whether there really was anything I could have done to save Jenny, Suzanne explained to me that the mind of a bereaved parent will go to extraordinary lengths to blame itself. She told me this patiently and repeatedly, until it finally began to sink in and give me some perspective on things.

In all honesty, if the tables had been turned—if I had been out of town and Jenny had died while under Suzanne's care—I would have wondered if Suzanne had committed a fatal error in procedure or judgment. And if I had wondered such a thing, I ask myself if I would have been insensitive enough to have added to her anguish by saying something about it. However, my feelings are not about judging Suzanne. I would have had such feelings regardless of who my wife was. Rather, my admission reflects my own shortcomings. Parents who have lost a child need to pay very close attention to any feelings, however subtle, they may have about the culpability of the other parent, justified or not. Such feelings need to be dealt with, but in the proper setting, because whether suppressed or expressed, they could destroy the bond between the parents.

If you know or suspect that your child died because of someone else's incompetence, pursue all available legal remedies. It will not bring your child back, but it may save someone else's. On the other hand, if you know that no one caused your child's death, be mindful, nevertheless, of the tendency to blame something or someone else because of your need to vent your grief, confusion, and anger. These emotions are natural and inevitable and, if unexpressed, are damaging to one's emotional health. But they are best expressed and dealt with in a nurturing setting such as that of a grief support group, in which you can find the right kind of understanding and fellowship.

Grief support groups can be invaluable. Like everything else, they are not for everyone. For many, they have been a salvation. I do not know exactly how new such groups are, but I suspect few, if any, existed fifteen or twenty years ago. They are definitely growing. An individual's temperament may resonate better with one group than another. Not only do various organizations differ, but small groups within a given organization vary in character. Do not give up on the whole idea if you do not feel comfortable in the first group you visit. Try another.

Some organizations meet only in members' homes, with each monthly meeting hosted by a different participant. Other groups may meet at a YMCA, a church, a hospital, or other institution. Also, larger organizations, in addition to having small groups that usually meet once a month, may host a larger monthly meeting at a hospital or somewhere else designed to accommodate a greater attendance. These meetings usually have established agendas and may include guest speakers or films. Organizations maintain membership rosters, supply names of individuals who may be called upon in times of crises, publish newsletters, have picnics and other outings, and offer an array of support services and activities.

If you attend such a support group, you may be put off by the first meeting. You may feel apprehensive and uncomfortable, both about going and once you arrive. After all, you have gone there to share what is most likely the most painful experience of your lifetime and to hear stories much like your own. After you leave, you may feel drained or exhausted, very sad, and you may have the conviction that this kind of setting will not help you. Do not make a hasty decision. You may feel differently by the next meeting. Despite the pain you focused on, you may soon realize that it did you some good, and that you want to go back. Also, others in the group will understand your initial reaction, because they probably had similar feelings.

Go for three or four months and then make an assessment. How do you feel? Better? Worse? Of course, the pain will still be there, but you may realize that you do not feel so alone—others can understand and support you. Between meetings, find one or two people in the group you can phone or meet over a cup of coffee. You may establish some deep and lasting friendships. Chances are the meetings will help you, and you will look forward to them. But if you attend one group for several meetings and things do not feel right, try another group or a different organization entirely before giving up. You may derive enough emotional benefits to warrant the effort of finding a group in which you feel comfortable.

If you become established in a support group, you will wonder how long you want to attend. Stay as long as you wish—as long as you are deriving benefit. Also, you may wish to help and support other members. Some people attend only a few times. Others stay with the group for years. The first time Suzanne and I went, we were very naive about the nature and length of the grieving process. We thought that it was normal to grieve for the departed, regardless of who they are, for perhaps a year. Both of us were somewhat taken aback to hear others in the group say that their child had been dead for two, three, or four or more years. At first, this seemed abnormal. Were these people emotional cripples?

When one has lost a child, the grieving process can continue for a lifetime. One does not really put such a loss behind them. Time simply enables one to heap more and more current experiences upon the mind and memory so that past hurts become buried or latent. But somewhere inside, the hurts remain ready to come forth with unbelievable energy and clarity if the right stimulus is applied.

This should not frighten anyone. It is simply the way human beings work emotionally. After the death of a child, one does not get on with one's life as before, and one does not get back to normal. That kind of "normal" is gone forever—gone with the death of the child who was loved so much. But hopefully, in time, the pain changes because it is accepted, not denied; and one learns gradually to readjust, to reshape one's existence around the undeniable reality of such a loss. Does one heal? Yes, over time—but not because of time. Hurt is buried by time. Hurt is transformed and healed by sincere inner work on one's self, by facing pain, by accepting it, embracing it, and working with it.

The passing of a child from this plane of existence to another does not end the relationship between that child and you. I believe that the relationship is eternal, that time and death do not limit the soul. Personally, I would prefer not to exist if I thought that Jenny's death was the end of our bond. I do not accept this. This does not mean that I cling to her. I must accept the physical separation. But there is an eternal link between our souls.

The soul is eternal; the personality is transitory and changeful. Recognize the difference. True union with one's self can only be found in the soul, and real unity with others is possible only on this deeper level. When I recognized this through extensive meditation, I discovered a new strength and self-reliance. Therefore, I attended support groups only for about six months.

Individual counseling with a psychiatrist, psychologist, or social worker is another avenue for working through the loss of a child, and one should never feel ashamed to pursue such possibilities. However, if I had to choose between individual counseling and a well-organized support group, I would opt for the group. There may not be one professional counselor in the group, but I guarantee you that everyone in the meeting will understand what you are going through. This can mean a great deal. I see nothing wrong with combining individual counseling and a support group. But if you seek private therapy, make sure the therapist is right for you.

Finding the right therapist is important. It is of paramount importance in dealing with something this heavy. I have heard terrible stories from people in grief support groups about therapists who were unbelievably insensitive and ill-equipped to deal with this kind of loss. I am not denigrating therapy or even implying that this kind of experience is typical; I am only advising you to be careful. This is another reason why the support groups are so useful. If you are seeing a therapist who is not equipped to deal with your loss, you will find it out right away in the group. Then, perhaps, you can try another therapist. Perhaps someone in the group can recommend one who is especially skilled. Such therapists do exist; in fact, some specialize in grief therapy. Suzanne and I saw a psychologist together—the same one—before and after Jenny's death. In fact, we took Jenny with us a couple of times while she was still alive. Dr. Wortz was an expert in biofeedback and taught Zen meditation. Although we did not attend his meditation classes, and despite the fact that he did not specialize in grief therapy, he was deeply sensitive to our loss and provided us with some wonderful insights. The therapy was helpful because of the resonance and communication that existed between us.

Even close friends or relatives may not really understand what you are going through if they have not lost a child. They may seem insensitive, especially as time goes on and they wonder why you have not gotten over it. Initially, my own mother had no concept of what Jenny meant to me. Only over time did she begin to comprehend the magnitude of my loss.

Perhaps, for any number of reasons, the mother and father of the dead child may not be able to support each other. They may blame each other, or they may have different emotional makeups that operate on completely independent time cycles and which require different kinds of support. Perhaps they are so overcome with their own grief that they simply have nothing left to enable them to help the other partner. Sometimes, in the midst of such grief, a mother who has lost one child will feel indifferent toward her other children for a time, or even resent them.

The death of your child may change your social life and your circle of friends. Relationships between adults often form because their children play together or go to the same school. In many cases, such relationships will fade away. This may seem sad, but it is true. The idea of death and dying is frightening to most people—and painful. And to a parent, nothing is more terrible than the idea of their own child dying. People do not want to be around death or other people who have been touched by it.

If a child of yours dies, you will find out who your true friends are. They will be the ones who will be around to support you regardless of the discomfort they feel because of the nearness of death. You may have to be stronger than those around you, not only in terms of negotiating your own grief, but in finding the maturity to forgive people who you thought would be there for you but turned out not to be. Sometimes they simply cannot help themselves. They are afraid and cannot understand, and they lack the maturity, insight, and strength to be what you would like them to be—which is not a sin, not something for which they can really be blamed. Let them fall away, if they must.

I was disillusioned when most of the contacts I had made at Huntington Memorial Hospital fell away immediately after Jenny's funeral. It closed a whole world for me, one I missed deeply. Some individuals there did not even respond to repeated phone messages and notes. I am not angry, and I blame no one. People were just being themselves and dealing with life as best they knew how. But it disappointed me very much. At first, I thought perhaps that they resented Suzanne and me for taking Jenny away or that they blamed us for her death. But in time I came to realize that they simply faded away. Only in one or two cases involving people who were very close to Jenny have I remained perplexed. Perhaps for them the pain was greatest, and that made it even harder for them to stay in our lives.

As with the death of any family member, there is the issue of what is to be done with a child's room and belongings. Be open and honest, most importantly with yourself, about your feelings of loss. Do not try to deny them or cover them up. It will not work, and it will block the healing that can otherwise be realized over time. Second, remember that you are unique and that you have your own emotional timetable for dealing with things. Do not let anyone coerce you into making decisions until you are ready.

Do not be in any hurry to dismantle your child's room or pack away clothing and toys. Also, do not be premature in giving anything away. Later, perhaps, you may choose to let go of some things, but if you do so too soon, you could regret the decision. Some people leave their child's room untouched for years, except to clean it. I see nothing wrong with this. It is a personal decision. There are no rules you must follow, and you need not care what others think.

I kept Jenny's clothes, shoes, toys, photos, paintings, drawings, medical supplies that were not carted off, and other possessions, except for a few things Suzanne wanted. I will never get rid of any of them. Physically, these things are all I have left of Jenny. They are sacred to me. I am happy to let Jessica—my goddaughter and Jenny's half-sister—play with Jenny's toys. I am sure that Jessica thinks the toys are hers, which is fine. But I will always keep them. After Jenny's death, people suggested I donate Jenny's clothing and toys to a charity. I told them emphatically to forget it. If there were a charity to which they really thought I should donate something, fine; I would buy something or give money, but Jennifer's things were staying with me.

I kept Jenny's room unchanged for a long time. In fact, I was adamant about leaving it untampered with, even with Suzanne. I am not ashamed or apologetic about this. I believe I had every right to feel that way. When it was suggested that perhaps I had turned it into a shrine, I said, "Fine. Maybe I have. So what?" If you feel defensive about the same issues, honor your emotions and instincts. Do not let anyone push you around. If you feel deeply it is best to dismantle things early, then do it. Just make your own decisions. You do not have to explain or justify them to anyone else. If someone else seems determined to "reason" with you or change your mind, just say, politely but firmly, "This is the way I want it. End of discussion." The shorter the response, the better.

I do not know how long I would have left Jenny's room unaltered (except that I began meditating in it), were it not that I finally felt forced to dismantle it in order to make more room and get our cars into the garage after they had been repeatedly vandalized. It was galling to have to destroy Jenny's room because of criminals who controlled the streets. At some point, I probably would have made some changes, but I was not ready then, especially not to dismantle it completely. If nothing else, I would most likely have left the room largely as it was for Jessica when she visited.

The day that I dismantled Jenny's room was indescribably painful. It was numbing and killing. There was nothing good or positive in the experience, or in the memory of it. I re-experienced my deepest grief, and part of me died that day. It was another reminder—a very anguishing and uncompromising one—that Jenny was gone forever. I am not convinced that I did the right thing, although at the time it seemed unavoidable. The room has never been the same since. The vibrations of love and happiness that were once there have, in my mind, been vandalized—torn asunder. Again, my advice is to allow yourself all the time you need, whether it is a month, or a year, or more, to make decisions about your child's room and other possessions. Do not be hurried. If you have doubts, wait, and reconsider the issue at a later time.

When I began spending time with Jenny on the pediatric ward at Huntington, I realized quickly how preciously fragile children are, that they are in no way exempt from disease and death, and that they are especially vulnerable to accidents and injuries. I saw or heard about many tragedies—children with cancer and other serious or fatal diseases, children with insurmountable birth defects, and babies who had failed to thrive because they were not loved by their parents. On some nights, I would go and sit for a while in the room of a young girl, probably not yet a teenager, who had bone cancer, and who would cry at night after her parents left because she could not go home with them. Coming back to the hospital after brief excursions home for holidays was especially hard for her.

Other children had suffered injuries, sometimes fatal, because of an adult's abuse, recklessness, or carelessness, or by a parent's unfortunate lapse of attention, possibly for only a few minutes or seconds—death or brain death from drowning, trauma from automobile accidents, accidental poisonings, and the like. I remember one poor little boy whose lower face, mouth, and neck were horribly disfigured from drinking a can of liquid drain cleaner that he accidentally got hold of. The inside of his mouth, his esophagus, and digestive tract were deeply scarred, and he had to breathe through a tracheotomy. I do not know how much reconstructive surgery was able to do for him. I saw another small boy brought in who had fallen unnoticed into a swimming pool. He did not recover. But I have only scratched the surface. I have only seen the surface.

In addition to urging parents to take every reasonable step to protect their children from accidental harm, I would advise them to be cautious when deciding to whom they will entrust their children. I do not wish to make anyone paranoid. However, all of us see or read daily what goes on in today's world. Children are targets for all kinds of predators, so parents must exercise responsibility in selecting day care facilities, baby sitters, and so on. Research the agencies and individuals you are considering. Get recommendations. Do anything you can to ensure that your children are in competent, safe hands. Any clever pervert can hide their activities for a while, but do your best to check people out.

Be vigilant about where your children play. I am appalled when I see things like young, unsupervised children running into the street in front of my car to retrieve a ball. How would you feel if your child was run down in the street and killed, or injured for life, because you had not taken sensible steps to keep them safe? Never let your children out of sight in public places such as shopping centers, stores, and parks. If they are in a swimming pool, watch them every second, and be able to rescue them if they get into trouble. Never, under any circumstances, allow a child in a boat without a certified life vest. Have them take swimming lessons at an early age from a qualified instructor. Learn CPR, and have them learn it. Water safety is a book in itself.

As soon as your children are old enough to understand such things, make sure that, in addition to teaching them basic principles of safety in the house, around traffic, water, and so on, see that they are taught how to respond to situations in which people are trying to take sexual liberties with them or abuse them in any way. I believe there are a number of crimes that should receive an automatic death penalty. These include hijacking and carjacking, certain kinds of terrorism, rape, and especially the most severe and indefensible cases of child molestation and kidnapping. Of all the crimes perpetrated today, the ones that confound me the most are those against children. What kind of individual would leave a newborn baby in a dumpster, or steal someone else's child because they did not have one of their own? How does a person become so twisted inside that they would have sex with a three-year-old or kill them? Modern culture and psychology obviously have failed us in many respects. Therefore, until we can evolve to the point where we do not do such terrible things, the best deterrent, I feel, is swift and sure punishment.

Children are precious and wonderful, and their childhood years should be something beautiful for them, full of adventure and wonder. Children are resilient and flexible, but they need structure, guidance, and protection. They especially need to feel secure, to know that they are loved by their parents, or by someone, and that the unconditional trust they give will not be violated. Early childhood is spent almost exclusively in learning. A child grows and learns best in an environment of love and trust. Whether a child is healthy or sick, or whether they grow to adulthood or die at an early age, they need to be loved. And their intelligence and ability to understand should never be underestimated. Although vulnerable in many ways, children possess an extraordinary wisdom. They need their parents' guidance, but they also need their respect. Their bodies may be small and fragile, but their souls, like our own, are unlimited.

Jenny—
My Final Thoughts

All relationships are temporary.
All relationships are eternal.

I believe that there is a design, whether comprehensible to us or not, that brings our children to us, whether through birth or adoption. To those parents whose children have special needs, whatever they are, or whose children die at an early age, I suggest that such children are a precious trust not given to everyone. When a soul is born into difficulties of various kinds, it is not a curse on that child or its parents. Such circumstances indicate that the child, and maybe the parents also, have unique lessons to learn, and the parents of such a child might well feel privileged to have been entrusted with this child. A rare and valuable opportunity for evolution has been provided to parents in such circumstances, an opportunity to look within and discover hidden strengths and resources, and not to recognize this opportunity and do everything one can to rise to it is a real waste.

Jennifer Pivaral was born under some very unique circumstances, and with extraordinary medical problems that sowed the seeds for a limited life span. However, despite its shortness—not quite three years and two months—I see her life as full and complete. I am able to say this because I believe totally that she accomplished what she came here to do, for herself and, if I may say so, for me.

237

I said previously that if I thought Jennifer's death meant the end of our relationship, I would prefer not to exist any more. Some might call this my inability to accept the finality of her death. I will not argue with them. They are right, in the sense that I maintain that our relationship, although interrupted physically, continues in some form in spite of her death. In addition, my solid belief in reincarnation and karma means that I accept that Jenny and I have lived uncounted past lives—and in our case, many of which I deeply believe have been together in various relationships. Therefore, to me, this lifetime, in which we spent such a short time together, was no accident or meaningless coincidence, no one-time occurrence. It was one link—and a very powerful, meaningful, and decisive one—in a chain of physical existences, many of which were spent together.

I expect that when I die, one of the first faces I see will be Jennifer's. Hers is the first face that I shall look for. I believe that after I am gone from here, even if God himself were to reveal his presence to me, my first concern would be, "Where is Jennifer?" I hope we would not have to reincarnate again, but if we do, that it will be together, and that it will be the last time. And if Jennifer should have to return, I have made up my mind to come back with her, if I have the choice. If she should come back without me, I would watch over her every step, and I trust that she would do the same for me. My commitment to Jenny is eternal.

There is a story in the Hindu *Mahabharata* about Yudhisthira, a royal saint, who, with his faithful dog, journeyed to the heights of the Himalayas to the abode of God. They reached heaven. Yudhisthira's spiritual nature was advanced to such a degree that Indra, the king of the gods, offered him entrance into paradise, but the dog would have to be left behind. Yudhisthira asked that his dog be allowed to enter paradise with him. When the wish was refused, Yudhisthira politely declined to enter paradise, saying that he would not desert his faithful pet, who trusted him and wished for his protection. A long argument ensued. Finally, Yudhisthira and his dog were allowed to enter paradise together. The dog is then revealed to be Dharma himself, the personification of duty and virtue. It has been a test for Yudhisthira. I relate the story here because it embodies my feelings for Jenny. Without her, there can be no real heaven. Wherever she is, that is where I want to be.

When the brief time that Jenny was allotted in this life ran out, although my grief was almost unbearable, I was deeply grateful, and remain so, that she left this world while she was in her own home, asleep in her own bed, near to me. I am so thankful that Jenny did not die in a hospital, perhaps in an intensive care unit, frightened or in pain, perhaps without my being there. I am absolutely convinced that the circumstances of her passing were no accident. For although she had to go on to another sphere of existence, some personal destiny of Jenny's and mine—or perhaps the design of some loving power—arranged things to happen the way they did. There is no doubt in my mind about this.

During the time Jenny was with me, the realization came that, given her medical condition, I might one day have to deal with her death. Although this possibility, which often lurked on the border of my consciousness, was agonizing to consider, I somehow accepted that it might come to pass and that I would then have to face it. At the same time, there was another possibility, at least in my mind, and however remote, that the Department of Children's Services would see fit, for some reason I cannot imagine, to take Jenny from my care. Things like that happen to perfectly good foster parents all the time, sometimes for reasons that seem rooted in little more than whimsicality on the part of the institutions in control.

As I have said, I regarded Jennifer absolutely as my own daughter. It was my intention to adopt her. Had Jenny been healthy and free to move from locale to locale without dependence on medical equipment and supplies, and had the institutional powers decided to take her from me, I would never have let her go, even if it meant fleeing the country. I would have died rather than let her go, healthy or not. Therefore, given the reality of her inability to move far from the medical equipment upon which she depended, if someone had tried to part us, I am convinced that I would not have lived with it.

If someone had chosen to take her from me, what would I have done? Would I have taken my own life? Possibly. Despite my philosophical convictions, I might have done so either in an act of desperation or after deliberation. But the question I am most afraid to ask myself is this: Would I have considered painlessly ending Jenny's life and then taking my own, so that we could have gone out of this world together in the hope that this would prevent our separation from each other? The only reason that I even raise such a deeply serious question is because the scenario has crossed my mind. I am not in any way saying that I planned to do this or that I even considered it in earnest—only that such images have come into my mind from time to time before and after her death.

I know that people sometimes do things in overwhelming desperation, probably because they feel trapped and can see no other way out of their predicament. Romeo and Juliet come immediately to mind. Personally, I also believe that the extreme acts people sometimes commit are the result of their having gone beyond even desperation—into some kind of mental or emotional "calm" beyond the storm, in which they are able to carry out normally unthinkable acts calmly, resolutely, and beyond the interference of emotion or thought.

I could never have been so selfish as to take Jenny's life along with mine if I knew she would be happy in a new home, deeply cared for, and traumatized as little as possible by her separation from me, even though losing her in this way would have broken my heart irreparably. I do not know if I could have survived it.

The possibility, however remote, of contemplating taking Jenny out of this world with me would have been something with which I would have had to wrestle if I had seen that her removal from me would deeply traumatize her and turn her world upside down. After all, I was "daddy" to her. We had bonded completely. She had given me her total, unconditional trust. How could I have allowed a situation to occur in which she felt that I had abandoned her? I have thought of her without me, wondering why I was not there, why I had left her with strangers. I remember the odd way Jennifer looked at me while she was still living in the hospital, when I returned after being gone for only a few days to visit my mother over the Christmas holidays—that look as if I had abandoned or betrayed her. I resolved then and there never to miss a single night coming to see her at the hospital.

Even at this moment, as I write this years after Jenny's death, I cannot imagine giving her up to anyone else if I thought it would make her unhappy—which it surely would have. And I must add here that Suzanne's doubts toward the end about keeping Jenny alarmed and outraged me the most because I feared, especially at first, that her acting on such doubts or even expressing them might cause Jenny to be taken from me. I felt that Suzanne was placing everything at terrible risk, and I do not believe that she has ever fully understood the agony that this caused me or the magnitude of the stakes. Perhaps I have said too much. I thank God circumstances were never such that I had to wrestle with such terrible decisions.

I recall a conversation Suzanne and I had soon after Jenny's death, after her return from Gethsemani, in which it became clear that she had talked about her feelings during her retreat with one of the brothers there whom she regarded as a special friend and confidant. In response, he had said something about the nature of love and how it was relevant to her dilemma. I inferred that his insight had convinced her that the right path for her was to remain with Jenny and me, and, as I choose to phrase it now, to cease in her struggle to tear free from the doubts and fears that she felt and surrender herself to the difficult and sometimes painful, but deeply rewarding task at hand of being Jenny's mother and working with me to heal the wounds in our marriage. I can only hope and choose to believe that this was the case.

One evening in September 1995, I called Suzanne and asked her to remind me what the brother had said to her. I felt that his words would have made a beautiful addition to the manuscript, and, perhaps more importantly, might have clarified Suzanne's position both for me and for those who would come to read this story of Jenny's life. However, she declined, politely, to refresh my memory, saying that her experience at Gethsemani had been deeply personal, that she felt it was best for her keep it so, and that, someday, she herself might write about the experience. I accepted her position on the matter and did not press further.

I am grateful that neither I nor anyone else ever had to make another agonizing decision—that of whether to continue or terminate life support for Jenny if she were critically ill in the hospital. If she had become septic and gone to the hospital, and her condition had eventually deteriorated to the point that her chances for survival looked grim or impossible, someone might have been called upon to decide whether her life support should be prolonged. Being empowered and called upon to make a life-and-death decision for any critically ill family member would be difficult and painful, but it seems to me that to have to decide whether your child lives or dies would be far worse. Thank God that, at some point in the past before I ever knew Jenny, Dr. Laurance had opted to give Jennifer every chance to fight under such circumstances. Had he not, Jennifer never would have come into my life.

While on the one hand it would have been agonizing for me to have to make such a decision about Jenny, I have also thought of how painful and frustrating it would have been not to have had any input, either way, into such a decision; for since Jenny was a ward of the State, life-and-death decisions would most likely have been made by a judge or even a bureaucrat. My hope would be that Dr. Laurance would have had a lot to say about such a decision, and I know that, in addition to having Jenny's best interests at heart, he would have been sensitive to our feelings. It would have been terrible for Jenny to suffer, without hope for recovery, because of some government employee or red tape. The state probably would have been more likely to prolong her life than to cut it short because of the human rights issues involved.

Suzanne and I were spared many tragic scenarios and difficult decisions. Shortly after Jenny died, another little girl with a condition similar to Jenny's got to the point where she simply ran out of access sites in her body where the doctors could place a catheter to feed her. Nothing more could be done for her. I remember this child well, because she used to be in and out of the pediatric ward when Jenny lived there. This sweet little girl was about Jenny's age, but blond, pale, and fragile. In the end, the doctors simply removed the old catheter and sent her home to die. Without proper nourishment and liquids, she slipped into a coma and died within a few days. How agonizing it must have been for her parents to sit by helplessly and wait for this to happen. I realized that the very same thing could have happened to Jenny in time. I regret that I found myself emotionally unable to attend this little girl's funeral. I did, however, call her parents afterward.

Before ending this book, I must speak a little more about Jenny's medical problems in light of my own personal views on reincarnation. What I have to say may provide food for thought for parents of children who have disabilities or who have died, and for anyone who questions why there seems to be so much injustice, inequality, and suffering in the world.

I have a serious problem with Western Christianity's concept of God. Christianity, to me, does not satisfactorily explain suffering and inequality. When applied to children, this inability to explain why one child is born healthy and another with a deadly disease, why one must endure want and starvation while another grows and prospers, results in a kind of spiritual shrugging of the shoulders, a default to the attitude that such conditions are simply a result of the infallible but indecipherable will of God, who moves in mysterious ways beyond human comprehension.

I can agree that there is much which the human mind, in its present state of evolution, cannot comprehend, although one can eventually find one's way to certain spiritual disciplines and practices designed to overcome such blindness. Nothing can compare with the direct intuitive perception of spiritual truth. But since few of us have access, at least for any length of time, to such infallible states of consciousness, I do not wish to deceive myself, however comforting it may be, into believing that my personal opinions and wishful thinking are in any way comparable to the clarity of perception experienced in such states. Therefore, as I strive for such realizations, let me admit to the limits of the intellect while at the same time using it as a tool to carry me as far as it can. In my opinion, rationality is not inimical to spirituality, and the idea of sheer blind faith unsupported by direct spiritual perception or by any attempt to use one's intellect and reason to examine life is unacceptable.

Some ideas go so much against my grain spiritually and intellectually that I simply cannot accept them. Therefore, I cannot accept a whimsical god, nor a universe based on some omnipotent Will or cosmic throw of the dice which dictates that one child is born a genius and another an idiot, or that one child comes into the world physically perfect while another must deal with conditions like the ones which Jenny faced. Such ideas are totally inimical to my idea of love. And I believe deeply that the ultimate creative and sustaining force behind and permeating all creation is a cosmic Love, although the true nature of such a Love cannot be fully understood until each of us attains that state of enlightenment wherein we can directly perceive those realities beyond the realm of the intellect.

How, then, can I intelligently explain how such things as Jenny's condition come to be? My answer is that the causes of Jenny's medical condition lie in her past lives and in the karma—the law of cause and effect—that was set into motion in those previous existences. First, Jenny was born a Siamese twin—a medical rarity. Siamese twins have very strong karmic bonds from previous lifetimes. Regarding Jenny and her twin, Wendy, I have often had the feeling that perhaps the two souls had fought to keep each other from reincarnating in the same womb. Perhaps this struggle killed Wendy before she was born, but not before she took so much nourishment from Jenny and from the mother that it deprived Jenny of her normal physical development and left her organism deeply flawed in some respects, eventually killing her also. This dramatic scenario indicates to me the strong possibility that Jennifer would have owed her twin some kind of karmic debt—apparently a heavy one. Although I have no idea what this debt might have been, I would hope that it is now repaid in full, that the scale is balanced, and that Jennifer is free of it and able to go on in her spiritual evolution. Such a scenario could easily suggest karma of a negative character. However, there is another possibility.

Without question, Jennifer was a very old soul, highly advanced, and near the end of her evolution in terms of rebirth in human bodies. Therefore, although it is certainly possible that she got into some kind of serious karmic difficulty that had heavy medical repercussions, even possible that this karmic debt was very old and had to be balanced before she could progress in her spiritual growth, it is also possible that her condition was the result of her having taken on a karmic debt of the twin and working it off for her. This latter possibility would suggest some kind of guru-disciple relationship between Jenny and her twin. Certainly, just from my experiences with Jenny in this lifetime and my knowledge of my own previous incarnations with her, I know that she was an advanced being and that one time she had even been a spiritual teacher to me. I may never know in this lifetime the real relationship between Jenny and her twin, Wendy, but one of the scenarios I have offered may be close to the truth.

As I have said, I have wondered from time to time if Jennifer reincarnated as Jessica, especially since Jessica was born only two months after Jenny died. There is to be remembered the strange slip of the tongue made several times by the astrologer whom I consulted shortly after Jenny's death, who repeatedly referred to Jennifer as "Tina." Two weeks later, Jessica Christina was born. I also call to mind the powerful dream vision I had of Jenny on October 10, 1993, just two days after the second anniversary of Jessica's birth, in which Jenny communicated to me by saying, "Yes, of course, I am really alive. I am resurrected. I have come back to you." These two incidents do not prove anything, but they are remarkable coincidences, if nothing else, at least in my mind. Oddly enough, the main reason I have dismissed them as indications of Jenny's rebirth as Jessica is that I have always felt that I surely would have recognized Jenny's soul in this new "Jessica" body if she had returned by that means. And although Jessica naturally reminds me of Jenny, I have never had any kind of experience that seemed like a recognition of Jenny's soul in Jessica's body. Perhaps one day such a recognition will occur, but I am not expecting it, and I have seen no indications in Jessica's behavior to indicate that she is Jenny reincarnated.

Perhaps Jessica is Wendy reincarnated. Why not? After all, the soul that was Wendy may have made a second attempt, this time a successful one, to reincarnate through the womb of the same mother. I cannot say, but such a possibility is not at all implausible. I do know that Jennifer, Jessica, and I are intimately bound together by strong karma created through associations in numerous past lives.

Jennifer and I were destined to meet in this lifetime to help each other, as we have done many lifetimes before. Jenny needed a daddy to love her, someone whose devotion to her was equal to the task of caring for her and dealing with her medical problems. Therefore her soul found its way to me, someone closely connected with her and who had been her father, caregiver, and protector in numerous past incarnations. She needed me, and I was there.

Likewise, as far as I am concerned, Jenny was my savior in this lifetime. She showed me, as no other human being has been able to, the kind of love possible between two souls. Before meeting Jenny, I never imagined that such beautiful love could be experienced with someone else. As a young man, I had been confronted with incredible perceptions and experiences that could only be called mystical, in which I encountered a cosmic love that is impossible to express. I have written about these experiences and the many years of spiritual searching they engendered in a previous book entitled *Darkness Is Light Enough*. Only through Jenny did I realize that such love could be experienced between two human hearts—a love that transformed me and enabled me to see the Divine in the eyes of every child.

Jenny also had a critical and permanent impact on my spiritual life and the direction of my path. It took something as traumatic as her dying to make me recognize the need to take up once again a daily spiritual discipline. It was her overwhelming presence and communication to me during my meditation on October 6, 1991, that brought about my commitment to practice kriya yoga daily from that time forward. This practice has had an immeasurable influence on my inner and outer life, and I would not have survived without it. The impact of her short but wonderful presence in my life, and her death, have changed me forever.

As I have said, the other participant in this living drama, the other soul to which both Jenny and I are linked, is Jessica. I am so deeply thankful that Jessica came along when she did—no accident, I am sure—and that she is such an important part of my life. Whether Jessica is just Jessica, or Wendy reincarnated, or whatever, is not ultimately important. What counts is that we love each other. We matter in each other's lives. In my mind, Jessica and I are also linked by past lives. Like Jenny, she has been my daughter before, although in Jessica's case the number and variety of past-life relationships are not as extensive as those I have shared with Jennifer. I believe that the two girls have been sisters before, possibly with me as their father. Once, during meditation, I had a vivid vision of Jessica in a past life. The setting was somewhere in South America. She was a beautiful, strong-willed young woman then—qualities clearly manifested in this lifetime.

I hope my words will help bereaved parents understand and deal with their pain, and I believe that only someone who has experienced such a loss can really empathize with the kind of grief that accompanies the death of a child. Let this book provide comfort and guidance, and let other grieving parents know that they need not be alone with their loss—that many others have walked this road and can offer support.

I eventually heard a quiet, tender, but unrelenting voice speaking in my heart, telling me this book must be written. The voice was an inescapable realization that something within my own being—a personal destiny—made its writing unavoidable. At the root of this calling was my love for Jennifer, which made me want to make her known, remembered, and immortalized in the minds of many people, even though I do not question the immortality of her soul. I wanted the message of her life to be heard, and to give voice to my consuming love for her.

I have vowed to love Jenny, to care for her in any way possible, for all time—for all the future and for all existence beyond this life, whether in incarnations to come, or on other planes, or wherever. It is my deepest desire that my path to realization, and its attainment, be fused irreversibly and forever with Jenny's path. My final word is to Jenny:

"I will not enter Heaven without you."

October 14, 1995

Epilogue

In September 1996, Suzanne left Los Angeles and returned to her family home in Kentucky.

To order books, please send full amount
plus $4.00 for postage and handling.

Send orders to:

GALDE PRESS, INC.
PO Box 460
Lakeville, Minnesota 55044

Credit card orders call 1–800–777–3454

Write for a free catalog!